IMAGES OF THE ALGERIAN WAR

IMAGES OF THE ALGERIAN WAR

French Fiction and Film, 1954–1992

PHILIP DINE

CLARENDON PRESS · OXFORD

1994

Oxford University Press, Walton Street, Oxford OX2 6DP
Oxford New York
Athens Auckland Bangkok Bombay
Calcutta Cape Town Dar es Salaam Delhi
Florence Hong Kong Istanbul Karachi
Kuala Lumpur Madras Madrid Melbourne
Mexico City Nairobi Paris Singapore
Taipei Tokyo Toronto
and associated companies in
Berlin Ibadan

Oxford is a trade mark of Oxford University Press

Published in the United States
by Oxford University Press Inc., New York

British Library Cataloguing in Publication Data
Data available

Library of Congress Cataloging in Publication Data
Dine, Philip.
Images of the Algerian War : French fiction and film. 1954-1992
Philip Dine.
Includes bibliographical references and index.
1. French fiction—20th century—History and criticism.
2. Algeria—History—Revolution, 1954–1962—Literature and the revolution. 3. Algeria—History—Revolution. 1954–1962—Motion pictures and the revolution. 4. War stories, French—History and criticism. 5. Motion pictures—France—History. I. Title.
PQ673.D55 1994
843'.91409358—dc20
94–12383
ISBN 0–19–815875–0

1 3 5 7 9 10 8 6 4 2

Typeset by Datix International Limited, Bungay, Suffolk
Printed in Great Britain
on acid-free paper by
Bookcraft Ltd.,
Midsomer Norton, Bath

For A. N.

Acknowledgements

I wish to thank all those friends and colleagues who, by their generous help, have made this book possible. I should like in particular to acknowledge the very considerable assistance and encouragement that I have received from Ian Lockerbie (who supervised the original research at the University of Stirling), Alec Hargreaves, William Kidd, Gilbert Meynier, and Walter Redfern. I am also grateful to Andrew Lockett and Jason Freeman of Oxford University Press for their invaluable guidance in bringing the project to fruition. However, my greatest debt of gratitude must, as always, be to my wife Carol.

Contents

List of Abbreviations

ALN	Armée de libération nationale: National Liberation Army
CNC	Centre national de la cinématographie: National Film-Making Centre
FLN	Front de libération nationale: National Liberation Front
OAS	Organisation armée secrète: Secret Army Organization
SAS	Sections administratives spécialisées: Specialized Administrative Platoons
REP	Régiment étranger de parachutistes: Foreign Legion Parachute Regiment
RCP	Régiment colonial de parachutistes: Colonial Parachute Regiment
RAS	'Rien à signaler': 'Nothing to report'
FFI	Forces françaises de l'intérieur: Internal (i.e. Resistance) French Forces

Glossary of Arabic and Military Terms

appelé	conscript
bidasse	(*slang*) conscript
bled	bush
contingent	the body of conscripts called up for national service (cf. US 'the draft')
corvée de bois	(*slang*) summary execution (literally 'wood-cutting duty')
crapahuter	(*slang*) to carry out military operations in difficult terrain
djebel	mountains or bush
douar	village
fellagha	Arabic term (literally 'road-cutter') adopted by the French army to refer to FLN fighters (also *fellouze*, *fell*)
gus	(*slang*) conscript
harki	member of a locally recruited Algerian force supporting the French army
katiba	FLN battalion
mechta	village
moudjahid	FLN combatant (literally 'holy warrior')
quadrillage	the military partitioning of Algeria for surveillance purposes
quille	(*slang*) demobilization
rappelé	recalled reservist
regroupement	the forcible relocation of Algerian civilians
zone interdite	forbidden (i.e. free-fire) zone

THE ALGERIAN WAR: HISTORY AND IDEOLOGY, MYTHOLOGY AND FICTION

History: The Logic of Military Confrontation

The Algerian war of national liberation is generally held to have begun on the eve of All Saints' Day, 1 November 1954, when the newly formed Front de Libération Nationale (FLN) launched its armed challenge to a century and a quarter of French colonial rule. However, the small-scale and amateurish execution of these first attacks on people and property meant that it was only with hindsight that their historical significance became apparent. Certainly the immediate response of the French press was to play down this latest manifestation of Algerian nationalist sentiment, presenting it as a mere footnote to troubles already being experienced elsewhere in France's North African territories. Yet, within just four years, the conflict in Algeria would come to dominate French political life to the exclusion of virtually all else. The institutional crisis which it provoked was to lead directly to the collapse not only of a succession of governments but also of the entire regime. Indeed, the moribund Fourth Republic was to follow a recent precedent as it voted itself out of existence and granted full powers to the hero of a previous war, in a desperate attempt to find a way out of the country's Algerian predicament.

The parallel between the dramatic events of May 1958 and those of June 1940 was inescapable, yet the return from the wilderness of General Charles de Gaulle was to prove essential to the final execution of France's belated and bloody retreat from overseas empire. Brought to power on the back of a threatened military coup, and in the full expectation that he would keep Algeria French, de Gaulle would take just another four years to rid the nation of its ruinous Algerian obsession. In order to do so, he would first establish the semi-presidential form of government so characteristic of the modern Fifth Republic, and would then have to overcome the armed challenges of both the European settlers of Algeria and the French military. Only in this way would France be free to complete the process of economic reconstruction and social renewal required for a new and Europe-centred national *grandeur*. These changes were arguably the most dramatic in the history of European decolonization, and to understand how they came about it is necessary to consider two more key dates.

The brutal repression of the nationalist riots which occurred in the Sétif region of Algeria on VE Day, 8 May 1945, was a clear sign that a France profoundly traumatized by the experience of defeat and occupation intended a swift return to business as usual in the colonies. This strategy for recovering the country's lost international status failed to take account of the wave of decolonization which was to sweep through the European empires from 1945 onwards, with the result that France engaged in a series of particularly unpleasant, and ultimately futile, colonial wars. Its first major challenge came not in Algeria, but in Indo-China, which the French had lost control of to the Japanese, and which had been liberated by a combination of American military might and indigenous nationalist resistance. After eight years of jungle fighting, the French forces were to be catastrophically defeated at Dien Bien Phu on 7 May 1954, and the peace agreements that sealed their withdrawal would be signed before July was out. However, neither the newly sovereign state of Vietnam nor the still unconsolidated Fourth Republic was destined to live in peace for long: the Vietnamese would only have a respite of a few years, France barely a few months. The failure of the United States to learn the lessons of this first Indo-China war is clearly beyond the scope of the present book. That of France, however, can be understood by considering the events of 6 February 1956.

On that day, the socialist Guy Mollet, recently elected at the head of a Republican Front government expected to end the still low-intensity conflict in Algeria, was pelted with tomatoes by an angry European crowd in Algiers. Shocked by this wholly unexpected reception, he would make a complete about-turn and commit the country to an all-out war in defence of *Algérie française*.[1]

[1] The term 'French Algeria' was coined by the European settler community and is a particularly loaded one, implying an inviolable link between the two territories. De Gaulle, very significantly, would avoid using it when he returned to power in 1958.

From this moment on, the logic of military conflict was to prevail in Algeria, and France itself would be brought to the brink of civil war as the army entered the political arena under the banner of a patent theory of *guerre révolutionnaire*. Produced in the wake of the Indo-Chinese débâcle, this strange blend of semi-digested Maoism, virulent anti-communism, and colonialist wishful thinking would encourage the 'activists' within the armed forces to disregard successive governments in their quest for a resounding military victory in Algeria.

The massive use of conscription, never resorted to in Indo-China, was only the most obvious aspect of the Mollet administration's new belligerence. The war which awaited the nearly three million young Frenchmen sent to serve in Algeria was one without fronts and with no major battles. The single confrontation subsequently to have been dignified with this name, the so-called 'Battle of Algiers', was a particularly unpleasant anti-terrorist operation which set the French army against the FLN's urban bombing networks. A military victory for the French, this campaign was to prove a political disaster, both in its hardening of Algerian support for the nationalist cause, and in its impact on metropolitan public opinion. As revelations about the army's systematic use of torture and summary execution gradually filtered back to France—in many cases through the eye-witness accounts of returning conscripts—a vigorous denunciation of French 'pacification' methods was mounted by a generation of intellectuals still haunted by the memory of France's own recent experience of occupation and resistance.[2]

Ideology: The Intellectuals' Last Stand

David Schalk has usefully reminded us that 'the noun *intellectuel*, demarcating a segment of society, became a part of everyday French vocabulary [only in] 1898, at the height of the Dreyfus affair, with the publication of Emile Zola's *J'accuse* and the manifestos and countermanifestos that followed'.[3] First recognized as a distinct social category in this specific historical context, the French intellectual class was to continue to take political sides in the

[2] See esp. M. Crouzet, 'La Bataille des intellectuels français', *La Nef*, 12–13 (Oct. 1962–Jan. 1963), 47–65; P. Sorum, *Intellectuals and Decolonization in France* (Chapel Hill, Univ. of North Carolina Press, 1977); J.-P. Rioux and J.-F. Sirinelli (eds.), *La Guerre d'Algérie et les intellectuels français* (Brussels, Complexe, 1991); D. Schalk, *War and the Ivory Tower: Algeria and Vietnam* (New York and Oxford, Oxford Univ. Press, 1991).

[3] Schalk, *War and the Ivory Tower*, 40.

decades which followed. Indeed, it was precisely this preoccupation with politics which would famously be denounced by the philosopher and novelist Julien Benda in his *La Trahison des clercs* [translated as *The Betrayal of the Intellectuals*] (1927). Yet in spite of this impassioned appeal for a return to the traditional detachment of the ivory tower, the intellectuals, at least on the Left, were to be confirmed in their collective belief in the necessity of political involvement by the multiple traumas of the 1930s and 1940s. The implications for literary producers of this conviction were given a systematic formulation for the first time in 1948, when Jean-Paul Sartre's *Qu'est-ce que la littérature?* was published.

In this important theoretical essay, Sartre addressed the politics of literary production, arguing the case for the radical political commitment or *engagement* of the producer of literature. His appeal for *une littérature engagée* has its roots in a revolutionary faith in the subversive potential of writing when carried out by a suitably *engagé* writer. Thus, as Rhiannon Goldthorpe puts it, 'the function of the committed writer can provisionally be characterised as that of revealing to the reader both his situation and his freedom to change it, in order that he might effect the critical *prise de conscience* [awakening or act of becoming conscious] necessary for a transcending of that situation'.[4]

However, the precise ways in which this revolutionary project of artistic *engagement* was to be implemented were by no means definitively identified in *Qu'est-ce que la littérature?*. On the contrary, this essay was merely the first formulation of 'an evolving theory of commitment, [which was] superficially assertive but potentially self-questioning',[5] and Sartre was to shift his ground significantly over the years. Moreover, his special use of the term 'commitment' in relation to francophone Black African poets in 'Orphée noir' (1948)[6] showed that the proclaimed duty of all committed writers to bear witness to the (political) world could be carried out in ways which were far more subtle and complex than the theory of *Qu'est-ce que la littérature?*, with its insistence on the transparent

[4] *Sartre: Literature and Theory* (Cambridge, Cambridge Univ. Press, 1984), 161. See also G. Brée, *Camus and Sartre: Crisis and Commitment* (New York, Dell, 1972), for a valuable comparison of the approaches to artistic commitment of the two most celebrated producers of *littérature engagée*.

[5] Goldthorpe, *Sartre*, 2.

[6] *Situations*, iii (Gallimard/NRF, 1949), 229–86. (First published as a preface to L. S. Senghor's *Anthologie de la nouvelle poésie nègre et malgache* (Presses Universitaires, 1948).)

character and instrumental function of literary prose, had suggested.

Sartre would be followed by Roland Barthes, Louis Althusser, Pierre Macherey, and Julia Kristeva as major commentators on the relationship between literature and the ideological as French writing continued to be discussed in primarily political terms for the next thirty years. More immediately, the group of literary innovators associated with the *nouveau roman* [new novel] found themselves obliged to argue the case for their brand of impersonal and apolitical objectivity in the face of Sartre's aggressive assertion of the need for artistic commitment (as, indeed, they would go on to engage with the debates inspired by each of the later theorists). It was Alain Robbe-Grillet who, in *Pour un nouveau roman* (1963) [translated as *Towards a New Novel*], most memorably riposted that, for the 'new novelist', the only possible commitment could be the commitment to literature itself, with all that this implied in the way of an awareness of the complex problems posed by the writer's own use of language.[7] Such a commitment did not, however, preclude an active involvement in politics; indeed, not only Robbe-Grillet, but also Nathalie Sarraute, Claude Simon, and Michel Butor were to join Sartre in signing the most celebrated intellectual petition against the Algerian war, the so-called 'Manifeste des 121' of September 1960. What their collective stand did mean for the *nouveaux romanciers*, however, was a radical separation of political causes and their patent version of literary practice.

The new novelists' flight from the artistic expression of politics—a response to historical events which was mirrored, to a certain extent, by that of the cinematic 'New Wave'—would thus, paradoxically, coincide with a last assertion of the need for the artist to enter the arena; either in defence of French Algeria or, more usually, to bury it. Although isolated from the mass of a French population which had rarely shown any great enthusiasm for the colonies, and never for any length of time, the intellectuals were to make the Algerian war their last great crusade, with the spirit of Captain Alfred Dreyfus regularly being invoked. Indeed, whether they saw themselves as Dreyfusards, Bolsheviks, or Tiersmondistes—to adopt Pierre Vidal-Naquet's taxonomy of the leftist intellectual opposition to the Algerian conflict[8]—these artists and academics

[7] *Pour un nouveau roman* (Minuit, 1963), 46–7; cited by M. Adereth, *Commitment in Modern French Literature* (London, Gollancz, 1967), 25.

[8] 'Une fidélité têtue: la résistance française à la guerre d'Algérie', *Vingtième siècle*, 10 (Apr.–June 1986), 3–18, 11.

would assert that what was at stake for France in North Africa was nothing less than national honour. In an age of collapsing ideological certainties, epitomized by the blows inflicted in 1956 on both the colonialist Right (Suez) and the pro-communist Left (Budapest), Algeria was to prove a final rallying point for the advocates of artistic commitment. True, French intellectuals would subsequently be involved in the political struggles associated with the de-Stalinization of the Soviet Union (Khrushchev's 'secret' denunciation of Stalin also occurred in 1956, at the Twentieth Congress of the CPSU); they would take to the barricades, metaphorically if not literally, in May 1968; and they would campaign to the bitter end against America's war in Vietnam. However, the French intellectual class would never again be so united as it was in its opposition to the Algerian 'cancer'. As Schalk puts it, following Bernard Droz: 'Once that cancer had been excised from the French body politic, and the battle of the word won, the solder melted, the energies of the French intellectual class dispersed, and there was a nearly instantaneous, widely noted, and sometimes lamented *dégagement* [disengagement]'.[9]

Variously described as 'an intellectuals' battle', 'a war of petitions', even 'Sartre's war', the Algerian conflict was undoubtedly, in Michel Crouzet's celebrated phrase 'une bataille de l'écrit' ['a battle of the written word'].[10] Indeed, the war has generated and continues to generate an enormous volume of histories, testimonies, polemics, memoirs, and, especially, works of fiction. Yet the impressive quantity and variety of this material should not be equated with a correspondingly high level of quality, still less with the unproblematic functioning of the French collective memory. For the Algerian war has for long been what the American John Talbott was the first historian to characterize as 'the war without a name';[11] officially

[9] *War and the Ivory Tower*, 110. Droz, 'Le Cas très singulier de la guerre d'Algérie', *Vingtième siècle*, 5 (Jan.–Mar. 1985), 89. Cf. Sorum, *Intellectuals and Decolonization*, 244: '[The war in Algeria] may prove to be the final great battle in the long tradition of France's "engaged" intellectuals'; also cited by Schalk, *War and the Ivory Tower*, 165.

[10] J.-F. Sirinelli, 'Guerre d'Algérie, guerre des pétitions?', in Rioux and Sirinelli, *La Guerre d'Algérie*, 265–306; A. Cohen-Solal, *Sartre* (Gallimard, 1985), 563, cited and discussed by Schalk, *War and the Ivory Tower*, 102–5; Crouzet, 'La Bataille des intellectuels français', 47.

[11] *The War Without a Name: France in Algeria, 1954–1962* (London, Faber & Faber, 1981). See also P. Mus (ed.), *Guerre sans visage: lettres commentées du sous-lieutenant Émile Mus* (Seuil, 1961).

denied throughout its duration, when it was referred to by a series of euphemisms such as 'operations to maintain order' or 'the events', the conflict has subsequently been all but forgotten. It is not commemorated with a national remembrance day or a memorial site, and its French victims (some 24,000 dead and 300,000 wounded)[12] go largely unmourned. Its three million veterans—a body much the same size as that produced by America's Vietnam war, but drawn from a male population only one quarter the size—are still not officially recognized as ex-combatants on a par with those of 1914–18 and 1939–45.

In the continued absence of both a state-sponsored ritual of mourning and a consensual history of the period, those involved in the conflict have looked to writing as a private substitute for the physical *lieux de mémoire* [places of remembrance] inevitably lost together with French sovereignty over Algeria. So intense has this process of individual commemoration been that Benjamin Stora, one of the principal historians of the French collective memory of the Algerian conflict, has talked of 'the war of a thousand and one books'.[13] Writing for themselves and their kindred spirits—old soldiers, exiled settlers, anti-war militants—the properly literary output of some of these deeply committed writers will form the backbone of the corpus of fiction examined in this book. Their commitment is not, generally speaking, the theorized and consciously political *engagement* recommended by Sartre, but rather an intensely personal investment in the literary text as a means of fixing and rendering comprehensible their sense of grief, be it individual or collective, or both.

Only in recent years have French historians seriously attempted to cut through the Manichaean discourse which typifies not only much of this fictional production, but also the majority of supposedly scientific studies of events in France and Algeria from 1954 to 1962. This legacy of bitterness and ill-will is of particularly pointed relevance to any attempt to understand the present relationship between the indigenous population of modern France and the country's large ethnic minority of North African origin, itself the most obvious and permanent reminder of past colonial adventures.

[12] Estimates of the total number of dead in the war are a notoriously vexed question, and range from less than 200,000 to over a million. See B. Stora, 'Le Bilan des pertes', in the same author's *La Gangrène et l'oubli: la mémoire de la guerre d'Algérie* (La Découverte, 1992), 180–4.

[13] See 'Le Livre: la guerre comme une affaire privée', in *La Gangrène et l'oubli*, 238–48.

Indeed, this failure of the collective memory is an important object of study in its own right for those French historians who have, at last, shown themselves ready to probe beneath the surface of a peculiarly troubled colonial past. To the fore in this enterprise has been the Institut d'Histoire du Temps Présent (IHTP), whose December 1988 conference on 'La Guerre d'Algérie et les Français' undoubtedly constituted a watershed.[14] This major gathering served to lay the ground for the mass of publications, exhibitions, conferences, films, and television programmes which were subsquently produced to mark the thirtieth anniversary of the Évian Accords, the agreements which had finally brought the war to a close in March 1962. It is my contention that the close reading and re-reading of now largely forgotten French works of prose fiction and film can make a significant contribution to this continuing elucidation of a historic occultation. Indeed, the present exercise in literary archaeology may not only help us to understand France and the French better, but may even cast light on the shadowy psychological processes of our own colonial past and post-colonial present. This is undoubtedly a large claim, and one which requires some explanation.

Mythology: La Guerre des Mythes

For the French, the *drame algérien*, as it is routinely described, came to symbolize the process of decolonization as a whole, and was infinitely more acutely felt than the country's successive withdrawals from the Levant, Indo-China, sub-Saharan Africa, Tunisia, and Morocco. The intense passions aroused by Algeria are to be understood in terms of the specificity of the French colonial enterprise on the one hand, and of the colony's unique status on the other. The accepted wisdom which contrasts a narrow British mercantilism with French colonial faith—on the rhetorical level if on no other—in 'assimilation' and 'the France of one hundred million Frenchmen', may be an over-simplification, but there can be little doubting

[14] See J.-P. Rioux (ed.), *La Guerre d'Algérie et les Français* (Fayard, 1990). This massive work represents the proceedings of the IHTP conference, and is without doubt the single most valuable study yet produced of the French role in the Algerian war. See esp. the following articles on the failure of collective memory: J.-P. Rioux, 'La Flamme et les bûchers' (pp. 497–508), and R. Frank, 'Les Troubles de la mémoire française' (pp. 603–7).

the commitment of French colonizers to the nation's self-appointed *mission civilisatrice* [civilizing mission]. Whether inspired by Jacobin universalism or Catholic evangelism, or both, it was this time-honoured conception of France's role in the world which led, in the immediate post-war period, to what Bruce Marshall has called the 'colonial myth': that is to say 'the vision, held by virtually all of the French élite, of an indissoluble link between France and the colonies'.[15] In the Algerian context, this 'symbolic language [providing] a common universe of discourse to virtually all segments of the political élite, both metropolitan and colonial'[16] was ultimately to have disastrous consequences. Indeed, the new Fourth Republic was not only born of the colonial myth, but was also destined to die by it.

Much of the responsibility for the regime's demise can be attributed to one very specific aspect of this all-embracing myth-system, namely the notion that Algeria was not a colony at all, but rather a province, and thus an integral part of a 'Greater France'. This legal fiction has been most fruitfully described by Emmanuel Mounier as 'the myth of the three *départements*', and dates from the 1848 juridical incorporation of France's principal overseas territory into the body of the French nation: it is to be regarded as the foundation myth of *Algérie française*.[17] It is in this more than anything else that the history of France in Algeria comes closest to that of Britain in Ireland; a fact which goes some way towards explaining why these two colonies should have constituted special cases in the histories of the two imperial powers.[18] As in 'British' Ireland, there was a demographic reality to go with the legal fiction of 'French' Algeria: that is to say, a process of civilian colonial settlement on a scale and in a ratio unknown elsewhere in the French empire. By 1954 there were just under a million *pieds-noirs*, as the settlers would become known, resident in Algeria, out of a total population of less than ten million.[19] By 1963 they would, with very few exceptions, be gone.

[15] *The French Colonial Myth and Constitution Making in the Fourth Republic* (New Haven, Conn., Yale Univ. Press, 1973), 2.

[16] Ibid. 4.

[17] E. Mounier, 'Impossibilités algériennes ou le mythe des trois départements', *Esprit*, July 1947.

[18] M. Kahler, *Decolonization in Britain and France: The Domestic Consequences of International Relations* (Princeton, NJ, Princeton Univ. Press, 1984), 367–8.

[19] Opinions differ widely as to the origin of the expression *pieds-noirs*, lit. 'black-feet'. The most plausible explanations are that the term refers either to the army boots worn by the first (military) French occupiers of Algeria or to the dirty bare feet of the impoverished European settlers who came after them.

It is undoubtedly difficult to imagine the occurrence of the Algerian war without the presence in the colony of this large settler population. However, at least as important in the calculations of successive French governments was the profound belief—sanctified by the Revolutionary principle of 'the one and indivisible Republic'—in the nation's right to administer the disputed territory. Indeed, as far as the French presence in Algeria is concerned, history is primarily understandable not in terms of rational economic or strategic interests, nor yet as a result of the shortcomings of a political system, but rather as a function of ideology.[20] Only within this ideological framework, in fact, is it possible to comprehend the often self-destructive impulses of many of the actors in the Algerian drama. This is not so much to imply a rejection of historical materialism as to acknowledge the Algerian question's importance as a generator of collective confusions, which we may variously refer to as phantasms, instances of false consciousness, or myths. Literary and cinematic texts, I shall argue, constitute a privileged and yet readily accessible site of ideological tension. This is particularly true of the fiction and film of the French colonial enterprise, and above all of the corpus generated in response to the traumatic experience of decolonization.

It is important to make clear at this point that whereas the term 'ideology' is intended to be value-free for the purposes of my analysis, the term 'myth' is not. Like Frederic Jameson, I 'take the term ideology here in Althusser's sense as a representational structure which allows the individual subject to conceive or imagine his or her lived relationship to transpersonal realities such as the social structure or the collective logic of History'.[21] Ideology is not, therefore, something which may be avoided, but rather a basic given of human existence; what is available to the individual in society can never be the absence of ideology, but only ever a choice between competing ideologies. However, it does not follow from this that all of the available ideologies are equally appropriate in a given historical context. On the contrary, an ideology which has been rendered obsolete by historical developments will be a dangerous liability both to the individual and to the society of which he/she is a member. Thus, in the Algeria of the post-war period, the

[20] T. Smith, *The French Stake in Algeria: 1954–1962* (London, Cornell Univ. Press, 1978), 23–30.

[21] *The Political Unconscious: Narrative as a Socially Symbolic Act* (London, Methuen, 1981), 30.

complementary ideologies of imperialism and colonialism would be tested to destruction. In the process, not only the various defenders of these redundant systems of thought, but also those who sought to distance themselves from them, if not always actively to overturn them, were called upon to suffer and very frequently to die for their beliefs; as, indeed, were very many Algerian men, women and children who by virtually any standard would be deemed wholly innocent. I shall argue that a major contributory factor in this pointlessly destructive end to the *présence française* in North Africa was the range of myths uttered by the French participants in the conflict, both metropolitan and *pied-noir*: myths about themselves, about Algeria, and about the territory's indigenous population.

A natural point of departure for any consideration of the 'mythical' element in the French experience of the Algerian war is the analysis of popular culture put forward by Roland Barthes in his 1957 collection of essays, *Mythologies*. In this seminal critique of the self-images communicated by the mass culture of the day, Barthes provided both practical examples of the mechanics of contemporary mystification, and a theoretical framework for the analysis of all such myths. In his later theoretical work, most notably *S/Z* (1970), Barthes would seek to explain this kind of transformation in terms of the literary text's systematic exploitation of a complex structure of linguistic and cultural codes.[22] Although not explicit in his earlier analysis of French mass culture, such thinking clearly underpins his proposed demystification of its signifying systems. Moreover, if Barthes sought, in *Mythologies*, to draw the attention of his readers to the covert manipulation of these codes, then nowhere was the disparity between image and event more apparent than in the depiction of the mother country's relations with her overseas empire. It is for this reason above all that Barthes's model of semiosis must remain a privileged point of reference for this discussion of what one of the critic's contemporaries memorably described as 'la guerre des mythes'.[23] However, as we shall see, Barthes's strategies for demystification may equally well be applied to the

[22] *Mythologies* (Seuil, 1957); see esp. the essays 'L'Opération Astra', 'Grammaire africaine', and the major theoretical piece, 'Le Mythe, aujourd'hui'. Barthes, *S/Z* (Seuil, 1970).

[23] J. Duquesne, *L'Algérie ou la guerre des mythes* (Desclée de Brouwer, 1958). For a good introduction to the role of myths in French political history see R. Girardet, *Mythes et mythologies politiques* (Seuil, 1986). For a useful survey of recent theoretical work on the mechanics of colonialist mystification, see R. Young, *White Mythologies: Writing History and the West* (London, Routledge, 1990).

colonialist Right and Centre—his own preferred targets—and to the Marxist, or at least Marxian, Left of which he himself was a member.

Fiction: The Undervalued Text and the Integrated Reader

The complex of myths generated by the final stage of French decolonization has historically been communicated by means of a wide variety of media: official pronouncements, parliamentary debates, newspaper articles, works of academic and popular history, personal memoirs, and the like. However, it is through the analysis of generally unappreciated works of fiction—both discursive narratives in the form of novels and short stories, and the performative variety represented by feature films—that I propose to consider the still uneasy Franco-Algerian relationship. A peculiarly rich source of ideologically motivated images, this corpus has only very recently been catalogued in anything like a coherent fashion, and has not previously been studied in depth.[24] There is, in consequence, no established canon of significant texts, either literary or cinematic. Yet the very real inadequacies of the existing bibliographical information are more than compensated for by the ample scope which remains for personal discovery, and a number of previously unidentified primary sources are discussed here. This said, the present analysis is emphatically not conceived as a comprehensive study, much less the definitive one. Rather, it presents a survey of some of the principal ideological myths communicated by a sample of prose fiction and feature films, together with a tentative analysis of their characterizing rhetoric.

The selected works are intended to be representative as regards their range of political affiliation and thematic orientation, their dates of publication, and, most contentiously, their literary merit. I do, however, restrict my study to the properly French literature of the Algerian conflict, as opposed to the equally valuable, but substantially documented, Algerian narratives of French expression

[24] A very helpful critical bibliography has been produced by M. Breton and J.-L. Gérard, 'La Guerre d'Algérie au miroir de la fiction française', in the collective *Trente ans après: nouvelles de la guerre d'Algérie* (Le Monde-Editions/Nouvelles-Nouvelles, 1992), 169–89. The most developed discussion of the literary corpus is A.-G. Slama, 'La Guerre d'Algérie en littérature ou la comédie des masques', in J.-P. Rioux, *La Guerre d'Algérie*, 582–602; 676–82.

which have been and continue to be inspired by the memory of what in Algeria itself is called 'the Revolution'.[25] As Albert Memmi explains in an anthology intended to bring together some of the better-known examples of these two very distinct bodies of writing, it was the revelation of the radical division of colonial society during the period of violent conflict which first necessitated this basic critical dichotomy: 'Il fallait . . . signaler le partage des eaux' [It was necessary to draw attention to the watershed].[26] The corpus of texts which constitutes 'Algerian literature of French expression' has been clearly catalogued and extensively analysed: it is of undoubted and undeniable importance. However, it is not the subject of this book.

The focus of the present study is rather upon the neglected final phase of a much older tradition: namely, French colonial literature, understood here as writing produced in, and/or dealing with, the nation's overseas empire. It was in the 'age of imperialism', the period of European expansionism between about 1870 and the Great War, that literature—and particularly fiction—was, like public education, first consciously conceived of by French imperialists as a weapon in their propaganda armoury. This overtly instrumental view of cultural productions became even more obvious as part of the process of French colonial consolidation which occurred between the wars. Indeed, what Jules Ferry had done for the schools of the Third Republic, periodicals such as *Outre-Mer* [Overseas] and contemporary prefaces did for *le roman colonial*, foregrounding its ideological aims as France continued to seek colonial compensation for domestic upheavals.

Colonial Algeria was thus by no means a case apart. However, as a result of the dedication and energy of its literary defenders, the territory became and remains the clearest possible example of the use of the novel as a political tribune: specifically for *la colonie de*

[25] For a useful introduction to this material see C. Achour, 'La Guerre de libération nationale dans les fictions algériennes', in the collective *Trente ans après*, 145–68; cf. C. Achour, *Dictionnaire des œuvres algériennes en langue française* (L'Harmattan, 1991); See also C. Bonn, *Le Roman algérien de langue française* (L'Harmattan, 1985); J. Déjeux, 'Essai de bibliographie algérienne, 1er janvier 1954–30 juin 1962: lectures d'une guerre', *Cahiers nord-africains* (ESNA), 92 (Oct.–Nov. 1962); J. Déjeux, 'Romans algériens et guerre de libération', *L'Esprit créateur*, 26/1 (Spring 1986), 70–85.

[26] *Écrivains francophones du Maghreb: anthologie* (Seghers, 1985), 12. Memmi himself previously edited 2 volumes which split the Maghreb's writers along the lines which I suggest: *Anthologie des écrivains maghrébins d'expression française* and *Anthologie des écrivains français du Maghreb* (Présence Africaine, 1964 and 1969). In this he followed the pattern established by Jean Déjeux's bibliographical and critical work, a model which has subsequently been adopted by commentators like Achour and Bonn.

peuplement [colonization characterized by large-scale civilian settlement]. In their rejection of the 'littérature d'escale' [port-of-call literature] of metropolitan tourists and their quest for aesthetic autonomy, the theoreticians of the 'Algérianiste' movement made particularly plain their commitment to exploiting the opportunities provided by fiction for ideological formation and reinforcement.[27]

To undertake an ideological analysis of the French literature and cinema of the Algerian war is, inevitably, to make a number of assumptions about the nature of the relationship obtaining between art and life. However, it is certainly not to suggest that French writers and film-makers were able to exert a direct influence on the process of decolonization. On the contrary, the contemporaneous literary and cinematic production was primarily remarkable for its political impotence. Indeed, to approach the question in these terms is surely to misunderstand the nature of all cultural products. For, if I, again following Jameson, 'will argue for the priority of the political interpretation of literary [and cinematic] texts',[28] this is most certainly not because I believe that French producers of fiction should, or could, have put a stop to the war or have exerted a comparable influence over its day-to-day conduct. Rather, I do so because I consider that narratives are possessed of a unique capacity to communicate ideology. Whether or not literature can change the attitudes of its readers, and if so how, has been the subject of continuous, intense, and frequently acrimonious debate since Aristotle; recent developments in critical and film theory have only served to fuel the speculative fire. For this reason, I shall limit myself to a very modest project: the present study seeks to identify and to explicate a range of literary and cinematic texts which may have tended to reinforce or, less frequently, to undermine the ideological stances of certain 'integrated' readers of both fiction and film.

[27] See P. Siblot, 'Pères spirituels et mythes fondateurs de l'Algérianisme', in M. Mathieu (ed.), *Le Roman colonial* (L'Harmattan, 1987), 29–59. Also see, among others, M. Astier-Loutfi, *Littérature et colonialisme: l'expansion coloniale vue dans la littérature romanesque française, 1871–1914* (Mouton, 1971); T. August, *The Selling of the Empire: British and French Imperialist Propaganda, 1890–1940* (Westport, Conn., Greenwood Press, 1985); A. Calmes, *Le Roman colonial en Algérie avant 1914* (L'Harmattan, 1984); H. Gourdon, *et al.*, 'Roman colonial et idéologie coloniale en Algérie', *Revue algérienne des sciences juridiques, économiques et politiques*, 11/1 (Mar. 1974; special number on this theme); H. Ridley, *Images of Imperial Rule* (London, Croom Helm, 1983); W. Schneider, *An Empire for the Masses: the French Popular Image of Africa, 1870–1900* (Westport, Conn., Greenwood Press, 1982).

[28] *The Political Unconscious*, 17.

The term 'integrated reader' I take from A. P. Foulkes, who defines it as: 'a reader [who] attributes to a text meanings which he[/she] considers to be totally natural and spontaneous, but which may in fact derive from . . . integration propaganda'. The concept of integration propaganda is itself drawn from the pioneering work of Jacques Ellul, who has emphasized that ideological messages have the greatest impact when they tend to reinforce the consumer's existing opinions and beliefs.[29] So, the model of reading proposed in this analysis is not the conspiratorial one of vertical political propaganda, in which wicked colonialist writers manipulate images in order to dupe an innocent French readership, but rather one of sociological integration propaganda in which the postulated reader is a willing accomplice in the self-justifying mystification of historical events.[30] This is a perspective which recognizes that narratives are cultural creations which cannot be convincingly analysed by means of a mechanical comparison of their images with historical 'reality': they must be understood rather in terms of the conditions of their production and consumption. To this end, and to obviate the need for the type of public-opinion-poll data which would be required for an analysis of the practical effects of fiction on public attitudes,[31] I combine Foulkes's model of the reading process with that proposed by the German reception theorists, including particularly Wolfgang Iser's concept of the 'implied' reader. Defined as the reader constructed by the text itself, a reader who 'embodies all those predispositions necessary for a literary work to exercise its effect—predispositions laid down, not by an empirical outside reality, but by the text itself',[32] it is this transcendental figure rather than 'real' readers that I shall invoke when discussing the ideological impact of the narratives under discussion.

The basis of my claim that a limited number of fictions may actually have been able to pierce the veil of false consciousness surrounding the Algerian war, as epitomized by the myths of the civilizing mission, the one and indivisible Republic, and the war

[29] A. Foulkes, *Literature and Propaganda* (London, Methuen, 1983), 28; see also 29–36. Cf. J. Ellul, *Propagandes* (Armand Colin, 1962), and see G. Jowett and V. O'Donnell, *Propaganda and Persuasion* (New York, Sage, 1992), 221–2.

[30] Foulkes, *Literature and Propaganda*, 31–2.

[31] See S. Chatman, *Coming to Terms: The Rhetoric of Narrative in Fiction and Film* (Ithaca, Cornell Univ. Press, 1990), 184–203.

[32] *The Act of Reading* (London, Routledge & Kegan Paul, 1978), 34; cited by C. Belsey, *Critical Practice* (London, Methuen, 1980), 35. See 'Readers and the Concept of the Implied Reader' in Iser, *Act of Reading*, 27–38.

without a name, is the belief that 'art can actively demystify, can catch the forces of integration unawares as it were, and induce a moment of self-reflection, however brief'.[33] This statement raises in turn the problem of the relationship between ideological defamiliarization and formal innovation, which must briefly be considered here.

It was the Russian Formalists who first drew attention to the processes of defamiliarization or 'making strange' (*ostranenie*) as the key to an understanding of artistic productions. However, as applied to the study of narrative, the group's insistence on the variety of 'literary devices' used to 'foreground' the *syuzhet* [discourse] at the expense of the *fabula* [story] served above all to emphasize the literary text's radical independence of the wider society in which it was produced. Predictably, the lack of a social dimension has prompted a number of vigorous Marxist critiques of the Formalist conception of literature, including particularly that associated with Mikhail Bakhtin. This language-centred model has been usefully summarized by Ann Jefferson, who, moreover, draws attention to its compatibility with later, 'post-Saussurean', literary theory:

> The main thrust of the interesting critique of Formalism made by the Bakhtin school . . . is based on the claim that all use of language, including a literary use, is both social and ideological. The advantage of this argument is that it allows one to define literature's relation to reality in a much more positive and coherent way: both literature and the reality which it represents are of the same order and, according to Bakhtin, this order is ideological. But although literature is necessarily ideological, its qualities as literature have a distancing effect on the ideologies that it represents, and so allows the reader to become aware of them as ideologies. The structuralist view of language also yields a much more flexible and wide-ranging view of the relationship between literature and reality. Both literature and social or cultural reality are defined by structuralist theory in semiotic terms, so that (as in the Bakhtinian theory) they are seen as belonging to the same order.[34]

This persuasive formulation is one which has important similarities with both the Althusserian Marxist model of Pierre Macherey and the arguments of semioticians like Roland Barthes and Julia Kristeva. So, on the one hand, Macherey's 'production' theory of

[33] Foulkes, *Literature and Propaganda*, 35.

[34] 'Russian Formalism', in A. Jefferson and D. Robey, (eds.), *Modern Literary Theory: A Comparative Introduction* (London, Batsford, 2nd edn., 1986), 24–45; see also D. Forgacs, 'Marxist Literary Theories', ibid. 166–203, and esp. 191–9.

literature holds that every text is inherently incomplete and contradictory, precisely because of its existence as a distinct ideological practice: the specific characteristics of the fictional narrative are such that it is distinct from and in conflict with the ideology which prompted its creation and to which it vainly attempts to give a coherent voice. While, on the other, Kristeva 'emphasizes the revolutionary nature of literary language, as one which renders explicit the total signifying process [*signifiance*] of language, something that is not acted out in automatized practical language'.[35]

It was in *S/Z*, previously noted for its seminal analysis of the literary text's existence as a network of linguistic and cultural codes, that Roland Barthes made his famous distinction between the *lisible* (readerly) work which is passively consumed and the *scriptible* (writerly) text which must be actively produced.[36] By establishing the 'plural' or 'polyphonic' text as the positive value in this differential model, Barthes did two important things. First, he emphasized the reader's creative role as the producer of meaning; a position which would also be adopted by Iser and the reception theorists, and which is arguably implicit in the concept of defamiliarization itself.[37] Second, he breathed new life into the Formalist tradition, which, as David Robey has argued, 'attaches overwhelming importance to the element of innovation in literature, thus reflecting the permanent revolution in poetic language, and in literary forms in general, brought about by the modernist movement from the later nineteenth century onwards'.[38] Indeed, for the Barthes of *S/Z*, it is only through radical formal innovation that a truly revolutionary discourse becomes possible: that is to say, a mode of writing that maintains the widest possible plurality or polyphony, and which may thus successfully oppose what he calls the 'imperialism' of cultural codes (and of the ideological assumptions which they both reflect and encourage).[39]

As we shall see, only a small minority of French producers of fiction and film have looked to radical formal innovation in order

[35] Ibid. 197; see also 177–83 for a summary of Macherey's position.

[36] p. 10. See Belsey, *Critical Practice*, 103–9, for a useful summary of Barthes's position, as well as for an intriguing analysis of Barthes's debt to Macherey. See also A. Jefferson, 'Structuralism and Post-Structuralism', in Jefferson and Robey, *Modern Literary Theory*, 92–121, and esp. 107–12.

[37] See Jefferson and Robey, *Modern Literary Theory*, 45.

[38] 'Modern Linguistics and the Language of Literature', in Jefferson and Robey, *Modern Literary Theory*, 46–72, 55.

[39] p.212; cf. 25–30.

to cast new light on the Franco-Algerian conflict; while the overwhelming majority have preferred the tried and trusted illusionism, closure, and hierarchy of discourses of what Belsey, following Barthes, refers to as the 'classic realist' narrative.[40] The extent to which these few writers and film-makers have succeeded in their pursuit of the minority cause of experimentation will be considered in due course, as will the impact of the realist majority. As for the basic distinction between fiction and non-fiction, this will itself be seen to be blurred in those narratives which take the Algerian war as their subject, with the best-represented *genres* being the highly autobiographical novel and the quasi-documentary film. This fact is a function of the clear primacy of ideology over artistic self-referentiality in what is very much a politically committed corpus.

Of the hundreds of literary texts spawned by the Algerian war, some fifty have been retained for more or less detailed analysis in the pages which follow. I shall propose elements both of a chronology and a typology for this body of writing without being a slave to either, preferring instead to follow the thread of ideological reference. The works in question are likely to be unfamiliar in many cases, a fact which underlines the importance of non-canonical fiction in the Algerian context. This is not to say that the work of a *monstre sacré* like Camus will not feature here, but it is to suggest that such celebrated literary figures will be very much the exception to the general rule.

My reading of the corpus will seek to focus critical attention on the range of ideological myths habitually associated with the principal parties to the Algerian conflict: the French soldier, the metropolitan observer, the European colonizer, and the colonized Algerian. As a reflection of its historical and thematic importance, the French military presence in Algeria will be further subdivided into the élite soldiers of the parachute regiments, the conscripted troops of the *contingent* [mobilized national servicemen], and senior army officers. Each of these categories of participant will be looked upon both as a socio-political entity and as a literary archetype; indeed, it is precisely in the tension between historical specificity and fictional image that I shall seek to identify both artistic mystification and demystifying art.

The discussion is divided into three sections: Part I concentrates on the problematic of *la sale guerre* [the dirty war], as articulated by

[40] *Critical Practice*, 70.

literary material produced during the conflict itself; Part II switches the focus to the problematic of memory in the literature produced since 1962; while Part III is devoted to the feature films inspired by the war. Chapter 1 thus introduces the central literary myth of the paratrooper, which I argue is a paradigm of the political imaging of the war as a whole. The critical arguments rehearsed in this opening section of the discussion will be applied in Chapter 2 to the literary myth of the *seigneur* [feudal lord] as uttered with reference to French staff officers. This rhetorical figure will lead, by way of the intellectual preoccupation with torture, to an analysis in Chapter 3 of the self-images proposed by liberal critics of the French war effort, both metropolitan and *pied-noir*. The rare images of the conflict produced by French Algeria's most renowned literary son, Albert Camus, will form the subject of Chapter 4, which concludes this analysis of contemporaneous fictional representations of the war. As the focus switches from the war as present politics to past trauma, Chapter 5 provides a survey of the literary role of the metropolitan French conscript as both producer and protagonist. Chapters 6 and 7 will complete the literary picture by drawing attention to the respective images of the two groups most directly and permanently affected by events in Algeria, namely the settler community and the territory's indigenous population. Chapter 8 will extend the discussion's coverage into the sphere of film by means of a chronological and typological survey of the cinematic narratives generated by the war, thus permitting both formal and thematic comparisons with the literary corpus.

In this way, I shall endeavour to show the contribution made by these variously communicated narratives to the collective memory of the most traumatic French experience since the Liberation. This is a project which is conceived as a modest contribution to that much wider scientific engagement with France's recent past which has as its ultimate goal, in David Schalk's peculiarly apt phrase, 'amnesty without amnesia'.[41]

[41] *War and the Ivory Tower*, 179.

Part I

Waging a Dirty War, 1954–1962

I

THE MYTH OF THE PARATROOPER

In his 1962 novel *Entre chiens et loups* [Between Dogs and Wolves],[1] the liberal Catholic writer Gilbert Cesbron describes the experience of a French schoolmaster who sets his class an essay on the ideal hero. Expecting a range of conventional answers, the teacher is horrified to discover that his star pupil has chosen a disturbingly contemporary subject:

> 'Il s'élance du ciel, tel un archange: mais dans sa tenue bariolée d'homme-léopard, il règne aussi sur la jungle. C'est donc à la fois la légende dorée et la sorcellerie primitive qu'évoque ce guerrier dont les exploits . . . (76–7)
>
> He leaps from the sky like an archangel: but in his mottled leopard-man uniform, he is also lord of the jungle. So both the lives of the saints and primitive sorcery are evoked by this warrior whose exploits . . . '

For the disgusted schoolmaster, we learn, the subject of this paean is to be regarded neither as an 'archangel', nor yet as a 'leopard-man', but rather as 'une brute' (78). The teacher's near-hysterical reaction draws the attention of the reader to the French paratrooper's status as a central mythical figure of the literary and cinematic imaging of the Algerian war. For by the time Cesbron wrote his novel, the *para* had become well-established as a focus for hero-worship; and, as John Talbott has pointed out, this was by no means confined to the impressionable young:

> Indeed, in the France of the 1950s, the paratrooper was as celebrated a figure as Brigitte Bardot. Like Bardot, he fulfilled escapist fantasies. As the retreat from empire created deep divisions in French politics and society,

[1] The title is a play on the expression 'entre chien et loup', meaning dusk or the twilight moment in which diurnal dogs give way to nocturnal wolves. It should be noted that page-extents for the principal literary texts cited are provided in parentheses in the main discussion. All translations are my own.

the paratrooper became as much a political symbol as one of sex, violence, and adventure. Some detected in his image the lineaments of fascism; others saw the last remnant of virtue in an otherwise decadent society. So prolonged and intense did the controversy become that one observer was moved to remark that the paratroopers had spilled more ink than blood.[2]

Just how had the French army's airborne troops acquired this central position in the nation's collective consciousness? Two main reasons suggest themselves. To begin with, the paratroopers came to the Algerian conflict with their collective heroism already well established. One of the youngest elements of the nation's armed forces—their roots went back only as far as de Gaulle's Free French—the *paras* came to Algeria virtually direct from the disastrous Indo-Chinese campaign. The great valour which they had undoubtedly displayed at Dien Bien Phu was only matched by the scale of their suffering, both in the catastrophic battle itself, and on the awful forced marches to the prison camps where they were to be 're-educated' by their Vietminh conquerors. Their bravery in the face of overwhelming odds and dramatically heavy losses were widely reported in the press and by the other media. This was not yet the televised combat of the second Indo-Chinese conflict (America's Vietnam war), but the 'blow-by-blow' coverage of the siege and eventual collapse of the Dien Bien Phu garrison undoubtedly brought about a comparable collective awareness of the fighting as it actually happened.[3]

In *Entre chiens et loups*, a whole chapter is devoted to describing the hero's reaction to the news of the garrison's surrender. His interpretation of the event in the light of earlier 'Great French Defeats', such as Sedan and the first battle of Verdun, is indicative of a wider preoccupation with what was, after all, 'the most humiliating defeat suffered by any western power since the Second World War'.[4] For Cesbron's schoolmaster, as for the French nation as a whole, the collapse of the army's principal Indo-Chinese fortress is a profoundly traumatic development, and one which must be rationalized if it is to be lived with. This is a process,

[2] 'The Myth and Reality of the Paratrooper in the Algerian War', *Armed Forces and Society*, 3 (Fall 1976), 69–70.

[3] See J. Dalloz, *Dien Bien Phu* (La Documentation Française, 1991). For a historical comparison of the conflicts in Algeria and Vietnam as the backdrop to intellectual commitment, see D. Schalk, *War and the Ivory Tower* (New York and Oxford, Oxford Univ. Press, 1991), 14–37.

[4] A. Horne, *A Savage War of Peace: Algeria, 1954–1962*, (London, Macmillan, 1977), 175.

Cesbron makes clear, which necessitates the urgent replacement of the dramatically discredited *imagerie d'Épinal* of the French imperial tradition with a new set of myths: 'L'héroïsme des vaincus et la cruauté des vainqueurs réussirent à inverser la balance: l'Indochine était perdue, mais l'honneur restait sauf—comme toujours!' [The heroism of the vanquished and the cruelty of the victors managed to tilt the scales in our favour: Indo-China had been lost, but our honour was still intact—as always!] (128).

The paratroopers' own rationalization of their defeat in Indo-China—their patent theory of 'revolutionary war'—was to become one of the primary reasons for the length and the intensity of the subsequent war in Algeria. Meanwhile, the public's identification of these particular troops with this most dramatic colonial reverse was such that the event's potential for inflicting damage on the collective self-image of the French nation was effectively neutralized: a truly historic defeat became a source of pride, thanks to the gallantry of the *paras*. Yet this means of maintaining national self-esteem was to prove extremely costly in the long term, as those members of the corps fortunate enough to survive what Bernard Fall has memorably described as 'Hell in a Very Small Place'[5] would seek to expiate their Indo-Chinese failure by winning a decisive military victory in Algeria: this, either with the support of a grateful government and an admiring nation, or, if necessary, in spite of them.

The public prominence of the parachute regiments became all the more marked with their move into the Algerian theatre of operations. This may be explained in terms of the division of labour characteristic of the French war effort. In contrast to Indo-China, which had been the exclusive preserve of career soldiers, the hostilities in Algeria were the affair of both regulars and conscripted troops. Indeed, the vast majority of the roughly half a million French soldiers committed to the territory at the height of the war were recalled reservists or national servicemen. Their duties were those associated with the strategy known as *quadrillage*, the spreading of large numbers of troops across Algeria in an effort to protect both people and property. Farms, roads, railway lines, and other such strategic installations were typical enough postings for very many *appelés* [conscripts]. Guarding the inhabitants and the economic infrastructures of *Algérie française* in this way may have been boring, but it was neither particularly demanding nor dangerous,

[5] *Hell in a Very Small Place: The Siege of Dien Bien Phu* (New York, Lippincott, 1966).

and consequently appealed to successive French governments anxious to avoid conscript losses in an undeclared colonial war.

The real fighting, in contrast, was done by the army's élite units: the paratroopers and the Foreign Legion, with the two overlapping in such regiments as the celebrated 1er REP (Régiment Étranger de Parachutistes). Just as with the public perception of Dien Bien Phu, it was the paratroopers who provided the media and thus the metropolitan French public with an image of colonial conflict that appeared to bear out their preconceptions. Thus it was that heroic images of the mobile war waged by these airborne troops quickly came to dominate news coverage of the conflict, in spite of the fact that the *paras* made up less than 5 per cent of the total French forces in Algeria. This was ultimately to prove a very costly form of national escapism as the parachute regiments became ever more closely associated, both in public opinion and, crucially, in their own minds, with the cause of *Algérie française*.

The combination in the person of the paratrooper of military romanticism and political activism is characteristic of right-wing treatments of the Algerian war. All such representations must attempt to reconcile this supposed romance with the rather more sordid historical reality of the *paras*' counter-insurgency operations in North Africa. Faced with an invisible guerrilla adversary on the one hand, and by a variously hostile Algerian population on the other, the paratroopers resorted to the use of torture to obtain essential military intelligence. This tactic was systematically applied during the Battle of Algiers, as was the summary execution of native 'suspects'. With the publication—and botched suppression—of *La Question* [The Question and/or Torture] (1958), Henri Alleg's account of his own experiences at the hands of the paratroopers of General Jacques Massu's 10th Parachute Division, and with the outcry over the disappearance of Algiers University lecturer Maurice Audin, it became clear that the use of such methods was by no means restricted to Algerians.[6]

The Battle of Algiers may properly be regarded as a watershed in the evolution of public and media attitudes towards the erstwhile heroes of Dien Bien Phu, and this on both sides of the Mediterranean. In metropolitan France, a torrent of accusations regarding

[6] *La Question* (Minuit, 1958). See also P. Vidal-Naquet, *L'Affaire Audin* (Minuit, 1958). The unprecedented defence *in absentia* of Audin's doctoral thesis at the Sorbonne on 2 December 1957 became a rallying point for intellectual opposition to the paratroopers' methods. See Schalk, *War and the Ivory Tower*, 68–9.

the paratroopers' methods marked the beginning of the intellectuals' campaign against torture, which was to contribute significantly to the polarization of public opinion. Feared and hated by the indigenous population of Algiers, and branded the French equivalent of the Gestapo by their metropolitan critics, the *paras* were nevertheless hailed as heroes and saviours by the *pieds-noirs*, understandably grateful for the removal of the threat of bomb attacks from the streets, cafés, cinemas, and dance-halls of the territory's capital. Thus was marked a crucial stage in the paratroopers' identification with the cause of *Algérie française*, a process which would lead many of their number to challenge the governments and institutions of both the Fourth Republic and its Gaullist replacement. In the case of the 1er REP, this commitment to the preservation of French Algeria would only end with the disbanding of the regiment and the execution of its most recalcitrant members (such as leading OAS figures Roger Degueldre and Albert 'Bobby' Dovecar): an outcome which can in large measure be attributed to the intoxicating effect on the officers concerned of their own paratrooper mythology.

We may go further and state that this particular myth is a paradigm of the politically motivated imaging of the Franco-Algerian conflict. This is clearly recognized by John Talbott, who concludes that 'as the French role in Algeria became the obsessive preoccupation of French politics, [the paratrooper] became a vehicle for comment on the political and social issues of the war, a means of simplifying them and stripping them of their ambiguities'. The complex reality of the conflict was thus replaced by two competing sets of apparent certainties, each with its patent version of the paratrooper myth: 'For the press of the Left, the *para démoniaque* became a symbol of the unequivocal opposition to the government's Algerian policy, just as the *para angélique* became in the columns of the press of the Right a symbol of *Algérie française*.'[7]

The mediatic 'split personality' of the paratrooper is primarily attributable to the dual policy of repression and reform pursued by successive French governments in Algeria, including that of de Gaulle himself up to September 1959.[8] What this approach entailed was the destruction of the nationalist guerrillas, while at the same time other members of the French army—most notably the suppos-

[7] Talbott, 'Paratrooper', 79–80.

[8] This dual approach was best symbolized by the (economic) Constantine and (military) Challe 'Plans' pursued under de Gaulle.

edly non-military *Sections administratives spécialisées* or 'SAS' units—sought, as part of a wider package of political and economic improvements, to better the lot of the native population from which the rebels sprang. As the spearhead of the authorities' repressive apparatus, the *paras* were, like the Legion, given considerably more scope for displays of military force than of reforming zeal. Nevertheless, the fact that they did come to see themselves as the incarnation of both aspects of the army's pacification effort cannot be doubted. The symbolic importance of the title chosen by paratrooper Pierre Leulliette for his 1961 account of service in Algeria —*Saint Michel et le dragon, souvenirs d'un parachutiste* [Saint Michael and the Dragon: A Paratrooper's Memoirs] (1961)—is clearly revealed against this backdrop. Part archangel (Michael was the *paras*' adopted patron saint), part monster; an image of the paratrooper which accurately reflects the deep ambivalence of the colonial authorities' response to the armed challenge of the Algerian nationalists.

Both versions of the myth of the *para* are, by definition, distortions of the historical role played by airborne troops in the Algerian war. However, this fact should not lead us to underestimate the mythical figure's touchstone status in the rhetoric of the French mass media. Indeed, the preferred image of the paratrooper provides the key to an awareness of the competing, and often violently antagonistic, positions adopted by groups and individuals on the Algerian question as a whole: once the relevant stance on the *para* has been discovered, the associated political and ideological framework can frequently be deduced (just as it can from the relevant attitude to torture). This is particularly true of the representations of the paratrooper communicated by fictional narratives (and, indeed, by film), with the result that an examination of the literary imaging of the paratrooper does not merely draw attention to the position occupied by the Algerian war in the French collective consciousness, but rather gets to the very root of that society's Algerian problematic. The *para* is either wholly good or wholly evil, much as his FLN opponent is either a barbarian or a valiant heir to the glorious tradition of the (French) Resistance. Hero or villain? Terrorist or freedom fighter? Such questions should not be dismissed as merely semantic considerations; for an historical tendency to Manichaeism is very much a given of the French cultural identity, and it is no coincidence that the spirit of Dreyfus should so regularly have been invoked both by contemporary critics of the

Algerian war and by later, less impassioned commentators. The directly competing versions of the *para* myth reveal this black-and-white way of perceiving and conceiving of the war, and the world, in a strikingly clear fashion. It is for this reason that we now begin our discussion of the literary imaging of the Algerian conflict by looking in detail at Jean Lartéguy's best-seller of 1960, *Les Centurions*, a novel that could be found on every railway bookstall, and which exemplifies the myth of the *para* more obviously than any other.[9]

The 'centurions' of the novel's title are a group of paratroopers, of differing opinions and from various backgrounds, brought together by the novel's central figure, Lieutenant-Colonel Pierre-Noël Raspéguy, in order to fight the FLN in Algeria. What these men share is a common experience of defeat in Indo-China, coupled with a sense of alienation from metropolitan French society. Taken in hand by Raspéguy, they will set about revitalizing a run-down colonial parachute regiment in order to produce a new breed of French troops for a new type of 'revolutionary' war: the 'Soldats de l'An Zéro' [Soldiers of the Year Zero], as another member of France's new model army was to put it.[10]

Raspéguy himself is transparently based on the historical figure of Marcel Bigeard, the most celebrated and 'mediatic' of all the *para* colonels. Like Bigeard, who was known personally to Lartéguy—himself a former *para*—he may usefully be considered in the same light as the commanding officer of another ex-paratrooper, Jean-Yves Alquier, 'qui est comme nous tous avant tout "para"' [who, like all of us, is a 'para' first and foremost].[11] With his junior officers, NCOs, and men, Lartéguy's colonel epitomizes the *soldat d'élite*, conforming to the right-wing stereotype of the paratrooper as the incarnation of military efficiency on the one hand and the quintessence of patriotic courage on the other. This is most clearly evidenced by his masterly orchestration of an operation against a particularly tough band of rebels. Having located the guerrillas, responsible for a fatal ambush on one of his officers and a conscripted man, Raspéguy sets about destroying them:

[9] *Les Centurions* (Presses de la Cité, 1960; refs. are to the 'Presses Pocket' edn., 1961). See D. O'Connell, 'Jean Lartéguy: A Popular Phenomenon', *French Review*, 45/6 (May 1972), 1087–97.

[10] P. Héduy, *Au lieutenant des Taglaïts* (La Table Ronde, 1960), 19.

[11] *Nous avons pacifié Tazalt* (Robert Laffont, 1957), 25.

Accroupi, les jambes croisées, à côté de son poste de radio, Raspéguy mâchonnait une vieille tartine de pain enduite de ce pâté des rations militaires qui semble avoir été fabriqué avec de la sciure de bois et des déchets. Devant lui une grande carte dans un étui de plastique sur laquelle il faisait des marques à grands coups de crayon rouge et bleu, à mesure que chaque compagnie lui donnait sa position.

Le commandant de Glatigny qui revenait des mortiers vint s'asseoir près de lui.

'Ça ne se présente pas trop mal,' dit Raspéguy. 'Le bouclage se resserre et les gars se tiennent bien. Les pertes?'

'Quatre morts et sept blessés. Les morts sont tous chez Esclavier.' (368)

Squatting cross-legged on the ground beside his radio set, Raspéguy chewed on a stale slice of bread spread with the sort of military ration pâté that seems to have been made from sawdust and scraps. Spread out in front of him was a large map in a plastic holder on which he drew with great strokes of his red and blue pencils as each company reported its position. Major de Glatigny who had just returned from the mortar batteries came and sat down beside him.

'It's not looking too bad,' said Raspéguy. 'We've got them surrounded and the lads are holding out well. What about the losses?'

'Four dead and seven wounded. The dead are all from Esclavier's unit.'

This image of the *para* officer is an interesting one in several ways. To begin with, the fact that Raspéguy should be seen to be roughing it with his men is obviously important. Here we see the new style of military commander, more concerned with results than formal hierarchies, and caring little for his creature comforts. That those results will be achieved is beyond doubt: his mastery of the situation is reinforced with every stroke of his symbolically coloured pencils. Such control is based on the obvious superiority of his 'lads', courageously and efficiently putting his plan into practice in spite of their losses. For Raspéguy, whose single-minded pursuit of victory accurately reflects the historical obsession of the parachute regiments with *efficacité*, the dead and wounded are only of significance in so far as their numbers may be a factor in the outcome of the battle.

It is Raspéguy's insistence that the deaths of his men should always be useful that sets him against the criminal blundering of the military traditionalists in Algeria, just as it leads him to condemn the French army's lack of mobility from Verdun to Dien Bien Phu. With his lightly equipped airborne troops, the colonel will aim at new standards of performance on the basis of a new military ethos. What is needed now, Raspéguy argues, is a new type of army for a new type of war: 'Tous dans la merde avec la même boîte de ration . . . une véritable armée populaire, commandée par des chefs qu'elle se choisit en quelque sorte' [Everyone in the shit with the same rations . . . a genuinely popular army, led by officers who are, in a way, chosen by the men themselves] (295–6).

His men are thus indoctrinated with a conception of warfare which lays a particular stress on death as a function of military utility. Such a cult of death is obviously by no means restricted to this particular corps in this particular theatre of operations: a similar insistence on the ever-present threat of death could be found in the military literature of any nation. However, in the creative writing generated by the Algerian war this theme was to take on an important political dimension. For to insist on *para* deaths was to invoke the heroic spirit of Dien Bien Phu and to underline the risks run, yet again, by the military defenders of France's overseas empire. Both that spirit and those risks would be contrasted with the 'decadence' supposedly tolerated by a metropolitan society from which the paratroopers had been physically excluded by their years of combat abroad, and from which they had consequently become wholly estranged.[12] The cult of death was thus a crucial element in the *esprit para*, as the paratroopers' patent view of themselves, the war, and the world was to become known.[13] The components of this internally coherent, but historically disastrous *Weltanschauung* may, for the purposes of analysis, be divided into the commonplaces of military romanticism on the one hand, and instances of a more specific political mythology on the other.

Perhaps the most obvious of these military-romantic clichés is the notion that the French paratrooper is somehow more masculine than his civilian counterparts: a 'real man'. This type of thinking is regularly demonstrated in Lartéguy's novel, which often dwells on the physical perfection of its heroes. In this way, a cult of the physique serves to stress the distance supposedly separating Colonel Raspéguy and his men from lesser mortals, and specifically the fictional representatives of all those who would 'abandon' the French population of Algeria and the friends of France amongst the

[12] The alleged decadence of metropolitan writing on the colonies—and particularly that of supposedly superficial travelogues, decried as 'la littérature d'escale' [port-of-call literature] in the Algerian context—is commonly referred to by French and other colonial writers. See P. Siblot, 'Pères spirituels et mythes fondateurs de l'Algérianisme', in M. Mathieu, (ed.), *Le Roman colonial* (L'Harmattan, 1987), 41. The theme of the decadence of the mother country is, of course, as old as colonialism itself.

[13] See esp. G. Perrault, *Les Parachutistes* (Seuil, 1961), 157–67.

indigènes [natives], together with the nation's valiant military defenders, simply because they judge it politically expedient to do so. The parliamentary schemers of the Fourth Republic thus join the bleeding hearts and fellow-travellers of the Parisian intellectual establishment in being contrasted physically as well as morally with Lartéguy's *para* heroes: a connotative dichotomy which reveals a properly fascistic line of reasoning. For it is by virtue of their superior physical fitness that the paratroopers' vigorous defence of *Algérie française* is magically deemed to be the only defensible political stance. As Roland Barthes once put it, physical plenitude is erroneously taken to establish a moral clarity: only the strong individual can be right.[14]

This sort of thinking underpins Lartéguy's depiction of the transformation of a group of recalcitrant conscripts into paratroopers, a metamorphosis which entails a moral elevation just as much as it does a physical improvement. The camp's radio station hammers this message home:

> 'Radio Raspéguy' insiste sur tout ce qui peut dégoûter le soldat de la vie civile. Le monde extérieur est présenté comme vil, pourri, sans grandeur, le pouvoir comme se trouvant aux mains d'une bande d'escrocs de petite envergure.
>
> Mes camarades disent déjà 'nous autres', par opposition à tout ce qui ne porte pas la casquette et la tenue camouflée. Ils sont propres, nets, ils deviennent agiles; ils sont purs, tandis qu'en France règnent la corruption, la lâcheté, la bassesse, 'le monde du péché' de nos monastères. (328)
>
> 'Radio-Raspéguy' insists on everything that is liable to disgust the soldier with civilian life. The outside world is presented as vile, rotten, and lacking in grandeur, with power concentrated in the hands of a gang of small-time crooks.
>
> My comrades are already saying 'we paras', as opposed to anybody and anything that doesn't wear our peaked cap [i.e. of the type designed personally by Raspéguy—like Bigeard—for his 'boys'] and our camouflage uniform. They have become clean, tidy, and agile; they are pure, whereas life in France is dominated by corruption, cowardice, and vileness, 'the world of sin' that they talk about in our monasteries.

This moral and physical health is similarly insisted upon in Lartéguy's regular celebration of *para* virility. In sharp contrast to the 'eunuchs' and 'females' who dominate Parisian political and intellectual life, Raspéguy and his men exert a powerful sexual attraction over all those women with whom they come into

[14] *Mythologies* (Seuil, 1957), 186.

contact—from Vietminh nurses to the wives and mistresses of the metropolitan bourgeoisie—and the text abounds with examples of their womanizing. In the Algerian context, this will mean *para* conquests at all levels of colonial society: Raspéguy has a fling with a Spanish beauty from Bab-El-Oued; Esclavier becomes involved with the wife of a pillar of Algiers high society; Glatigny wins the heart—and with it, crucially, the conversion to support for the French colonial cause—of a glamorous FLN militant; handsome young soldiers charm the veiled Algerian women whom they transport to work in army trucks to break a nationalist-ordered strike.

Lartéguy's glorification of his heroes' sexual exploits should not be dismissed as merely cheap eroticism, for it has a profoundly political character. Indeed, this image of *para* virility is an important element in the narrative's denigration of any attitude which hinders the fulfilment of the army's imperial aspirations, serving to stress the naturalness of both the men themselves and the ideas which they represent. Conversely, those who challenge the *paras*' political opinions are shown to be lacking in virility themselves and to advocate 'sexless' political systems.[15] This explains Lartéguy's permanent equation of love with the French colonial cause, and especially the ability of that love always to triumph over (anti-colonialist) politics: in the fictional world of *Les Centurions*, love may not conquer all, but it certainly conquers all Algerian nationalist sentiment. As depicted by Lartéguy, in fact, *para* sexuality makes as great a contribution to the cause of *Algérie française* as anything achieved by the paratroopers in their days and nights in the *djebel* [mountains or bush].

My comments thus far will have drawn attention to Lartéguy's continual confusion of political order and natural order, a tendency which, as Barthes has famously explained, is characteristic of mythical discourse. At the root of this politically motivated confusion, Barthes goes on to argue, is a mistaken essentialism, which typifies the Right's way of thinking (about) the world.[16] So in the case of Aïcha, the aristocratic de Glatigny's FLN lover, Algerian nationalism becomes one particular activist, who in turn becomes Woman in need of Love. This characteristically mythical reduction of a collective politics to essentialized individuals is nowhere more apparent than in Lartéguy's extensive use of animal imagery to describe his paratrooper heroes.

[15] Cf. Perrault, *Les Parachutistes*, 154–6.

[16] *Mythologies*, 135–6.

It will be recalled that we opened this discussion of the *para* by citing Gilbert Cesbron's reference to the theme of the leopard-man as a commonplace of the French literature of the Algerian war. Central to this apect of the *para*'s mystique is what John Talbott has described as the 'talismanic' function of the *tenue léopard*. It was the distinctive camouflage pattern of the paratroopers' uniforms which, together with their special regimental berets, visibly set them apart from the rest of the French forces in Algeria. These mottled outfits were, along with the *paras*' supposedly cat-like way of walking, generally held to have given rise to the 'leopard-man' tag. As Talbott rightly suggests, 'the *paras*' camouflaged combat fatigues cast a spell that in retrospect seems extraordinary, and even faintly ridiculous'.[17] Nevertheless, the affective power of this attire was such that even the paratroopers' military critics could not entirely avoid it.[18]

While the paratroopers' effectiveness as fighters can hardly be denied, it is possible to criticize the terms in which that military efficiency is evoked. The *paras*' small numbers, isolation from the main body of the army, experience of combat, and airborne transportation all contribute to their heroic image, as does the suggestion that their battle with the FLN is a straight, one-to-one contest. This is a view which is commonly echoed, but which conveniently ignores the historical disparity between the armed forces involved in the Franco-Algerian conflict. For while the notion of a contest of enemy equals may have a strictly limited numerical validity, it effectively ignores the might of the military apparatus backing up the French combatants. The *paras* may well have been the army's tiny operational fringe, but these few thousand 'real soldiers' had the support of a huge army of occupation to fall back on, with all that this implied in the way of transport, supplies, medical care, and facilities for rest and recuperation.

Exclusivity and isolation, action and purity: these are basic givens of the *para* myth, as, indeed, is the suggestion that the paratroopers and their FLN counterparts share a common identity as *fauves* [wild beasts]. The leopard is the usual choice of the writer seeking to imbue the paratrooper with the dangerous charms of the wild

[17] 'Paratrooper', 73.

[18] See e.g. Colonel Georges Buis's references to 'les hommes peints' [the painted men] and 'les bariolés' [the rainbow men] in his novel *La Grotte* (Julliard, 1961), 50–1. Also of interest is a fictional celebration of the 'painted men' by Bigeard's official photographer, M. Flament, *Les Hommes peints* (Pensée Moderne, 1962).

beast, and it was thus no coincidence that the first, very journalistic, attempt at an academic history of the Algerian war should have included a volume entitled *Le Temps des léopards* (1969).[19] Other feline referents are to be found in the corpus,[20] but the mythical impact of such metaphors is essentially the same: by appealing to the idea of animal savagery, elements of the demonic version of the *para* myth may be exploited in a pragmatic fashion in order to further the idea that the paratrooper is a superman. Moreover, such antithetical references conform to that pattern of thematic tension which characterizes the literature of the French paratrooper as a whole. Whether he be a wild animal, or an avenging angel, or both,[21] the *para* is clearly not like lesser mortals.

One important way in which *Les Centurions* serves to encourage this reading is through the depiction of its *para* heroes as members of a militant sect. In Lartéguy's novel, Raspéguy and his men live independently of the rest of the world: self-contained and self-sufficient, their 'clan' seems more like the rebel bands of the FLN than traditional French military units.[22] Simply calling the roll of its principal members, its officers and NCOs, brings to mind other, similarly clannish, communities: Raspéguy, *le patron* [the boss]; the aristocratic de Glatigny and the iron-hard Esclavier; cheeky little Lieutenant Merle and his best friend, the huge, red-headed Lieutenant Pinières; the mysterious Captain Boisfeuras, the regiment's intelligence officer, and Min, his oriental batman and bodyguard; 'Boudin', the quartermaster, and 'Polyphème', a tough little NCO who wears a black patch over his blind eye and is responsible for drill; and last, but by no means least, Dia, the X^{e} RPC's magnificent Negro *toubib* [medical officer]. What is this but a paratrooper version of Robin Hood and his Merry Men, with the Algerian *djebel* substituted for Sherwood Forest? For Raspéguy and his *paras*

[19] Y. Courrière, *La Guerre d'Algérie, ii: Le Temps des léopards* (Fayard, 1969).

[20] Buis e.g. likens the camouflaged *paras* to tigers and their FLN opponents to jackals (*La Grotte*, 179 and 176 respectively). Cf. J. Brune, *Cette haine qui ressemble à l'amour* (La Table Ronde, 1961), which also dwells on the tiger image, 180–1. Cesbron appeals both to the tiger and the panther when describing his schoolmaster hero's confrontation with a *para* lieutenant (*Entre chiens et loups*, 102); while the jackal is commonly taken to characterize the FLN's fighters. See e.g. F. Valmain, *Les Chacals* (Fayard, 1960), a crime thriller set against the background of the nationalist insurrection.

[21] For Cesbron, the *paras* are 'des anges de proie': *Entre chiens et loups*, 349. While Cesbron also images the *paras* as wolves—most obviously in his title—it is rather their various opponents that Héduy sees in this light, with the paratroopers themselves being imaged as lions: *Au lieutenant des Taglaïts*, 36.

[22] See Perrault, *Les Parachutistes*, 98–106. See also P. Williams, *Wars, Plots and Scandals in Post-War France* (Cambridge, Cambridge Univ. Press, 1970), 93.

are very much outsiders, even if they are not quite the *hors-la-loi* [outlaws] that their nationalist opponents are deemed to be. As for the villainous Sheriff, who better to play this part than de Gaulle himself? This is precisely his role in *Les Prétoriens* [The Praetorians] (1961), Lartéguy's inferior sequel to his principal treatment of the *para* theme, in which his heroes become ever more involved in the political side of the Algerian problem, and are thus brought into direct conflict with *la grande Zohra* [the *pieds-noirs*' abusive nickname for the General] and his post-1959 plans for *une Algérie algérienne*. In the meantime, the men under Raspéguy's command will be isolated from civilian society and its distractions, with their individual identities suppressed in favour of a quasi-monastic mode of existence, complete with its own peculiar rites, and requiring both sobriety and chastity.

As for jump-training, the *paras*' most obvious rite of passage, this is presented in *Les Centurions* in terms of a myth of expiation. More specifically, the initiatory jump focused on by the novel is depicted as an appropriate penance for the paratroopers' retaliation against the adult male inhabitants of a native village in the wake of the murder and ritual mutilation of two of their number. Not only are the paratroopers' reprisals rationalized as the minimum necessary palliative for the dead soldiers' comrades, their precise mode—the paratroopers use their knives only—is put forward as the inevitable result of the barbarism displayed by the throat-cutting and genital-removing Algerian enemy. As Raspéguy explains:

> J'aurais peut-être préféré les grenades et les mitraillettes et qu'ils nettoient tout. Le couteau transforme la guerre en assassinat. Et voilà que nous faisons comme eux, que nous nous salissons les mains comme eux.
>
> Mais peut-être que c'était nécessaire et qu'il fallait commencer, parce qu'on nous a obligés de descendre des pitons dans la plaine, et parce que nous avons été outragés dans notre honneur d'hommes par la mutilation de Merle et de Fleur de Nave. C'est l'homme primitif et non le soldat qui a réagi en faisant cet holocauste. (355)

> I might perhaps have preferred them to clean up the place with grenades and machine-guns. Knives turn war into murder. And here we are doing the same as them, dirtying our hands like them.
>
> But perhaps it was necessary and we had to make a start somewhere, because they've made us come down from the mountain-tops to the plains, and because our manly honour was outraged by the mutilation of Merle and Fleur de Nave. It was the primitive man in us all and not the soldier who retaliated by carrying out this massacre.

So Lartéguy's paratroopers would have preferred to have used their 'clean' modern weapons rather than having to resort to the knife of the Algerian murderer. The fact that they have had to come down, both literally and metaphorically, to the level of their FLN opponents is wholly attributed to the methods employed by the enemy: the *paras* have not been able to 'act like soldiers' because they are locked in a life-and-death struggle with 'primitives'. As Esclavier will reflect a little later in a further rationalization of French military brutality: 'Peut-être pourrions-nous empêcher l'empire de s'écrouler en nous transformant nous-mêmes en barbares . . . ?' [Perhaps we can prevent the empire from collapsing by transforming ourselves into barbarians . . . ?] (378).

Within this preferred perspective, those (conscripted) paratroopers involved in the massacre of the unarmed civilian inhabitants of Rhalem are deemed to be haunted by a guilt which is more imagined than real. This is the main point of the expiatory rite of parachute-jumping as depicted in *Les Centurions*. It falls to Boisfeuras to underline the whole episode's mythical message with a self-congratulatory toast: 'Je bois au saut de Leucade [an ancient Greek expiatory rite] que firent aujourd'hui les deux cents rappelés d'Esclavier pour se laver d'une faute qu'ils estimaient avoir commise' [I drink to the leap of Leukas performed today by Esclavier's two hundred conscripts to cleanse themselves of a sin which they felt they had committed] (384). As for the question of FLN throat-cutting and mutilation, the general literary (and journalistic) insistence on this practice serves to institute the rebel as a barbarian: the theme functions as a kind of mythical shorthand for the presupposed savagery of the French army's colonial adversaries.[23]

By presenting the nationalist guerrillas as barbarians, the French military is inevitably cast in a favourable light. Indeed, as the title of his novel suggests, Lartéguy relies on the *Algérianiste* notion of North Africa's Latin heritage[24] to justify his developed appeal to the myth of the *barbare*. The narrative itself fulfils the mythical promise of the title by making it plain that the French paratroopers fighting in North Africa are most definitely to be regarded as 'centurions', defending a decadent Rome against the hordes amassing on its frontiers:

[23] In an ironic inversion of this tradition, ex-paratrooper Benoist Rey entitled his own account of service in the corps *Les Égorgeurs* (Minuit, 1961).

[24] The significance of the colonialist literary insistence on Algeria's supposed Latin heritage is discussed further in Ch. 6.

Vingt siècles plus tôt, un centurion romain avait rêvé près de cette colonne et guetté au fond du désert l'arrivée des Numides. Il était resté là pour défendre . . . l'Empire, pendant que Rome pourrissait, que les barbares campaient aux portes . . .

Les centurions d'Afrique allumaient de grands feux sur les crêtes de l'Atlas saharien, pour faire croire aux Numides que les légions montaient toujours la garde. Mais un jour les Numides apprirent qu'ils n'étaient plus qu'une poignée, et ils les égorgèrent . . .

Le centurion Philippe Esclavier du Xe Régiment parachutiste, chercha les raisons qu'il avait d'allumer, lui aussi, des feux pour contenir les barbares et sauver l'Occident. (377–8)

Two thousand years earlier, a Roman centurion had dreamed near this column as he kept watch, waiting for the Numidians to surge up out of the desert. He had stayed on to defend . . . the Empire, while Rome rotted and the barbarians camped at the gates of the city . . .

The African centurions would light great fires on the crests of the Saharan Atlas mountains, to make the Numidians think that the legions were still mounting guard. But one day the Numidians found out that there was only a handful of them left, and cut their throats . . .

The centurion Philippe Esclavier of the 10th Parachute Regiment tried to think of the reasons that he too had for keeping back the barbarians and saving the West.

Taking as his starting-point the presence of Roman remains in North Africa, Lartéguy proceeds to build a coherent and plausible Latin myth of the Algerian war.[25] This particular rhetorical figure inevitably raises the question of the appropriateness of an ancient colonial defeat as the model for a reading of history designed to permit a modern colonial victory. It also leads us to go a step further than Esclavier and to ask why, if the whole of Western civilization is as rotten as the *paras* suggest, they should bother fighting for it at all.

Lartéguy's references to Rome draw attention to the theme's double value as an instrument of mystification, for both the Rome of antiquity and that of the Catholic Church are mythically exploited in *Les Centurions*. Predictably, the latter approach is very closely associated with the notion that the Algerian war is in some sense a crusade. However, this particular holy mission is not restricted to the combating of a long-perceived Muslim fanaticism, being rather the continuation of a more modern and genuinely global struggle. This began with the defeat of Germany in 1945,

[25] Cf. Perrault, *Les Parachutistes*, 74–6.

then flared in Korea and, above all, in Indo-China, and is nothing less than the defence of western civilization against the spread of communism: 'cette défense de l'individu . . . cette nouvelle forme de croisade' [this defence of the individual . . . this new form of crusade] (216). The belief that the Algerian conflict constituted an integral part of a world-wide pattern of Moscow-backed aggression may appear hopelessly mistaken thirty years after the event, but was widely accepted in the climate of the Cold War.[26] As Raspéguy himself puts it to a doubter: 'Et l'Algérie? C'est la même guerre qu'en Indochine. Vous n'avez pas lu Mao-Tsé-Toung?' [And what about Algeria? It's the same war as in Indo-China. Haven't you read Mao-Tse-Tung?] (301–2).

So when we read that, in order to win in Algeria, the *paras* will have to become 'des missionnaires . . . qui prêchent la main sur leur crosse de revolver' [missionaries . . . who preach with a hand on the grip of their revolvers] (286), we can be sure that it is their own anti-communist gospel that they have in mind. Indeed, the collective determination of the colonel's historical counterparts to avenge their defeat in Indo-China is regularly reflected in the fictional Algeria of *Les Centurions*. In particular, and like the German *Freikorps* of the interwar years, the *paras* see themselves as having been 'stabbed in the back' by both politicians and intellectuals, a groundless rationalization which would historically encourage the growth of *activiste* praetorianism and thus bring the French polity to the very brink of collapse.

The *paras*' peculiar sense of mission ties in very straightforwardly with the text's monastic imaging of the troops' communal existence: in return for their isolation, asceticism, and surrender of individuality, Lartéguy's paratroopers become military supermen, and thus finally equipped to win 'their' war in Algeria. The 'tourment et bagarre' [torment and fighting] of the famous 'paratrooper's prayer'[27] are primarily repaid by an improvement in *efficacité*: the paratrooper becomes a more effective combatant as a result of the dietary and other restrictions in force. However, on a second level, we can inventory a number of rather wider-ranging benefits, complete with their attendant mythologies.

[26] In fact, this reading of the Franco-Algerian confrontation was accurately identified as mythical as early as 1958: J. Duquesne, *L'Algérie ou la guerre des mythes* (Desclée de Brouwer, 1958), 105.

[27] Quoted in full in E. Bergot, *Les Paras* (Balland, 1971), 148–9. Cf. J.-M. Curutchet, *Je veux la tourmente* (Robert Laffont, 1973).

Basically, what we discover in Lartéguy's novel is a celebration of his paratrooper heroes' transcendence of every aspect of civilian social relations. The *paras*' regular surpassing of accepted physical and military norms is less remarkable than the text's insistence on their rejection of the materialism so characteristic of the civilization which they claim to be defending. This notion appears particularly clearly in the case of Boisfeuras, who, as Glatigny points out to Aïcha, is far above all such venal considerations: 'Il est très riche . . . mais l'argent ne l'intéresse pas; il préfère rester avec nous' [He's very rich . . . but money doesn't interest him; he'd rather stay with us] (475). As Boisfeuras explains to his father, money would be a barrier to his understanding of a deeper truth: 'je ne suis pas à l'aise avec l'argent, j'ai l'impression qu'il me sépare de quelque chose d'essentiel' [I don't feel comfortable with money, I get the feeling that it's keeping me from something essential] (218). Only hinted at here, the nature of this supposedly essential reality will shortly become clear. Meanwhile, it is worth noting that the presence of this mythical theme does not prevent the author of *Les Centurions* from depicting his heroes as mercenaries on occasion. In particular, he self-consciously likens Raspéguy and his men to the mercenaries sacrificed by an ungrateful and fearful Carthage in 238 BC, an event graphically described in Gustave Flaubert's exotic masterpiece *Salammbô* (1862) (421–6).

Even more significant, given the colonial situation in which they find themselves, is the paratroopers' claimed lack of racism. Their community includes Dia, their black doctor, as well as Aïcha's brother, Mahmoudi. Moreover, they have not come across the Mediterranean to praise *Algérie française*, we learn, but to bury it: 'Nous ne sommes point venus ici pour défendre le colonialisme; nous n'avons rien de commun avec les gros colons qui exploitent les musulmans, nous sommes les défenseurs d'une liberté et d'un ordre nouveau [*sic*]' [We have not come here to defend colonialism; we have nothing in common with the big colonists who exploit the Muslims, we are the defenders of a new freedom and order] (328).

The heroes of *Les Centurions* may be above colonialism, but their stand is by no means to be equated with support for Algerian independence. On the contrary, Raspéguy and his men are committed to maintaining French rule over the territory, and, as the spearhead of the military efforts directed towards this end, are able to make particularly good use of one further aspect of their transcendent condition. It is, in fact, the *paras*' much vaunted overcoming of bourgeois morality which is put forward as a rationalization of their use of 'exceptional' methods in Algeria. Given that torture and summary execution constitute essential tools in the *guerre révolutionnaire* in which Raspéguy and his comrades find themselves engaged, they must therefore, if they seriously wish to achieve a military victory in Algeria, be prepared to go beyond received notions of acceptable military practice. As Raspéguy puts it when recruiting his group: 'Nous allons faire une guerre en dehors de tous les règlements' [We are going to fight a war which breaks all the regulations] (308–9). This outlook may set the paratroopers against both the military traditionalists and the metropolitan liberals, but its validity is underlined by their rebel opponents. So at the height of the Battle of Algiers, Boisfeuras will supervise the torture of an FLN bomber before having him disposed of, an approach which would be condemned in Paris, but which is plainly appreciated by the Algerian nationalist:

> Si Millial comprit alors qu'il allait mourir. Ce capitaine qui le regardait, la tête appuyée sur les deux coudes, en avait ainsi décidé.
>
> A sa place il en eût fait autant et, pendant quelques instants, il eut pour lui une bizarre estime car, de tous ces officiers, celui-là était le plus proche de lui. Boisfeuras appartenait à son univers efficace et juste, juste d'une justice qui ne s'embarrasse pas des hommes égorgés, des femmes violées, des fermes brûlées. En même temps, Si Millial eut pitié de cet autre lui-même qui continuerait de vivre sans amis, sans femmes, dans la solitude glacée des hommes qui font et défont l'histoire. (472)

> At that moment Si Millial understood that he was going to die. The captain who was looking at him, with his head propped on his elbows, had decided that that was the way it would be.
>
> In his place he would have done the same, and, for a few moments, he had a strange respect for him, because, of all the officers, he was the one who most resembled himself. Boisfeuras belonged to his effective and just universe, just with a justice that was not frightened to cut men's throats, rape women, or burn farms. At the same time, Si Millial felt sorry for this *alter ego* who would go on living without friends or women, in the icy solitude of those men who make and unmake history.

The ultimate benefit of the *paras*' renunciation of the world of men, Boisfeuras's 'quelque chose d'essentiel', is here revealed to be nothing less than the power to make History: the soldiers' asceticism effectively transforms them into key players in the global power struggle between communism and the Free World. For several of Lartéguy's heroes, the attainment of this higher and more essential plane of existence occurs during the Battle of Algiers, an event which is thus shown to constitute a peculiarly Algerian *dépucelage* or loss of virginity. This is most obviously true in the case of Glatigny, who, having hitherto sought to avoid the unsavoury aspects of the conflict, is forced by his relationship with the FLN militant, Aïcha, to confront the unpleasant reality of *la sale guerre*. As the authoritative Boisfeuras explains for the benefit of a comrade and the integrated reader:

> Le voici à son tour dans le bain! Aucun de nous ne pourra y échapper, jusqu'au moment où nous serons de plain-pied avec les fellagha, aussi couverts de boue et de sang qu'ils le sont. Alors nous pourrons les combattre; nous y laisserons notre âme, si nous en avons une, pour que là-bas, en France, des petits rigolos continuent à s'éventer avec leur bonne conscience. (475)

> Well now it's his turn to be thrown in at the deep end! None of us can avoid it, right up until the time when we are all on a par with the fellagha, and are just as covered in mud and blood as they are. Then we'll be able to fight them; we'll lose our souls in the process, if we've got any, so that back in France, the little frauds can congratulate themselves on their clear consciences.

As a best-seller, *Les Centurions* is a particularly important site of literary mystification: the novel's sheer popularity ensured that it did more than any other comparable work to further the pro-colonial version of the *para* myth. In combination with the negative stereotype projected by the Left, this rhetorical distortion of the parachute regiments' historical role in the war may even have contributed to a basic confusion as regards ultimate responsibility for events in Algeria. After all, as John Talbott reminds us, 'the paratroops were the executants of policy, not policy makers'.[28] This is as true of the counter-mythology of the *para démoniaque* as it is of the paeans to the *para angélique*; so such consciously oppositional testimonies as Henri Alleg's *La Question* (1958) and Benoist Rey's *Les Égorgeurs* [The Throatcutters] (1961) were at least as wide of the historical mark as Lartéguy's fictional celebration of *para* virtues. To suggest that all such politically motivated variations on the theme may have contributed to prolonging the war would almost certainly be to overstate the importance of the myth of the paratrooper. Nevertheless, the *para* was one of a number of such preoccupations which effectively distracted metropolitan public

[28] 'Paratrooper', 78.

opinion from the principal issue at stake in the Algerian war, that is to say the colony's future status. As we shall see, the political campaign against conscription and, above all, the intellectuals' campaign against torture fall into the same category of misleadingly francocentric methods of imaging the conflict in North Africa.

2

THE MYTH OF THE *SEIGNEUR*

Having considered the preoccupation, as much journalistic as artistic, with the élite combat units which formed the cutting edge of the French military presence in Algeria, it is now possible to examine the literary imaging of the men responsible for deploying both these forces and the mass of drafted military manpower: that is to say, the senior officers in charge of the paratroopers' search-and-destroy missions and the conscripts' *quadrillage* duties. Of these senior ranks, that of colonel is by far the most important, both in literary and historical terms: a fact which may straightforwardly be understood in terms of the post-Indo-China politicization of the French officer corps, and especially of those colonels commanding the parachute regiments in Algeria. For as the survivors of Dien Bien Phu increasingly rejected the traditional conception of the army's role—the unquestioning obedience summed up by the term *la grande muette* [the great mute]—the resulting tensions were to manifest themselves most obviously at the level of the individual regiment: with a colonel as its commanding officer, this was the largest unit upon which those suffering from *le mal jaune* [the 'yellow fever' of political activism] could impose their new vision of the French army. Above this level, power continued to reside with the general staff, whose collective attitudes were perceived to derive in equal measure from an uncritical reliance on precedent and a highly developed sense of the demands of personal advancement. The aristocratic products of Saint-Cyr and the École de Guerre would thus be brought into ever more regular conflict with such brash upstarts as the real-life Raspéguy, Colonel Marcel Bigeard, who rose from the ranks to become perhaps the most romantic figure of the Algerian war.

The power and prestige of men like Bigeard, both inside and

outside the army, derived from the fact that in a war which the politicians were ever anxious to deny, and in which the large-scale use of conscripts for combat was deemed politically unacceptable, he and his 'boys' actually did the fighting and other dirty work. The combination of an élite combat role and a high media profile, the latter shortsightedly encouraged by Paris, was to confirm the *para* colonels in their belief both in the special nature of their units, and in their mission to preserve French Algeria. When the governments of the Fourth Republic attempted to depart from what the colonels saw as their Algerian vocation, they would plot the downfall not only of individual administrations, but also, eventually, of the regime itself. The introduction of a stronger form of government under de Gaulle's Fifth Republic would see such men as Argoud, Godard, and Lacheroy seek to preserve their power to wage war in Algeria as they saw fit, a process that was to result in the abortive April 1961 *putsch*, and thus in their own downfall. Both militarily and politically, then, these men would come, in Alistair Horne's words, 'to bestride the Algerian scene like demigods'.[1]

It is with the specific contribution made by fiction to the propagation of the colonels' popular image—that of noble, and ultimately tragic, heroes—that I shall concern myself in the present chapter. To this end, I shall examine three developed literary treatments of the senior army officer, presenting these fictions as a progression from narrative mystification to thematic enlightenment. As all three texts date from 1961, they offer a suitably synchronic sample for the purposes of this analysis. Moreover, in spite of their considerable diversity of political inspiration and literary execution, they are all examples of a broad tendency discernible in the fictional imaging of the senior French officer between 1954 and 1962: specifically, a common appeal to the primary mythical figure of the *seigneur* or feudal lord. In its Algerian incarnation, this archetype may be said to be characterized by a combination of features which include chivalry, mission, creation, judgement, self-sacrifice, and paternalistic service. Indeed, the regular literary insistence on such qualities is only fully understandable on the basis of a properly informed reading of this underlying myth.

The first of these texts for consideration is *pied-noir* activist Jean Brune's best-known work *Cette haine qui ressemble à l'amour* [This

[1] *A Savage War of Peace: Algeria, 1954–1962*, (London, Macmillan, 1977), 167.

Hatred which Resembles Love] (1961), which the campaigning historian Pierre Vidal-Naquet has accurately identified as a major literary focus for the mythology of French Algeria.[2] The central figure in Brune's narrative is an unnamed colonel whose individual identity is, as the lack of a name suggests, entirely constituted by and subsumed in his rank. This character will completely dominate the action of the novel, and it is his perspective which will be adopted from the outset. Indeed, from the novel's opening image of the officer—the reader joins him late at night at his desk, as he pores over a set of files on FLN activists (9)—to its close with the successful completion of his mission against the nationalists' local guerrilla leader, the point of view of the narration coincides to a very large extent with that of the protagonist: we see the world in general, and the Algerian war in particular, through the eyes of Brune's colonel.

More specifically, information about the story-world is communicated by a narrative voice which systematically aligns itself with the novel's principal character and undoubted hero. There is thus a minimal disparity between the protagonist's point of view (whether understood as 'the physical place or ideological situation or practical life-orientation to which narrative events stand in relation')[3] and the position adopted by the third-person narrator. The uniformly sympathetic articulation both of what the character says and thinks, and what he is unable to say or think for himself (most notably the opinions held of him by others, whether friend or foe) serves in turn to construct a position of identification with the character for the reader. Our first view of Brune's Algeria is thus symptomatic of a wider process of pro-military alignment and mediation, in that our immediate access to the colonel's consciousness is, like our admission to any fictional character's thought-processes, 'the standard entrée to his point of view, the usual and quickest means by which we come to identify with him. Learning his thoughts insures an intimate connection.'[4] We may consequently be permitted occasional privileged glimpses into the thoughts of other characters, but

[2] P. Vidal-Naquet, *La Torture dans la République* (Minuit, 1972), 196. This work includes an excellent critical bibliography on the French use of torture in Algeria. On the same subject see R. Maran, *Torture and the Role of Ideology: The French-Algerian War* (London, Greenwood Press, 1989).

[3] S. Chatman, *Story and Discourse: Narrative Structure in Fiction and Film* (Ithaca, Cornell Univ. Press, 1978), 153.

[4] Ibid. 157.

never for long, and only ever to cast a positive light on the thematically and formally dominant central figure.

The Algerian conflict is thus reduced to this select individual's security problem, for the files described in the text's opening paragraph contain clues towards the possible solution of the military puzzle which will preoccupy the colonel—and with him the integrated reader of *Cette haine qui ressemble à l'amour*—for the remainder of its over 700 pages. The object of the colonel's obsessive attention is his immediate counterpart in the FLN, Kim ben Kim. His hunt for this clearly identified adversary gives the novel its basic shape, with the *traque* [manhunt] formula providing ample scope for the elucidation of the text's preferred interpretation of the war. In view of Brune's background of *ultra* [pro-colonial] militancy, it is only to be expected that his principal spokesman should throughout take the side of *Algérie française*, before firing the novel's parting political shot. Following the death of Kim ben Kim and the destruction of his band, the colonel thus reflects authoritatively, if somewhat unoriginally, on Algeria's destiny: 'Nous sommes tous au fond d'un tunnel . . . et tous ensemble . . . nous marchons désespérément vers la lumière!' [We are all deep in a tunnel . . . and together we are desperately walking towards the light!] (706).

The figure of the colonel dominates the novel's fictive space throughout and presides over its narrative and political closure. But what of the character himself? Let us consider the description provided by Ben Driss, an Algerian officer in the French army who deserts in order to join the FLN:

> Le souvenir du colonel l'obsédait. Il lui gardait un respect qu'il n'avouait pas, mais dont la secrète conscience le grandissait à ses propres yeux. Il méprisait l'ordre que servait l'officier, mais il admirait la façon dont celui-ci le servait, l'indomptable énergie tempérée par une indulgence puisée aux sources de l'amour et accessible à la pitié et la souriante simplicité de grand seigneur qui dissimulait à la fois derrière la même élégante mesure de l'humeur, la détermination ou la lassitude, la colère, l'affection, l'impatience, ou la résignation. Ben Driss devinait où se nouait chez le colonel le secret de cette noblesse. Le guerrier cédait toujours devant l'homme et l'homme donnait un sens à la guerre parce qu'il l'empêchait de se dégrader dans l'atroce férocité des combats de bêtes fauves. Le rebelle avait vu trop d'assassinats, trop d'égorgements, trop d'inutiles mutilations. (506)

> He was obsessed by his memories of the colonel. He had maintained a respect for him that he would not admit, but which subconsciously made him loom even larger in his own eyes. He despised the order which the

officer served, but he admired the manner in which he served it: his indomitable energy, tempered by a humanity that sprang from love and had room for mercy, and his good-hearted yet lordly simplicity, which, behind the same elegant façade of irritation, could just as easily conceal determination or weariness, anger, affection, impatience or resignation. Ben Driss could guess where the secret of the colonel's nobility had its roots. The warrior always gave way to the man, and the man gave war a meaning because he prevented it from deteriorating into the atrocious ferocity of a fight between wild beasts. The rebel had seen too many murders, too many throat-cuttings, too many needless mutilations.

Here we see the myth of the *seigneur* appealed to in an exceptionally overt fashion. Yet, revealingly, the examples of savagery cited by way of contrast with the protagonist's self-imposed and ennobling code of military conduct all relate to rebel atrocities: no member of the French forces is actually accused of any particular impropriety. Not that humanitarian considerations always take precedence over military ones for the colonel; very early on Brune's hero is revealed to be a 'military realist' of the purest stripe.[5] As such, he is prepared to countenance both the torture and the summary execution of FLN suspects in order to protect innocent lives, with the arguments in favour of this stance being regularly rehearsed throughout the novel. The relevant rationale is particularly to the fore in an extended argument between the colonel and a liberal priest, referred to simply as 'le Père'. Once again, the lack of an individual name is indicative of the character's representative status, and the confrontation between the two men is very much a set-piece debate in which military realism defends itself against the criticisms of the liberal humanists. Characteristically, the primary theme is that of the military's determination to protect innocent lives whatever the cost. As the colonel vows menacingly: 'J'arracherai la vie des innocents à la souffrance des suspects!' [I shall tear innocent lives out of the suffering of suspects!] (266).

The colonel's robust theoretical defence of torture is duly borne out in practice, or, more accurately, in a carefully contrived 'concrete' situation which conveniently meets all the usually proclaimed preconditions for its use: the certain guilt of those involved, the

[5] A term suggested by Paul Clay Sorum, used in contrast to the 'liberal', 'humanist', or 'moralist' (in the English rather than the French sense) critics of the French army's methods in Algeria. *Intellectuals and Decolonization in France* (Chapel Hill, Univ. of North Carolina Press, 1977), 105–15.

clear and specific threat to innocent lives, the urgent need to know, and the effectiveness of torture in extracting the required information. Yet the fact that Brune's hero should only sanction this scrupulously justified use of torture does not relieve him of the burden of guilt. On the contrary, the *seigneur* suffers for his high-minded sacrifice of the civilized values which he has been brought up to revere (266–7). Indeed, in the name of military efficacy, and in order to preserve western civilization for lesser mortals, the senior army commander has no choice but to take upon himself the heavy burden of this temporary suspension of accepted moral imperatives. The French army's systematic recourse to such aids to interrogation as *la gégène* and *le bain* [electric shocks and prolonged submersion], together with even more inhuman and degrading methods of extracting information from prisoners, is thus transformed into a duty which cannot be shirked: *noblesse oblige*, as it were. By the same token, the colonel is prepared to circumvent judicial procedures in deciding not only the guilt of these same native suspects, but also the punishment which they should receive. The case of a café bomber—whose guilt is, once again very conveniently, beyond any possible doubt—is typical of this rough and ready justice:

> Le colonel revoyait la scène . . . la fureur de la mère et la petite fille couchée dans le café au milieu d'une mare de sang. . . .
>
> C'était toujours le même problème. D'un côté la même carence . . . le même temps perdu . . . de l'autre la guerre et la mort qui frappaient partout à la fois . . . plus vite . . . toujours plus vite . . .
>
> 'Fusillé,' dit le colonel. (88)

> The colonel could still see the scene . . . the distraught mother and her little girl lying on the café floor in a pool of blood. . . .
>
> It was always the same problem. On the one hand, the same inefficiency . . . the same lost time . . . and on the other, the war and death which could strike anywhere and at any time . . . and faster . . . ever faster . . .
>
> 'Shoot him,' said the colonel.

It will now be clear that Brune's narrative seeks to square the celebration of *efficacité* with the claim that the colonel is an exponent of a brand of warfare which may be perceived as noble. The source of the colonel's mythical *grandeur* resides in the text's insistence that the protagonist does not enjoy having to make use of uncivilized methods in the defence of civilization, but rather suffers gravely for it. The characterizing ethical dilemma of every military response to insurrectionary violence in the colonies post-1945 is thus resolved to the satisfaction of Brune, the diehard supporter of *Algérie française*. The hero of his novel deceives, tortures, and murders: methods which may genuinely have had a certain, short-term, military efficacy, but which are invariably surrounded in myth. In particular, the colonel's supposedly monastic sacrifice of the comforts of this world in return for the salvation of those lesser mortals, both French and Algerian, who have been placed in his paternalistic care (336) is quite as spurious as that of Lartéguy's *paras*.

This reading of the French army's pacification effort as an Algerian version of Alfred de Vigny's *Servitude et grandeur militaires* [Military Servitude and Grandeur] (1835) is even more apparent in Brune's treatment of the potential perils of seigneurial power, and specifically the suggestion that the colonel pays for military efficacy not only with his honour, but also with his soul.[6] The risk of perdition supposedly run by the *seigneur* provides one more indication of his essential nobility: by chancing his soul, he proves its mettle. This theme adds mythic spice to the novel's description of the colonel's omnipresence, omniscience, and omnipotence. Consider his surprise arrival—alone, as befits his elevated status—at a lonely mountain village:

> 'Dieu soit loué!'
>
> 'Dieu soit loué!'
>
> Un homme montra du doigt les crêtes de Yemma Halima.
>
> 'Nous t'attendions de l'autre côté,' dit-il, 'au bout de la route ... Et voici que tu tombes du ciel ... Tu est le Diable! ... *el chitane*!' (478)

> 'God be praised!'
>
> 'God be praised!'
>
> A man pointed to the peaks of Yemma Halima.
>
> 'We were expecting you on the other side,' he said, 'at the end of the road ... And here you are, descended from heaven ... You are the Devil! ... *el chitane*!'

Like the devil, the colonel is everywhere present within his sector, and may pop up whenever and wherever he is least expected.

[6] See e.g. Brune, *Cette haine*, 265, 364. Cf. Lartéguy's aristocratic paratrooper, de Glatigny, who, during the Battle of Algiers, accepts the loss of both his 'honour' and his 'soul' in order to dismantle the FLN's bomb networks: *Les Centurions* (Presses de la Cité, 1960), 478–9. However, the most developed working of this theme is to be found in Vladimir Volkoff's celebration of the military *seigneur*, *La Leçon d'anatomie* (Julliard/L'Âge d'Homme, 1980). This novel, the 2nd vol. of Volkoff's tetralogy, *Les Humeurs de la mer*, will be discussed in Ch. 7.

Meeting native representatives in the mountains, or visiting their European counterparts on their farms; handling his troops on the ground, or directing operations from his headquarters; whisked over the rugged terrain by helicopter, bounced over it in a jeep, or slogging through the bush on foot, he is everywhere the complete man of action, seemingly in command of everything and everyone at all times. His omniscience—not to mention his Solomon-like impartiality and wisdom—is as obvious in his dealing with the settlers as it is with the Algerians, whether it be a question of the former group's clandestine payments to the FLN, or those of the latter. Small wonder that the local population should be prompted to think that 'décidément ces Français sont des diables . . . Ils savent tout . . . Des chitanes . . . Des diables . . . Comment peuvent-ils savoir?' [There's no doubt about it: these Frenchmen are devils . . . They know everything . . . Devils . . . How on earth do they find out?] (483). Needless to say, the brutally simple answer to this question—they find out by torturing suspects—is not provided here.

To this all-seeing knowledge of his sector and those who live in it, we must add the characteristically seigneurial ability to provide certainty: the colonel has only to assure his listeners that France will not leave (492), and the wish becomes the subject population's new reality. The fact that his assertion was to be denied by subsequent historical developments serves to highlight the text's utterance of this myth of French colonial permanence, a theme which is reinforced by the narrative's depiction of the *seigneur* as a city-builder. 'Sohane', the colonel's model village, has little in common with the sordid *camps de regroupement* [relocation camps] which were its historical counterparts. Indeed, the community's mythical antecedents are soon established to be the city-states of the classical past, as the colonel's plans for 'his' city make clear: 'Il rêvait de rendre Sohane à son passé romain et de la reconstruire comme ces castellae dont les ruines jalonnent encore les djebels et les steppes d'Afrique' [He dreamed of restoring Sohane to its Roman past and of rebuilding it like the castellae whose ruins still stretch across the mountains and the steppes of Africa] (585).[7] For this fictional representative of the French army's upper echelons, the typically seigneurial tendency to engage in personal empire-building represents an individual contribution to the creation of a new colonial order in

[7] See Ch. 1, n.25.

Algeria.[8] Indeed, the colonel's plans for Sohane reflect those of the military hierarchy for the country which it is deemed to represent in microcosm: an Algeria which will prove to the world that a European–African synthesis is possible (673). Provided, that is, that the old vision of paternalist colonial advance is never challenged by the indigenous majority of Algeria's population. So much for the brave new world of Jean Brune's anonymous hero.

Brune's extended expression of his faith in the colonial enterprise may productively be contrasted with the variously critical images of the senior officer put forward by two other novels produced in 1961, Georges Buis's *La Grotte* [The Cave] and Roger Ikor's *Les Murmures de la guerre* [The Whispers of War]. For all their differences in style and scope, these two works reveal a common political project: that is to say, the demystification of the French military *chef*'s role in the Algerian conflict.

At first sight, the French colonel depicted by Ikor would seem to fit very straightforwardly into the seigneurial mould: 'Il agissait en chef indiscuté et indiscutable, parfaitement sûr de lui, parfaitement indifférent à l'opinion d'autrui' [He acted as an unquestioned and unquestionable chieftain, perfectly self-assured, and perfectly indifferent to the opinion of others] (114). Yet in the pages which follow this first reference to the figure, Berriou's seigneurial persona will be both established and demolished: the narrative will simultaneously erect a monument to this senior French officer and show the subject's feet of clay. This second-level critique of the mystique of Berriou, and those like him, begins immediately the character has been introduced. Indeed, the treatment accorded to the colonel displays throughout a profound ambivalence: specifically, a pattern of tension between political appearances and military realities.

Ikor's colonel is described as a bear-like individual, whose cuddly exterior belies his real ferocity. Indeed, toughness is combined with valour and an obvious integrity to produce Berriou's seigneurial legend. Renowned as a character throughout the army,[9] the colonel is quite simply 'le "patron"' [the 'boss'] (201) for those troops who come under his direct command; a group which notably includes

[8] Colonel Jasson, the hero of Cécil Saint-Laurent's novels *L'Algérie quand on y est* (Le Livre Contemporain, 1958), *Les Passagers pour Alger*, and *Les Agités d'Alger* (Presses de la Cité, 1960, 1961), is a comparable city-builder.

[9] In this he resembles the Bigeard-inflected Colonel Grass in Jules Roy's *Le Tonnerre et les anges* (Grasset, 1975).

the novel's central figure, conscripted sergeant Ludovic Fenns. For better or worse, then, the protagonist is most certainly in complete control, a position justified by his obvious ability to motivate lesser mortals, and thus—like Lartéguy's Boisfeuras—to make history:

[Berriou] appartenait à cette race d'hommes à vues larges et ardeur impatiente qui ne permettent pas à l'humanité de s'endormir dans son confort présent. Homme des cavernes, Berriou eût poussé ses congénères vers la construction de huttes; anthropoïde, il les eût poussés vers l'humanité. Il vous faisait éprouver concrètement que l'Homme est encore en pleine croissance, que l'Évolution continue . . . (244)

[Berriou] belonged to that far-sighted and fiercely impatient race of men which refuses to allow humanity to slumber comfortably in the present. If he had been a caveman, Berriou would have pushed his fellow creatures into building huts; as an anthropoid, he would have pushed them in the direction of humanity. He gave you the concrete feeling that Man is still making rapid progress, that Evolution is still going on . . .

So much for the officer's credentials as a *seigneur.* What, then, of his fall from mythic grace? To answer this question we must turn now to the novel's handling of the problem of torture. While we are left in no doubt that, for Ikor's colonel, *le renseignement* [intelligence] is the key to the Algerian war, the precise nature of the methods which he uses to gather this crucial intelligence is far from obvious, and thus becomes the subject of considerable speculation on the part of the liberal Fenns. The sergeant's increasingly obsessive preoccupation with this central issue is the focus for an extended discussion of the problems raised by the Algerian nationalists' recourse to terrorist violence in their fight for independence. For Berriou, like Brune's anonymous colonel, does not merely impose his will upon his fellow soldiers, he also brings his brand of order to a town.

This patent version of the *pax gallica* consists, first and foremost, in the restoration of security for the town's European inhabitants. So while uncertainty reigns elsewhere in the sector, Berriou's town is relatively free of trouble. However, while the grateful *pieds-noirs* may feel inclined to ask no questions about the means used to restore order, Fenns is compelled to know more. With very little to go on in the way of personal experience, and dissatisfied with official accounts of the anti-terror campaign, Ikor's hero is left with a few bare facts, some worrying rumours, and a set of ever more nagging doubts:

Les faits nus? Berriou . . . avait pris en main le secteur de Descartes; quinze jours plus tard, le terrorisme urbain, qui faisait rage jusque-là, était muselé. Par quels moyens? . . . Et qui torturait, si torture il y en avait? . . .

Comment? Comment? Comment?

Et par qui? (234–5)

The bare facts? Berriou . . . had taken over the Descartes sector; a fortnight later, the urban terrorism which had raged unabated until then had been checked. By what means? . . . And who did the torturing, if indeed there was any torture? . . .

How? How? How?

And by whom?

In practice, the reader becomes aware of the simple answer to the hero's questions long before he himself learns the truth. The eventual 'revelation' that Berriou uses torture to extract information from Algerian suspects is thus anything but a surprise. This confirmation of the sergeant's darkest fears gives rise, nevertheless, to a set-piece confrontation between liberal humanism and military realism, much as in Brune's novel. Fenns thus states his total opposition to the use of torture, while Berriou makes out the familiar case for exceptional methods against an exceptional enemy. This confrontation enables Ikor both to contribute to the wider intellectual campaign against torture and to cut through the prevailing mythology of the military *seigneur* as the pacifier of Algeria.

Interestingly, the formal structure of this climactic final meeting appears initially to favour the colonel rather than the sergeant. For the only time in the novel, in fact, the narrative adopts Berriou's point of view in preference to that of Fenns. Hitherto a combination of non-intrusive third-person narration, conventionally reported dialogue, and the sergeant's interior monologue, the narrative now shifts its centre of focus away from the conscript and towards the career officer. This switch of perspective performs an important defamiliarizing function in the dramatic confrontation which follows. We thus 'see' the opening exchanges through the older man's eyes and within his preferred frame of reference. His is the voice of experience and sweet reason, while the sergeant's verbal assault is merely the latest in a long line of similarly self-righteous onslaughts; he maintains his affability in the face of an objectively intolerable breach of military discipline; his is the calm of the father-figure, to be contrasted with the impetuosity of his young adversary. The scene itself is at the beginning of a chapter, and opens as follows:

'On ne torture pas. C'est tout.'

Fenns se tenait au garde-à-vous, très droit, très haut, face au colonel Berriou assis derrière son bureau. Il avait refusé de s'asseoir, malgré l'aimable insistance de son chef, et tout de suite attaqué . . . A vrai dire, Berriou avait deviné dès l'arrivée du sergent qu'il se passait quelque chose, et ce qui se passait . . . le petit flairait depuis longtemps que papa Berriou savait appuyer sur le champignon quand il le fallait. Il serait instructif de voir ses réactions . . . Et le colonel Berriou s'était disposé à entendre, avec la résignation convenable, et sa propre argumentation toute prête, les belles indignations auxquelles l'avaient habitué les pauvres types des commissions d'enquête et autres journalistes; curieux par surcroît de voir comment le petit s'en tirerait.

Ma foi, le petit ne s'en tirait pas mal du tout. (277)

'You don't torture. That's all there is to it.'

Fenns was standing to attention, very straight, and very tall, across from the colonel seated behind his desk. He had refused to sit down, in spite of his chief's friendly insistence, and had immediately gone on the offensive . . . In truth, Berriou had guessed as soon as the sergeant arrived that something was up, and what that something was . . . the youngster had for a long time suspected that old man Berriou knew how to put his foot down when the need arose. It would be instructive to see his reactions . . . Colonel Berriou settled down to listen, with the necessary resignation, and his own counter-arguments ready and waiting, to the pretty indignation which he had grown accustomed to hearing from the sad cases appointed to commissions of enquiry, together with journalists and those of the same stripe; he was curious into the bargain to see how the young fellow would acquit himself.

Well, well, the young fellow was not acquitting himself badly at all.

This passage opens with what might reasonably be regarded, on the basis of Gérard Genette's famous distinction between 'showing' (*mimesis*) and 'telling' (*diegesis*), as a shown or mimetic narrative element: specifically a conventionally punctuated, but untagged and unattributed, piece of direct speech. We are at once in the thick of the action, and someone is clearly making an important declaration. However, the speaker's initial anonymity precludes our immediate identification with the unidentified character: on the contrary, it is as if the reader is the character's interlocutor, and as such is being spoken to, or even spoken at. This impression is reinforced as the speaker is identified, described in physical/visual terms, and located on the far side of the desk at which Berriou is sitting, and at which the reader too is apparently seated.

Although both the colonel and the sergeant are initially referred to in the third person by an overt (if conventionally unobtrusive) narrator, the narration soon switches to free indirect style and is consequently aligned with the senior officer. The textual signal for this narrative shift is the adoption of Berriou's ideolect (his pet names for Fenns and himself, his preferred euphemism for torture), and there can be little doubt that the reader is being permitted a privileged glimpse into his thoughts as he settles down to 'see' how the sergeant will react. In the conventionally reported reflections which follow (note the return to the third person and the shift to the pluperfect), Berriou's heavily ideologically slanted terminology is maintained ('belles indignations', 'pauvres types'); while the omission of the pronoun and verb before the adjective 'curieux' signals a partial return to the oral style—and the identification with the character—of the free indirect section.

The final comment ('Ma foi, le petit ne s'en tirait pas mal du tout') is neither tagged nor punctuated as the colonel's own words (or, more accurately, his own verbalized thoughts), but is clearly to be regarded as having this status. Once again the report is made in the free indirect style, a form of narration characterized by its generation of ambiguity. However, the relative lack of ambiguity as regards the identity of the narrative voice in this particular instance only leads us all the more urgently to ask which of the two basic perspectives permitted by the free indirect style is being exploited here: are we witnessing a sympathetic fusion of the narrative voice with that of the character, or, on the contrary, an ironic undermining of the latter by the former?[10] In the light of what follows, it is clear that the whole confrontation is weighted against Berriou. Moreover, the subsequent ironic deflation of the colonel's self-image, and with it his previously untroubled world-view, is strongly hinted at by the attention paid by the narrator (when most obviously distanced) to the officer's complacent respect for the polite rituals of a debate which has long ceased to have any real significance for him: his 'aimable insistance', his 'résignation convenable', and his 'propre argumentation toute prête'.

For the fact of the matter is that Fenns has captured the moral high ground with the first shot of the exchange: thanks to his categorical denunciation of torture, Berriou is henceforth on the defensive. Indeed, the colonel's slick line of argument will be seen as not so much made-to-measure as off-the-peg, its glibness only

[10] This dichotomy is persuasively argued for by Seymour Chatman; see *Story and Discourse*, 206–8.

underlined as the sergeant's anticipated 'belles indignations' signally fail to materialize. The lack of an appropriate moral dimension in Berriou's character, hinted at throughout the narrative, will thus be underlined in the dramatic contrast between the ease with which the career soldier considers the question of torture and the emotional turmoil experienced by the conscript. He will rehearse the standard military-realist arguments about innocent lives, but it is Fenns's unswerving refusal to countenance torture which must ultimately prevail in the mind of Ikor's reader.

Perhaps one of the most fascinating literary demystifications of the role played by the senior French officer in Algeria is to be found in Georges Buis's 1961 novel *La Grotte*. Unlike both Brune and Ikor, *le colonel* (later General) Buis had first-hand experience of the conflict, coupled with a remarkable ability to see through the mystifications uttered both by his fellow officers and by the French colonial authorities. It is this unique combination of insights which explains the rare power of *La Grotte*, and which makes the work 'as vivid a description of military operations as exists in the literature of the war'.[11] This vividness is attributable in no small part to Buis's treatment of his central figure, *le commandant* [major] Enrico.

Like *Cette haine qui ressemble à l'amour*, and, indeed, like much of the French military literature of the Algerian war, *La Grotte* focuses on a single operation: in this case, the location and destruction of a major rebel headquarters (the cave of the title), together with its occupants. The scale of this operation can be gauged from the fact that the cave houses nothing less than an entire *katiba*, a batallion-sized force of *Armée de Libération Nationale* (ALN) regulars. The novel opens, *in medias res*, with the latest in a long succession of frustrating near-misses for major Enrico and his men in their struggle against an adversary who is typically hard to pin down. The reader's first information about the story-world thus comes over the military's walkie-talkies, complete with interference and crackle, as directly reported speech. This is a common device for establishing both a sense of immediacy and also an impression of intimacy with the French military heroes, and is regularly used throughout the novel. Moreover, the device allows importance to be attached to the technical details of the operation (by its insistence on call-signs, specialist vocabulary, and military slang), while the physical difficulties of communication caused by the intense cold

[11] J. Talbott, *The War Without a Name: France in Algeria, 1954–1962* (London, Faber & Faber, 1981), 187.

and howling wind serve to draw attention to the harshness of the soldier's lot.

However, the very first words of the narrative—"Ah! négatif, négatif!" ["Oh! negative, negative!"] (11)—are much more than simply a situating reference to the conventions of military communication. Indeed, the first half of the narrative will be devoted to an account of the ten futile months which have preceded this particular exchange: a strategy which serves gradually and cumulatively to situate what is, in fact, an emphatic statement of French military failure in Algeria. The latest disappointment in the narrative present thus gives rise to a developed anachronous summary of events which have occurred in the narrative past: that is to say, the fruitless months spent combing the mountains and caverns of the major's sector, together with an equally futile large-scale operation organized by army corps headquarters, are presented in an extended flashback or, to use Genette's more accurately literary term, *analepsis*.[12]

As the soldiers' string of failures is 'remembered', the narration consistently adopts the point of view of the French soldiers in general and of the increasingly obsessive major Enrico in particular. Free indirect speech is here used to fuse the narrative voice and the central figure's perspective, with the most frequently used grammatical subject being the apparently impersonal but actually sympathetic pronoun 'on'. So, for instance, we read at the end of one more vain operation:

> Oui, c'était fini, pour cette fois. . . .
> On partait. On savait qu'il faudrait revenir. On reviendrait. (29)

> Yes, it was over, for this time. . . .
> We left. We knew that we should have to return. We would return.

It is symptomatic that I should have been obliged in my translation to render 'on' as 'we'; the only obvious alternative, 'they', would simply not convey the systematic alignment of the narrative voice with the soldiers' perspective. This sympathetic effect is reinforced by the apparently omniscient narrator's mental access being limited for the most part to the consciousness of the central figure, who, as the officer in charge, is very much the focus of the narration. However, this pattern of identification with Enrico will, crucially, be replaced by an objectification of the officer in the

[12] See Chatman's discussion of Genette's celebrated analysis of the time-relations between story-time and discourse-time in Proust, *Story and Discourse*, 63–79.

novel's final lines: the major's death and the mutilation of his body are witnessed by a reader who, as the narrative ends, is finally given a fleeting insight into the minds of his ultimately victorious Algerian opponents (317).

In the meantime, Enrico remains convinced of his own unique ability to influence events. The very personal nature of his search for the elusive *grotte* is underlined as the analepsis is completed and we return to the narrative present:

> Enrico se rendait compte à présent qu'il avait ausculté, tâté cette montagne, des mois durant . . . Sous tous les croissants de lune, par des temps de glace, ou, encore, sous les cataractes nocturnes tendues à l'horizontale par le vent . . . Il se révéla sur l'énorme calotte du sommet par de petits matins limpides, sous un ciel qu'aucun peintre n'aurait osé peindre tant il était, d'un seul coup, au lever du jour, uniment turquoise. Alors le soleil se levait sur une terre élastique au pas des brebis et chaque avoine folle était un joyau.
>
> Mais surtout, cette montagne, il l'avait vécue et elle l'avait envahi. . . .
>
> Il lui semblait parfois n'avoir été créé que pour deviner quelle roche de ces étendues revêches révélerait à l'apposition de la main l'ouverture . . . (147–8)

> Enrico now realized that he had been listening to this mountain, feeling and examining it for months . . . Through all the moon's phases, in freezing conditions or in nocturnal downpours blown horizontally by the wind . . . He appeared on the vast bonnet-shaped summit in the clear early morning, under a sky that no painter would have dared paint, so flawless was its sudden turquoise hue as the new day dawned. Then the sun came up on a land which was springy under the sheep's hooves, and every wild oat became a jewel.
>
> But above all, he had lived this mountain, and it had penetrated his being. . . .
>
> It sometimes seemed to him that he had only been created to discover which of the rocks in this barren expanse would reveal the opening to the cave when he placed his hand upon it . . .

The image of Enrico the commander, alone on the mountain-top, in the sight of God and the face of the rising sun, is particularly suggestive of those qualities that we have sought to characterize as 'seigneurial'. The crystallization of the French military effort in Algeria into a campaign personally waged by a single, exceptionally gifted, and chronically solitary senior officer is a characteristic literary ploy, while the appeal to a notion of superior destiny will by now be familiar. In the event, the circumstances leading to the eventual discovery of the rebels' hide-out are to provide ample evidence of Enrico's ability to assume his elevated responsibilities to considerable military effect.

Seizing upon a much-needed stroke of luck—the capture of FLN documents revealing the presence of a number of major nationalist leaders in the area—Buis's protagonist makes use of a suitably magistral ruse in order to trick the rebels into revealing the location of the elusive *grotte*.[13] Once this breakthrough has been achieved, the *commandant* is able to besiege the cave, thus pitting his talents and resources directly against those of his FLN opponents. As omniscient as he is omnipresent, Enrico leads his forces to the inevitable victory after seventeen days of bitter fighting. The account of this polished implementation of his plans often draws attention to the character's seigneurial qualities, but nowhere more obviously than in the description of his regular helicopter flights over the battle-zone and the surrounding area. Leaving the ground—'divinité mineure voletant à grand tapage sur cette Ilion étriquée' [a minor divinity fluttering about in a terrible din above this cramped Troy] (219)—Enrico enters what is supposedly another universe:

> Le sien, actuel, était celui, supérieur et condescendant, de la Very High Frequency, plus familièrement: V.H.F. Là, règnent les leaders-hélicoptères et autres seigneurs. (123)

> His present one was the superior and condescending one of Very High Frequency, more commonly known as VHF. It is here that helicopter-leaders and other lords reign.

The airborne Enrico is similarly seigneurial in his dealings with the local Algerian population. A cavalry officer, he likens the inhabitants of the native villages below him to a horse which, in its own best interests, must be ridden with a firm hand (133). However, this properly cavalier attitude does not prevent Enrico from recognizing a number of fundamental truths about that same population, nor about the war as a whole. Indeed, it is in his dissent from the prevailing orthodoxies that the character reveals a brand of nobility not previously noted. For the primary given of Enrico's analysis of the situation in his sector—and, come to that, in Algeria as a whole—is that the Algerians constitute a profoundly political entity. This is a view which inevitably sets him apart from, and at odds with, the majority of his peers, and particularly the theorists of *la*

[13] *La Grotte*, 44–52. Enrico thus manages to avoid the thorny problem of torture, which is effectively sidestepped in *La Grotte*.

guerre révolutionnaire. Having realized that the local villagers, for all their denials, are thoroughly implicated in the nationalist revolt—'Ils sont dans la rébellion jusqu'aux yeux' [They're involved in the rebellion up to their necks] (63)—he can have little sympathy for those who advocate a decisive show of military force to win over Algerian hearts and minds to the French colonial cause:

> Pauvres gens—désespérés sans doute—que ceux qui, ne pouvant mordre sur ces paysans depuis des années que durait la révolte, feignaient de ne voir en eux qu'une masse politiquement inculte à la remorque innocente ou terrorisée d'une poignée de meneurs! Sur cette analyse incroyablement fausse ils se fondaient à croire qu'une autre minorité—la leur, celle des augures durs—pouvait gagner à elle ce tiers-état par l'affichage d'une détermination plus grande et par la magie d'un slogan.
>
> Enrico songeait que la réalité—quotidiennement assenée depuis quatre ans—se situait exactement à l'opposé. Ces paysans constitueraient, peut-être, dans dix ans, dans vingt ans, une société économique dépolitisée, maniable, à prendre et à encadrer. Pour l'instant, ils étaient des politiques, même s'ils n'étaient pas politisés. (228)
>
> They were sad cases—desperate, no doubt—those people who, having been unable to get to grips with these peasants over the years since the revolt broke out, now pretended to see in them only a politically backward mass which could be swept along, either in innocence or in terror, by a handful of agitators! It was on the basis of this incredibly misguided analysis that they founded their belief that another minority—their own, hard-headed variety—could win over this third estate through a show of superior determination and through the magic of a slogan.
>
> Enrico reflected on the fact that the reality of the situation—which had been hammered home on a daily basis for the past four years—was exactly the opposite. These peasants would, perhaps, in ten or twenty years' time, make up an economically ordered and depoliticized society, which could then be manipulated, taken in hand, and shaped. But for the time being they were political animals, even if they were not politicized.

It is this remarkable awareness of the political culture of the indigenous population of Algeria which sets Enrico apart from the other *seigneurs* considered in the present chapter, as is made particularly clear by the major's outspoken stand against the army high command's policy of clearing the countryside of its native inhabitants in order to set up what the Americans would call 'strategic hamlets' and 'free-fire zones' (*camps de regroupement* and *zones interdites* in the French military's vocabulary). There is no 'Sohane' to be found in *La Grotte*, but rather an impassioned denunciation of this historically counter-productive, but media-celebrated, French variation on the theme of strategic hamlets: 'J'ai compris à présent! Ce n'est pas autour du fortin qu'il faut mettre les barbelés: c'est autour du village!' [Now I understand! We mustn't put the barbed wire around the camp now, but around the village instead!] (240–1). Heretical views of this kind will, inevitably, bring Enrico into direct conflict with his hierarchical superiors: his punitive posting back to France will be the price which he has to pay for his political insight. Not that such official retribution in any way diminishes the character's power to persuade: on the contrary, his critical opinions are rendered that much more attractive by their evident nuisance value. Undoubtedly the most important of these criticisms of the prevailing military *doxa* is Enrico's properly historical appreciation of the durability of the Algerian nationalist rebellion. In an army obsessed with *le bilan* [counting enemy dead and captured weapons], Buis's hero can see beyond these reassuring totals to the structural flaws in the colonial project: a military *seigneur* to the core, he is nevertheless able to recognize that the decisive master-stroke dreamed of by himself and other senior French officers must always remain a fantasy (310). His rejection of the convenient interpretation of the disappearance of a number of key FLN commanders known to have been trapped in the cave is typical of this systematic refusal of the easy political option: he is inclined to suspect that the rebels, against all the odds, but in keeping with their popular legend, will in time appear somewhere else (296).

It is against this background that the little spring which continues to flow in the darkness of the cave—'une source qui ne tarirait jamais' [a spring which will never run dry] (197)—can be seen to stand as a symbol of Algerian nationalism. Enrico's subsequent death at the hands of Tahar Marseillaise, one of the rebel leaders supposedly asphyxiated in the cave, performs a similarly symbolic function. Ironically, the fatal ambush occurs shortly before Enrico is due to leave Algeria: out exercising his horse one morning, the *commandant* is killed instantly by a burst of machine-gun fire. Though himself a clear-sighted dissenter from the orthodoxy of pacification, Enrico thus falls victim to the wishful thinking of lesser men.[14]

There can be little doubting that Enrico dies as he lives: as a *seigneur*. But neither can the real importance of Buis's contribution to the Algerian debate, through the mouth of this lordly character,

[14] See Talbott, *War Without a Name*, 191.

be reasonably denied. For this particular *chevalier* distinguishes himself by attaining something very close to enlightenment before he dies. Written in the heat of the battle, yet displaying a political insight conspicuously absent from many later works, *La Grotte* is to be regarded as one of the most historically significant novels of the Algerian war.[15]

[15] The work's recent republication in Seuil's 'Points' series is an indication that its abiding relevance to the historical debate about the Algerian war has been recognized in France itself.

3

NI VICTIMES NI BOURREAUX: THE LIBERAL DILEMMA

In the previous chapter, I drew attention to Roger Ikor's tale of the stand taken against the army's use of torture by a conscript sergeant. In fact, this action is prompted by that of a lieutenant, who, having been obliged to interrogate an Algerian suspect, leaves the army and enters a monastery. The character's decision to devote himself henceforth to the imitation of Christ is explained by his belief that the Son of God is the ultimate victim of any use of torture (267). This attitude reflects the views consistently expressed by François Mauriac in his influential 'Bloc-Notes' column in *L'Express*,[1] while the officer's consideration in turn of the murder of his superior, suicide, and madness serves to draw attention to the properly ontological pretensions of such liberal Catholic soul-searching. Indeed, for Plaa and those he represents, torture is not primarily a military tactic, to be accepted or rejected—either for practical reasons, or on ethical grounds, or both—but rather an existential dilemma which must be suffered even unto death. The lieutenant thus leaves the Algerian stage, having rejected the modalities of French repression, but, crucially, nothing else.

Given the abiding liberal faith in the French nation's civilizing mission,[2] such a response is only to be expected: Ikor's lieutenant

[1] The relevant articles have been usefully collected as *L'Imitation des bourreaux de Jésus-Christ* (Desclée de Brouwer, 1984). As the intro. and commentary by Lacouture and de la Morandais make clear, Mauriac's concern with the issue of torture became markedly less acute after the return to power of de Gaulle in 1958. This is a theme which is approached from an altogether more polemical perspective in J. Laurent, *Mauriac sous de Gaulle* (La Table Ronde, 1964).

[2] As I shall describe in Ch. 6, this civilizing mission is regularly contrasted with what Frantz Fanon identified as the perceived 'pre-colonial barbarism' of the Algerian nationalist movement: *Les Damnés de la terre* (Maspero, 1961; refs. are to the La Découverte edn., 1984), 153. Also of interest is his 1957 essay 'Les Intellectuels et les démocrates français devant la révolution algérienne', in *Pour la révolution africaine* (Maspero, 1969), 72–86.

may see enough of the Algerian war's horrors to convince him that he does not wish to continue his active service in the French cause, but he cannot be exposed to enough of the conflict's politics to transform that strictly limited opposition to military means into a more thoroughgoing rejection of colonial ends. To do so would be to accept the necessity of Algerian independence: a conclusion which was historically rejected by all but a few liberal commentators.

It is convenient that Ikor's anti-torture campaigners are both able to quit the Algerian conflict once they have come to their 'moralist'[3] conclusions about the unacceptability of the French army's pacification methods: the regular officer can resign his commission, while Fenns has only a few weeks remaining before the end of his military service. They are thus able to evade the war itself, and with it the underlying dispute over the future status of the territory. Once this issue has been honestly addressed, the appropriate response to torture, summary execution, and the like, effectively ceases to be a problem: either Algeria must remain a French colony, in which case 'exceptional means' are to be looked upon as a necessary evil; or Algeria is destined for independence, which means that such tactics are as unjustifiable as the rest of the pacification effort in Algeria. Viewed in this light, it is clearly no coincidence that the lieutenant's adopted retreat should be symbolically closed: a walled domain from which troublesome political questions are magically excluded, the monastery allows the tortured representative of military humanism to take refuge in a splendid isolation, his individual crisis of conscience unhampered by a collective Algerian politics. What is more, Ikor's novel conforms to a wider pattern of liberal evasion of the conflict's central issue.[4] This may be demonstrated by examining a number of comparable literary manifestations of intellectual hand-wringing, beginning with Pierre-Henri Simon's *Portrait d'un officier* [Portrait of an Officer] (1958).[5]

A member of that group of Catholic humanists which became

[3] See Ch. 2, n. 3 on the use of this term.

[4] As Sorum explains, '[the moralists] took the increasingly untenable position of desiring the goal of a French Algeria but despising the necessary means'; *Intellectuals and Decolonization in France* (Chapel Hill, Univ. of North Carolina Press, 1977), 128. His account of the Catholic intellectuals' campaign against torture may usefully be complemented by that in F. Bédarida and E. Fouilloux, (eds.), *La Guerre d'Algérie et les chrétiens* (*Les Cahiers de l'Institut d'Histoire du Temps Présent*, 9, Oct. 1988).

[5] (Seuil; refs. are to the 'Livre de Poche' edn.).

associated with Emmanuel Mounier's campaigning review *Esprit*, Pierre-Henri Simon first came to public prominence in the wake of the Battle of Algiers, as one of the foremost metropolitan critics of the French army's systematic use of torture for the gathering of intelligence. With the memory of the atrocities perpetrated by the Nazis still fresh in their minds, he and other liberal Catholic intellectuals were spurred into leading the denunciation of abhorrent pacification methods in Algeria. Simon's personal response centred on his influential pamphlet *Contre la torture* (1957), which made a major contribution to the increasingly heated debate on the subject.

Yet *Contre la torture* was only one aspect of the moralist thinker's political agitation. He was also active in the 'Comité de Résistance Spirituelle', a body which included amongst its members such leading Catholic figures as Mauriac himself and Hubert Beuve-Méry, the founder of *Le Monde*, and which sought to coordinate Christian opposition to military atrocities in Algeria. In addition, Simon produced his *Portrait d'un officier*, a short novel which transparently functions as a vehicle for the wider circulation of those liberal attitudes previously voiced in *Contre la torture*. In what follows, I shall seek to show that this text embodies an ideological contradiction which the author and other such 'men of two minds' experienced as the 'liberal dilemma'.[6]

As its title suggests, *Portrait d'un officier* focuses on a single military man, the aristocratic Jean de Larsan. From a long line of career soldiers, the protagonist sees service in the European and North African theatres of World War II before being sent to fight the colonial revolutionaries in both Indo-China and Algeria. It is the trauma occasioned by his involvement in these conflicts which will eventually lead him to resign his commission, thus following in the footsteps of such celebrated figures as Colonel Jules Roy and General Jacques Paris de Bollardière.

The key to a demystified understanding of Simon's short novel lies in its ambivalent attitude to military romanticism, particularly as manifested in that ancient confusion of French military exigencies and divine order encapsulated in the myth of the Christian knight.

[6] J. Talbott, *The War Without a Name: France in Algeria, 1954–1962* (London, Faber & Faber, 1981), 248. See also Talbott's 'Terrorism and the Liberal Dilemma: The Case of the Battle of Algiers', *Contemporary French Civilization*, 2/2 (Winter 1978), 177–89. Cf. A. Hargreaves, 'Caught in the Middle: The Liberal Dilemma in the Algerian War', *Nottingham French Studies*, 25/2 (Oct. 1986), 73–82.

For Larsan, we learn, the army is a sacred entity (57), much as it was for the Crusaders, and his military career was consequently embarked upon in an appropriately vocational fashion, just as if he had taken holy orders (16). However, this version of the myth of the saintly warrior will not be presented as an image of the French army in Algeria, but rather as its antithesis. Moreover, the potentially dangerous inappropriateness of such an anachronistic conception of war will be insisted upon as soon as it is uttered: Larsan, the self-confessed last of the Christian knights, will readily accuse himself of a quixotic sentimentality and lack of realism in an age when war has become—if it was not always—sordid and cruel, 'une espèce de boucherie scientifique où ce ne sont plus des soldats qui affrontent des soldats, mais des ingénieurs qui écrasent des villes, qui brûlent des foules' [a sort of scientific slaughter in which soldiers no longer face soldiers, but rather where engineers flatten towns and incinerate crowds] (16–7).

The fundamental ambivalence of *Portrait d'un officier* is hinted at here, for the narrative simultaneously utters a familiar myth and only part of the necessary antidote to it. So while Larsan's romantic belief in a noble brand of warfare may never be completely debunked, the radical discrepancy between this personal code and the conduct of the mass of the French forces in Algeria will be used to criticize the historical campaign there. This unresolved tension between two contrasting approaches to the waging of war is symptomatic of an unavowed contradiction at a deeper level, and one which takes us to the heart of the liberal dilemma. For what Larsan is really seeking in Algeria is a 'clean war', in direct contrast to the *sale guerre* which is actually being fought out there. Thus regarded, the hero of *Portrait d'un officier* stands revealed as a representative of the tortured liberal conscience, which historically supported the ends of colonial repression in Algeria, but could not bring itself to accept the brutal means necessary to crush the nationalist insurrection. Just as Larsan is only too keen to fight in Algeria, but not in this particularly unpleasant war, Simon and his fellow Catholic intellectuals, while continuing to believe in France's *mission civilisatrice*, were unable to countenance the methods actually used by the army in an attempt to preserve that 'civilizing' ascendancy. Effectively ignoring the pivotal question of how best to respond to terrorist violence in Algeria—whether to accept torture as a necessary evil in order to preserve the greater good which *Algérie française* supposedly represented, or to reject such methods completely and thereby resign oneself to Algerian independence—the moralist intellectuals would for long pursue the chimerical goal of a humane pacification effort. It is against this background that Simon's account of Larsan's Algerian war is to be set.

Larsan's initial optimism is rapidly modified by his first contacts with the reality behind the official myth of pacification, which is soon revealed to be an impossible balancing act between military repression and social protection. In the face of this fundamental contradiction, all the protagonist's attempts to remain *au-dessus de la mêlée* are destined to prove futile, as he too is obliged to confront the stock dilemma which sets the temporary suffering of guilty men against the loss of innocent lives. In the event, he will refuse to sanction the use of torture, for the simple reason that 'un officier d'une nation baptisée et civilisée ne torture pas, ne laisse pas torturer un homme désarmé' [an officer of a baptized and civilized nation neither tortures nor allows the torture of an unarmed man] (112).

The Catholic Larsan's single inflexible principle inevitably recalls that of the Jewish writer Roger Ikor's Sergeant Ludovic Fenns, and is similarly rooted in a rejection of rationalism. In place of reason, the Christian conscience is, like Pascal's 'heart', installed as the ultimate source of ethical authority. Yet this philosophical base will be found crucially wanting in the inevitable set-piece debate with the advocates of military efficacy. This time the theorists of revolutionary warfare include both the usual activist colonel and a regimental chaplain, but the confrontation is remarkable not so much for the arguments voiced as for the profound lack of confidence which it reveals in the liberals' anti-torture case. Indeed, it is in the full knowledge of the certainty of his own theoretical defeat that Larsan embarks on his critique of abhorrent pacification methods. His avowedly irrational and essentially mystical problematic is duly revealed to be no match either for the robust materialism of Colonel Dhagondange or the muscular Christianity of *le père* Legouey. Indeed, the priest will be able to develop a totally self-consistent version of the Algerian conflict which the hero may challenge occasionally, but which he is radically incapable of demystifying.

For Legouey, it is the Algerian war's specificity which inevitably determines the character of each individual's participation in it. Seen as a crusade against the twin evils of Islam and communism, themselves perceived to be readily compatible, the conflict makes its own harsh rules; and those liberals who refuse to apply 'effective methods' are themselves guilty of a bleating and pseudo-Christian sentimentality, a costly scruple which must be paid for in innocent lives. Opposing the vengeance-theology of the Old Testament to the non-violence of Tolstoy, Gandhi, and Romain Rolland, the priest thus challenges Larsan to find a flaw in the grim logic of military realism. This the idealistic officer cannot do, and his despairing parting criticism of the priest's lack of a sense of being torn apart (*le déchirement*) (125) is thus emblematic of the profound contradictions inherent in the liberal position. For what Larsan is really objecting to is not the substance of the priest's views, but rather the manner of their expression. He could, he admits, accept the clergyman's statement of the military-realist case if only it were accompanied by some display of grief: 'quelque chose de tendu, de déchiré' [some sign of strain, of being torn apart] (125). Indeed, the liberal officer's bemoaning of Legouey's untroubled acceptance of harsh military realities relies for its effect on the latter's perceived failure to participate in what was a common obfuscation of the Algerian war: the labelling of the conflict as a product of *le déchirement*, with all that this implied in the way of tragic inevitability, and thus the rationalization of events in Algeria as the expression of a global Evil rather than of a specifically colonial, and thus avoidable, evil.[7]

Larsan's preoccupation with the modalities of expression betrays a wilful blindness to underlying goals: verbal forms are focused on, to the exclusion of political ends. Given that the basic premises of the French colonial project were, in fact, accepted by the realists and the humanists alike, Simon's narrative can only chart the officer's decline as he fails to come to terms with the unpalatable military exigencies of the Algerian campaign. Faced with the spectacle of the French army's brutality and destruction, Larsan believes himself to be neither personally responsible, nor wholly innocent of guilt. To adopt the terms used by Albert Camus in his celebrated series of articles for *Combat* in 1946, he is neither one of the war's victims, nor yet one of its executioners.[8] He is therefore characteristically torn when considering reprisals carried out against the local Algerian population by soldiers under his command: 'Je ne

[7] The political implications of this liberal hand-wringing were first identified by Roland Barthes in his celebrated analysis of French colonial rhetoric, 'Grammaire africaine', *Mythologies* (Seuil, 1957), 137–44.

[8] 'Ni victimes ni bourreaux', in *Essais* (Gallimard/Calmann-Lévy, 1965), 329–52. See also Barthes's critique of liberal 'neither-norism' (*le ninisme*): *Mythologies*, 241.

pouvais ni les [les musulmans] accabler sous la terreur de représailles que je n'avais pas voulues, ni blâmer publiquement la colère explicable de mes hommes: seul, au cœur de la tragédie obscure, je portais en silence ma honte et mon chagrin' ['I could neither terrorize them [the Muslims] with reprisals that I had not ordered, nor publicly denounce the understandable anger of my men: alone, at the centre of the obscure tragedy, I silently bore my shame and my suffering'] (141).

In the absence of an appropriately political response, Simon's hero will—again like Camus[9]—seek temporary refuge in silence, before withdrawing definitively from the Algerian arena. As he retreats from the war and its horrors, the would-be Christian knight makes one final appeal to the notion of historical irresponsibility in order to deny his own guilt as an agent of colonial repression:

Le drame nous dépassait l'un et l'autre, et le jugement suprême n'appartient qu'à la souveraine intelligence qui regarde d'en haut, avec pitié je l'espère, les hommes s'agiter et souffrir au fond de leur nuit . . . dans un tragique qui ne jaillit pas, créateur d'héroïsme et de poésie, d'un conflit d'absolus, mais, destructeur et désespérant, d'un mélange d'absurdités. Pas commode de vivre Corneille au siècle de Kafka! (152–3)

The drama was bigger than both of us, and the ultimate judgement of it can be made by no one but the sovereign intelligence, who looks down, with pity, I hope, upon mankind as it scurries and suffers in the depths of its night . . . and in the midst of a tragedy which does not spring, with its attendant heroism and poetry, from a conflict of absolutes, but rather, bringing destruction and despair, from a mixture of absurdities. It isn't easy living out Corneille in Kafka's century!

The most striking feature of the hero's exit from this version of the cruel Algerian drama is, once again, its total exclusion of politics. In particular, Larsan's claim that the hostilities in Algeria do not constitute the site for a conflict of absolutes serves to deny the total nature of all such colonial conflicts, as argued most obviously by Frantz Fanon.[10] In this context, the primary distinction to be made is that between colonizer and colonized, the irreducible elements of a historical dialectic reflecting the diametrically opposed interests of the only social categories admitted by the conflictual

[9] Camus's silence on the Algerian question from 1958 onwards has been much discussed. See e.g. H. Lottman, *Albert Camus: A Biography* (London, Weidenfeld and Nicholson, 1979), 620–33; cf. M. Robin, *et al.*, 'Remarques sur l'attitude de Camus face à la Guerre d'Algérie', in J.-Y. Guérin, *Camus et la politique* (L'Harmattan, 1986), 185–202.

[10] *Les Damnés de la terre*, 186.

economy of colonialism: either victims, or executioners, as it were, but not both, and not neither. Indeed, the characterizing wish to avoid all forms of 'extremism' articulates a mythical duality which serves to transform the liberal commentator from a political agent into an ethical arbiter, and thus projects a preferred image of an unholy alliance between opposing men of violence which the moralist nobly, if vainly, attempts to thwart.

Larsan, the 'bad priest', will seek a way out of the liberal dilemma by quitting the military 'church' (153). In common with very many metropolitan French observers—including François Mauriac, the most celebrated voice of the liberal Catholic conscience—Larsan leaves this apparently insoluble problem to the latest in a long line of national saviours. Like the moralist intellectuals, Larsan demonstrates the ability to glimpse, but not properly to comprehend, the quite devastating implications of humanist thinking for the future of the colonial order.[11] That the explosion of revolutionary violence in Algeria inevitably resulted in the subordination of metropolitan sensibilities to more elemental historical forces was never fully grasped by the moralists, who consequently sought to escape from their predicament by artificially opposing FLN barbarism and military fascism: they could then imagine themselves to be the incarnation of moderation between the two. This aspect of the liberal perspective is best exemplified by Gilbert Cesbron's very significantly titled *Entre chiens et loups* [Between Dogs and Wolves] (1962).[12]

For Cesbron, a prolific producer of best-selling novels with a strong sense of their author's Catholic social conscience, the Algerian conflict never became the all-consuming passion that it did for some of the better-known liberal commentators. Instead, the war was perceived as one of a range of ills afflicting contemporary French society, and which his writing sought to place in a properly Christian context. Algeria thus becomes a setting for the author's exploration of the theme of the difficult path to self-knowledge and spiritual enlightenment. Not that Algeria is a mere backdrop to this modern version of *Pilgrim's Progress*, nor is the text's treatment of the conflict politically neutral.

Roland Guérin, a schoolmaster turned political columnist, is the central figure in this tale of Christian self-discovery. Confronted

[11] Sartre made this point particularly forcefully in his preface to Fanon, *Les Damnés de la terre*, 14–15.

[12] See Ch. 1, n. 1.

with evidence of the military's use of torture in Algeria, the protagonist resists his natural inclination to sit on the fence, endeavouring instead to 'Prendre parti sans devenir un partisan' [To take a stand without becoming a partisan] (139). Rooted in Cesbron's liberal humanism, this tenet is the key to an understanding of his portrayal of the Algerian conflict. More specifically, it explains the author's attempt to combine criticism of the nation's involvement in a self-evidently futile colonial war with the most sympathetic possible analysis of the motives and actions of individual French participants, and thus to further the process of Christian reconciliation.

Yet Cesbron's rejection of the partisan mentality and what he perceives to be the socially disastrous politicization of the Algerian question is less a solution of the liberal dilemma, and more the epitome of its literary expression. For the fact remains that the principal contention of the 'realists', both the anti-war radicals on the Left and the theorists of *la guerre révolutionnaire* on the Right, was the one borne out by history: the war in Algeria could not be made more humane, since the conflict's political and military logic defied all attempts to impose moral limits upon it. Cesbron's espousal of the cause of moderation can, in consequence, only result in a retreat from the brutally conflictual politics of Algeria, most obviously reflected in his narrative's insistence on the war's 'fratricidal' nature.

For Cesbron, the Algerian conflict is to be regarded as a cancer in the French body politic, the avoidable product of chronic colonial mismanagement and neglect (136–7). Such an interpretation has its roots in the liberals' faith in an improvable colonialism, and is typically phrased in terms of the opportunities which have been missed for avoiding the present historical crisis. Moreover, by seeking so determinedly to avoid the partisans' one-eyed vision, a text which is overtly committed to spreading the gospel of Christian pacifism comes to utter the foundation myths of military romanticism, such as the transcendent nature of the combat experience, the brotherhood of arms, and the communion of enemy equals. Indeed, much as in the case of Pierre-Henri Simon, the principal ideological 'error' made by Cesbron is to underestimate the extent and the resilience of the military-romantic tradition. For in the historical context of colonial war, to pursue an illusory golden mean of moderation was inevitably to run the risk of uttering the standard themes of the military's apologists.

The text's case against partisan ways of conceiving the Algerian war is most dramatically illustrated when Roland, the scourge of the pro-military and pro-colonial Right as the vitriolic columnist 'Fabrice', is finally brought face to face with his left-wing audience at a rally against torture. Appalled by the partisan audiences which he encounters both at this meeting and at a rival one, which he wanders into by mistake, Cesbron's hero will undergo a major shift in his thinking:

Belle soirée! En ce moment même, des musulmans dont il confond les noms, geignent de souffrance dans des cachots infects et leur corps, jusque dans leurs secrets, porte témoignage des tortures subies. En ce moment, de jeunes officiers veillent ou prient, se demandant où est leur devoir et si l'honneur commande vraiment de faire tuer leurs hommes pour épargner des terroristes. Mais les bourreaux dorment tranquilles, et les politiques se font applaudir, et les partisans recuisent leur haine mutuelle. Tous sont à leur affaire—oui, une belle soirée. 'La France', 'l'Honneur', 'l'Occident'—on lance en l'air les mêmes mots, ici et là: ils ont perdu leur poids entre les mains de ces jongleurs qu'on applaudit. Mais le visage d'un musulman et celui d'un officier qui ont fermé les yeux parce que l'un souffre et que l'autre s'interroge, qui se les représente, ici ou là, jusqu'à ce que son coeur batte à l'étouffer? Qui, sauf Roland l'imbécile, lequel s'est laissé prendre au piège des roués? (162)

What a lovely evening! At this very moment, Muslims whose names he gets mixed up are moaning with pain in stinking cells, and their bodies, even in their most intimate regions, bear witness to the tortures which they have suffered. At that moment, young officers cannot sleep or are praying, as they ask themselves where their duty lies and whether honour really does require them to allow their men to be killed in order that terrorists should be spared. But the torturers sleep soundly, and the politicians are applauded, and the partisans nurse their mutual hatreds. Everyone is doing what they do best—yes, a lovely evening alright. 'France', 'Honour', 'the West'—the same words are tossed around here as there: but they have lost their weight in the hands of these jugglers who always manage to get a clap. But who, here or there, imagines the faces of a Muslim and an officer, both with their eyes closed, one in pain, the other in self-doubt, until his heart thumps fit to burst? Who, if not Roland the idiot, who has allowed himself to get caught in a trap set by cunning individuals?

It is on the basis of this classic crisis of conscience that the protagonist will himself volunteer to serve in the Algerian war: a conflict which he has hitherto merely commented on at no personal risk and in the most socially divisive fashion. Carried out by *bourreaux* who are as conveniently anonymous as they are uncaring, rather than by the pious young officers who are clearly to be regarded as its French victims, the torture of terrorists is weighed against the lives of innocent servicemen. France, honour, and western civilization are meanwhile reasserted as abiding values by means of the familiar neither-nor double negation, while a note of Cornelian tragedy is introduced with the idea of a despairing choice between moral—but not, crucially, political—absolutes. The intensity and authenticity of the military experience are thus contrasted with the shallowness and mendacity of civilian politicizing, as Roland's beating—or perhaps bleeding?—heart points unequivocally to the text's proposed solution to the liberal dilemma: Christian love of one's fellow human being. His attempt to communicate this humanist insight to his left-wing audience may be an absolute failure, but Cesbron's hero is thus spiritually armed for his personal experience of the military struggle in Algeria.

Having been prompted to enlist by the news of the death of a *para* lieutenant with whom he was acquainted, Roland soon finds himself involved in a major operation against the FLN. This metamorphosis may be highly implausible, but it does allow the expression of the characterizing liberal preoccupation with torture, as Roland now makes a direct attempt to halt the practice. Overcoming his instinctive cowardice, he attempts to put a stop to a fellow officer's muscular interrogation of an Algerian suspect, but only succeeds in getting himself badly beaten up. Nevertheless, as soon as he recovers consciousness, our hero resolves to try again:

> Oui, c'est pour l'honneur du lieutenant Mansart qu'il va retourner gifler ce salaud et se faire rouer. Il remet à plus tard de comprendre lui-même pourquoi, mais respire encore une fois jusqu'au ventre et marche vers la porte qu'il ouvre toute grande . . . (273)

> Yes, it is to defend the honour of Lieutenant Mansart that he will go back and slap that bastard's face and get himself beaten up again. Putting off until later the task of working out for himself just why he is acting as he is, he takes another, really deep breath, strides towards the door and swings it wide open . . .

This passage may be regarded as a masterpiece of liberal mystification, for Roland's stand against torture actually contrives to transform the figure historically responsible for its perpetration—the French paratrooper—into the principal reason for avoiding its use. Clearly, *paras* do not torture in the Algeria of *Entre chiens et loups*, only 'bastards'. Although Roland will continue to fight in the war after this episode, the stage is now set for his final transformation, which sees him complete his spiritual development by becoming a persecuted advocate of Christian non-violence. It is thus as an opponent not of the Algerian conflict, but rather of all war that Roland returns to France: an ingenious evasion of that specific struggle's political dimension which, moreover, is both given a spurious moral weight by Roland's final martyrdom at the hands of an OAS-style commando, and made to appear definitive through the formal pressure of narrative closure.

A global pacifism is thus preferred to a properly specific, and inevitably traumatic, critique of French colonialism: bemoaning the human condition replaces the painful, but practical, politics of Algeria. As Sartre argued, metropolitan non-violence could never be radical, still less a solution to colonial conflict: those liberals who advocated it failed to appreciate their objective community of interests with the colonialist *bourreaux* and against the colonized *victimes*.[13] Roland's response to the liberal dilemma finally amounts to conscientious objection in the classic mould: it is a basically state-tolerated—because formalized, controllable, and self-limiting—type of dissent. Historical dynamism thus gives way to mythical stasis in Cesbron's narrative. Ordered progress may be a feature of the narrative's structure, but only in the sphere of the numinous; political advance is consistently mystified and effectively frozen. The 'neither-norism' at the heart of Cesbron's broad-spectrum pacificism provides evidence of the durability of the liberals' rhetoric, and also serves to underline its direct ideological descent from the Camus of the 1946 *Combat* articles. Moreover, it reveals, once again, how easily liberalism may be recuperated by a more robust and more coherent myth-system. All of which leads us now to consider the literary images of the Algerian conflict produced by a celebrated triumvirate of *pied-noir* liberals: Jean Pélégri, Jules Roy, and Albert Camus himself.

It is in terms of the key liberal myth of missed opportunities that we must consider the contributions made to the Algerian debate by Jean Pélégri and Jules Roy. Born, intriguingly, in the same small

[13] *Les Damnés*, 18. In Sartre's own allegorical literary treatment of the Algerian conflict, *Les Séquestrés d'Altona* (Gallimard, 1960), 'Frantz', a German officer traumatized by his role in atrocities during World War II, is plainly to be equated with 'France'. This work is usefully analysed in C. Brosman, 'Sartre, the Algerian War, and *Les Séquestrés d'Altona*', *Papers in Romance*, 3/2 (Spring 1981), 81–9. Also of interest is A. Cohen-Solal. 'Camus, Sartre et la Guerre d'Algérie', in Guérin, *Camus et la politique*, 177–84.

village—Rovigo, in the Algérois—these two contemporaries put forward strikingly similar critiques of colonial society. Without ever meeting, the two writers became equally conscious of the need for a major reconsideration of their community's position in the new Algerian reality. The most obvious candidate for this task was the world-renowned voice of the French liberal conscience, Albert Camus. He, however, had ruled out further public comment on the Algerian question in April 1958, following the failure two years earlier of his idealistic plan for a 'trêve civile' [civilian truce] in the colony. Both Jean Pélégri's *Les Oliviers de la justice* [The Olive-Trees of Justice] (1959) and Jules Roy's *La Guerre d'Algérie* [translated as *The Algerian War*] (1960) are to be regarded as attempts—overtly stated in the case of the latter—to fill the moralist void left by Camus's celebrated 'silence' and subsequent death in 1960.

In his own essay, Jules Roy notes with approval the contribution made to the Algerian debate by Pélégri's autobiographical narrative, praising it as a 'noble' work (58). An account of Pélégri's attempts to explain Algeria's current predicament to his dying father, the text may be shown to make an important statement about the social roots of Algerian nationalism, without ever being able to use its genuine insights to draw properly political conclusions either about the present strife or the future status of Algeria. As the author-narrator struggles to cope with the trauma of his father's death, he will thus come to a partial understanding of the changes occurring in his native land, but cannot achieve a full appreciation of the demise of the colonial order and its replacement by a nationalist one. As a result, Pélégri's work is unable to escape from a liberal problematic that comprehends Algerian suffering in terms of a failure of fraternity, rather than as an integral part of the colonial system. This way of reading the socio-political situation reflects an abiding belief in the reformability of *Algérie française*, in spite of the fact that earlier opportunites to achieve this end had consistently been squandered. The text's insistence on the need for 'justice' in Algeria appears in this light to be little more than the author's preferred alternative to what the nationalists were actually demanding in 1959: the full independence of an FLN-led Algeria.

Set in 1955, Pélégri's narrative turns precisely on the notion of a fraternity capable of transcending racial barriers in Algeria. This is exemplified by the atmosphere prevailing on the little farm where the author-narrator grew up. Throughout the work, this period and place are nostalgically evoked as a golden age, which might point the way forward to a new Algeria. The pastoral evocation of 'le bonheur du crépuscule' ['the bliss of the evening'] is typical of this aspect of the work:

> Oh! Je le sais, ces grandes familles qui s'endormaient dans la paix n'étaient, ne pouvaient être qu'un commencement: l'homme ne peut rester toujours dans sa famille, si juste soit-elle. Mais elles auraient pu . . . être le commencement de tout.
>
> Elles auraient pu faire oublier l'injustice première. (124)
>
> Oh! I know, those great families nodding off peacefully were only, could only ever be a beginning: man cannot stay forever within his family, however just it may be. But they could have . . . been the start of everything.
>
> They could have made people forget the first injustice.

Here, Pélégri combines a partial insight into the nature of colonialism—its foundation on injustice, characterized as 'la faute originelle' [the original offence] (123)—with a good deal of liberal wishful thinking. For the image of 'one big happy family' is a profoundly misleading one in the colonial context, characterized as it was by a radical separation of colonizer and colonized.[14] Moreover, colonialism's expropriation of the indigenous population is not in the nature of a single, properly punctual, injustice; it is rather a process, a continual denial of the colonized's natural rights. It is, in consequence, not liable to be forgotten, still less forgiven; it exists or it does not, it cannot be rendered more humane.

The Algeria of *Les Oliviers de la justice* is deemed to possess a dual cultural heritage, half European and half Algerian. These strands are perceived to be complementary rather than competing, and are variously symbolized. The most significant metaphor used by Pélégri is that of the vine and the palm tree, a dichotomy which is mirrored in the social domain by his father and Embarek, the local *marabout* [holy man or saint]. After a stormy first encounter, the two men arrive at a tacit agreement about their respective rights and duties, and are thus able to become friends. For the author-narrator, the relationship of this European and this Arab is symbolic of a broader division of responsibilities in colonial Algeria:

> Maintenant qu'ils sont morts tous les deux, à la même heure matinale, je ne peux les séparer dans ma mémoire, de même que je ne peux, dans le paysage, séparer la vigne du palmier.
>
> Tous les deux, chacun à sa manière, avaient donné un sens à ce paysage.

[14] This subject is discussed in detail in Ch. 6.

Toi, mon père, tu avais défriché, assaini. Dans les caniveaux douteux et peuplés de moustiques, toi, c'était du soufre que tu faisais brûler—comme pour le diable. Quand tu grelottais, hagard, dans ton lit, au moment de tes accès de paludisme, ne me semblais-tu d'ailleurs comme possédé? . . .

Et peu à peu le paysage était devenu fertile. (141–2)

Now that they are both dead, having passed on in the same morning hour, I cannot separate them in my memory, any more than I can separate the vine from the palm tree when I look at the landscape.

They had both, each in his own way, given a meaning to this land.

You, father, had cleared the scrub and cleaned up the land. It was you who burned sulphur in the stinking, mosquito-infested ditches—as if you were trying to ward off the devil. And, come to that, when you lay suffering from malaria, haggard and shivering in your bed at the height of the fever, did you not seem to me possessed? . . .

And little by little the land had become fertile.

Et toi, Embarek . . . que dirai-je de toi? . . . Toi, à ce paysage, tu avais donné une âme—ce qui est aussi important que le reste. En effet, je le sais maintenant, il n'y a point d'amour sans cela. . . . Toi, dans ce paysage de vignes, tu étais le palmier. (145)

And you, Embarek . . . what shall I say about you? . . . You gave this land its soul—which is just as important as everything else. In fact, as I now know, no love is possible without it. . . . You, in this land covered with vines, were the palm tree.

The two men's 'concordat tacite' [unspoken agreement] (141), dividing the world into the secular and the spiritual, is a particularly convenient one for the *pied-noir*, in that it posits a notional equality while upholding existing property relations: the ownership of the land—the real Algerian problem—is not here in question. Yet, elsewhere in his narrative, Pélégri is at pains to stress the violence inherent in the colonial system. Indeed, his account of the death of a starving Algerian in a European vineyard is amongst the most striking literary images of that endemic brutality:

Entre deux rangs de vigne, un Arabe d'une vingtaine d'années était étendu sur les mottes, immobile, enroulé sur lui-même comme un lièvre touché en pleine fuite. Le gardien l'avait surpris en train de voler du raisin et l'avait tué, au lieu de tirer en l'air. Sur les mottes fraîchement retournées, luisantes, s'étalaient des taches de sang déjà sombres, et autour de sa main, qui serrait encore ce qu'il restait de la grappe, des grains s'étaient éparpillés, des raisins verts. Il avait été tué pour une grappe de raisins verts! . . .

Depuis ce jour-là, la vigne a perdu pour moi son innocence. (126–7)

Between two rows of vines, an Arab of about twenty lay sprawled on the earth, quite still, and rolled up in a ball like a hare shot in full flight. The guard had caught him stealing grapes and had killed him, instead of firing in the air. The freshly turned soil shone where the already darkened bloodstains had spread over it, and around his hand, which still clutched what was left of the bunch, were scattered the unripe grapes. He had been killed for a bunch of unripe grapes! . . .

That day, the vine lost its innocence for me.

The fact that the Arab's executioner is a fellow Algerian serves to add a bitter irony to what is already a powerfully demystifying treatment of a major mythical theme.[15] Nevertheless, Pélégri remains emotionally attached to the vine and its symbolism, and thus, as he himself recognizes, complicit with the rest of the European community in Algeria (232). Ethnic affiliations thus conflict with, and eventually prevail over, liberal goodwill in what is a peculiarly intense version of the dilemma, memorably characterized by Albert Memmi as 'la danse tourmentée du colonisateur qui se refuse, et continue à vivre en colonie' [the tormented dance of the colonizer who rejects himself, and yet continues to live in the colonies].[16]

Much as the metropolitan liberals had urged a more humane form of the pacification programme designed to preserve French Algeria, so the more liberal-minded members of the settler community sought not to put an end to the colonial system, but rather to render it more 'just'. This perspective—in which 'injustice' was the preferred euphemism for an increasingly negatively perceived colonialism—did not prevent some very scathing criticism of the liberals' fellow settlers, or, indeed, of themselves, but it did preclude serious consideration of the only real alternative to *Algérie française*: namely *une Algérie algérienne*. So, throughout *Les Oliviers de la justice*, Jean Pélégri levels criticisms at French Algeria's habitual indifference to the culture, suffering, and nationalist aspirations of the territory's indigenous population. In particular, Pélégri's emphasis on the Algerian war's ideological dimension—its challenge to the settlers' vision of the world (229–30)—is of undoubted value, as is his drawing of attention to the colonizer's objectification of the colonized. Altogether less convincing, however, is his explanation of

[15] See J. Berque, *Le Maghreb entre deux guerres* (Seuil, 1962), 35, on the symbolism of the European farmhouse surrounded by vineyards. Several pro-colonial writers dwell on the bringing of vines to Algeria, especially from the 'lost province' of Alsace.

[16] *Portrait du colonisé précédé du portrait du colonisateur* (Corréa, 1957; refs. are to the Gallimard/NRF edn., 1985), 70.

this acutely observed colonial reality in terms of a failure of paternalism and of missed opportunities.

Such criticism can only ever be of abuses of the colonial system, rather than of colonialism itself. So while the author may rightly identify as the root cause of the Algerian revolt 'cette injustice quotidienne que l'on respirait comme un siroco' [this daily injustice, which we breathed like a hot desert wind] (33), he will be unable to recognize that this institutionalized abuse of the colonized is the very essence of French Algeria, and not some remediable failure on its part. By the same token, Pélégri will fail to appreciate the inevitability of European racism in the colonial context: the native must be perceived as the lazy and cowardly representative of 'Cette sale race qui veut nous chasser d'ici et prendre nos terres' [This dirty race which wants to kick us out and take our land] (26). This for the simple reason that, by 1955, an end to the colonial system of property relations was precisely what the Algerians sought, not the voting rights refused to earlier generations of nationalists and now offered belatedly in an attempt to defuse the colony's crisis. In short, Pélégri is unable to appreciate that, once triggered, this popular rising can only end in the demise of *Algérie française*, and so he will continue to express his faith in the settlers' future prospects in Algeria.

The basic premise of such thinking is a belief in the *tendresse* [fondness] which, it is maintained, underpins the relationship between the territory's European and Algerian communities (259–60). With the introduction of this theme, our attention is drawn to the liberal problematic itself. Put simply, inter-ethnic relations are to be understood in terms of the primary opposition of love and hate, with the liberal 'solution' to the present hostilities consisting in an extension of that fraternity often experienced at the level of the individual to Algerian society as a whole (249–54). Such a reading ignores precisely that historical indifference of the *pieds-noirs* to the surrounding Algerian masses so accurately identified by Pélégri, an absence of emotional interest which, as every student of French Classicism knows, is the true contrary of both love and hate.[17] The influence of this myth of supra-ethnic fraternity is best appreciated in Pélégri's developed statement of his hopes for Algeria's future.

[17] Interestingly, this image of the Franco-Algerian relationship appealed right across the political spectrum, and the communist writer André Stil is just as happy to state that *Nous nous aimerons demain* (Editeurs Français Réunis, 1957) as the *pied-noir* activist Jean Brune is to evoke *Cette haine qui ressemble à l'amour* (La Table Ronde, 1961).

His point of departure is their common experience of service in the Second World War, and its legacy of missed opportunities:

> Ah! si nous l'avions eu, ce courage, au retour de nos victoires, à ce moment unique où tout était possible, puisque cette Algérie juste et fraternelle dont nous rêvions, nous l'avions connue et vécue à notre tour sur les champs de bataille. Quel exemple nous aurions donné, nous les Africains! . . .
>
> Pour la première fois, des hommes de races et de religions différentes, triomphant de la haine et de l'injustice, se seraient unis librement, donnant ainsi au monde l'exemple de la fraternité future . . .
>
> Mais il n'est pas dit que nous ne la vivrons pas, un jour, cette histoire. Cela dépend de notre courage. (244–5)

> Oh! If we could only have had the necessary courage when we came back from our victories, at that unique moment when everything was possible. Because the just and fraternal Algeria that we dreamed of had already existed, we had lived it ourselves on the battlefield. What an example we would have set, us, the Africans! . . .
>
> For the first time, men of different races and religions, overcoming hatred and injustice, would have come together of their own free will, and so given the world an example of future fraternity . . .
>
> But who is to say that we will not live that history one day? It just depends on our courage.

Pélégri's typically liberal combination of diagnostic acuity and prognostic wishful thinking is nowhere more clearly underlined than here. So the Second World War may be rightly identified as a watershed in the history of French Algeria, but the only 'solution' urged is an undefined Algerian harmony, to be achieved by unstated means, at some unspecified point in the future. Mistaking the cultural superstructure of colonial Algeria for its politico-economic base, Pélégri is even able to suggest that a greater European awareness of Algerian traditions could have brought about a radical change in relations between the two communities:

> Nous étions, malgré les injustices, malgré les coups de feu qui crépitaient depuis plusieurs mois déjà dans les campagnes, nous étions si près de la réussite, de la communauté, de la victoire . . .
>
> Peut-être aurait-il fallu, tout simplement, que les petits Européens apprennent eux aussi, sur les bancs de l'école, des chansons arabes et kabyles . . . Il y en a de si belles—qui chantent la plaine, la montagne, l'amour. (262–3)

> We were, in spite of the injustices, and in spite of the gunfire that had

already begun to crackle in the countryside over the past several months, so near to success, to a community, to victory . . .

Perhaps all that would have been needed, quite simply, was for the little Europeans to have learnt, in the schoolroom, some Arab and Kabyle songs . . . There are such pretty ones—which sing of the plains, the mountains, and love.

Love and a few native songs are all that is required, then, to right colonial wrongs, and to bridge the gulf between colonizer and colonized. Jean Pélégri's goodwill is beyond question here; but so, unfortunately, is his liberal self-delusion as regards both the reformability of colonial Algeria and the extent of the changes that would be necessary to bring about such a transformation. In short, he reveals himself to be precisely that 'colonizer of good will' or 'colonizer who denies himself' described by Albert Memmi.[18] For what the author fails to grasp is the total nature of his community's reliance on colonial exploitation of the Algerian. Such a situation could never be made more just, any more than the French army's pacification effort could ever be rendered more humane. It was thus not a question of missed opportunities, still less of chances yet to come. The only real choice was between *Algérie française*, complete with its inherent injustice, or an FLN-led *Algérie algérienne*. When pushed, Camus was to opt in 1957 for the former, infamously preferring his 'mother' to 'justice'.[19] For his part, Pélégri attempts to evade the issue, languishing instead in the nostalgic evocation of a childhood golden age dominated by his now-dead father. It would thus fall to Jules Roy to argue for the latter option. Such *pied-noir* support for the cause of Algerian nationalism is not without its problems, inevitably, but it does show just how far the liberal conscience was prepared to go in the pursuit of 'justice'. As Roy explains in an apostrophe to his dead friend:

Il ne s'agit pas de préférer sa mère à la justice. Il s'agit d'aimer la justice autant que sa propre mère. (215)

It is not a question of preferring one's mother to justice. It is a question of loving justice as much as one's own mother.

With Jean-Jacques Servan-Schreiber's *Lieutenant en Algérie* (1957) and Henri Alleg's *La Question* [The Question or Torture] (1958), Jules Roy's *La Guerre d'Algérie* (1960) is one of the very rare books which may be said to have exerted a direct influence on French

[18] *Portrait*, 47–69.

[19] *Essais*, 1881–2.

public opinion regarding the conduct and, crucially, the continuation of the Algerian war.[20] As both a retired air force colonel and a *pied-noir*, Roy was uniquely placed to comment on military and political developments in the land of his birth, which helps to explain why his highly critical work quickly became a best-seller. Where such an attack would almost certainly have been seized by the authorities before the watershed of 16 September 1959, when de Gaulle expressed his belief in the necessity of Algerian self-determination, it now contributed to the shift in metropolitan attitudes away from the previous colonial orthodoxy.

Notwithstanding my introductory comments on both the blurring of generic distinctions and the primacy of ideology over self-referentiality in the literature of the Algerian war, the question possibly arises as to the relevance of this celebrated piece of non-fiction to the present discussion. Without invoking the spirit of Montaigne, I would suggest that even the most brief examination of Roy's deeply personal essay will serve to underline its relevance both as liberal testimony and as demystifying art. Indeed, in this little book, Jules Roy used his considerable literary talents to address the big political questions, taking to task both his former comrades-in-arms and his fellow *pieds-noirs*. Foremost amongst the latter was the dead Camus, despite Roy's repeated claim that he would never have had to produce *La Guerre d'Algérie* had his great friend still been alive (13–4; 205–6). For, in fact, Roy's study of the conflict in his native land is very much his own, and has as its foundation a political stand which had already proved to be beyond his illustrious contemporary and many other observers. This is not to say that Roy is any more able to break free of the love-hate problematic than was Jean Pélégri. However, he does push the liberal perspective to its limits, and thus produces its most persuasive account of the Algerian war and the colonial reality that gave rise to it.

Like Pélégri, Roy is preoccupied by the injustice of *Algérie française*, which he similarly identifies as the root cause of the current hostilities. Moreover, the current suffering of the native Algerians is recognized as being the same in kind as that endured by generations of Algerians in the face of the studied indifference of the *pieds-noirs*. So, if Roy returns to his own childhood, it is not to revel nostalgically in happier days gone by, but rather to focus

[20] On the impact of Roy's book, see Talbott, *The War Without a Name*, 175–6.

attention on the European child's indoctrination into the communal myths of the colonized's inferiority and animal-like 'otherness', which must scrupulously be maintained if the colonizers are to continue to be able to live comfortably with the daily spectacle of native misery.[21] By the same token, and without fully taking his accurate social observations to their logical political conclusions, Roy recognizes the effective segregation of the two communities in colonial Algeria. He is consequently well-placed to see through such rare displays of Pélégri's inter-ethnic fraternity as do, in fact, occur:

> Quand la situation était sérieuse, il y a trois ans, les colons prenaient les ratons dans leurs voitures. La fraternité régna tout à coup. On les plaçait à l'avant, bien en évidence. Il fallait les aimer puisqu'ils semblaient avoir gagné. Et puis, le barrage mis en place, les fellagha se firent plus rares et les choses redevinrent ce qu'elles étaient auparavant. La fraternité s'estompa puis disparut. (118)

> When the situation got serious, three years ago, the settlers started taking the wogs in their cars. Fraternity reigned all of a sudden. They would stick them in the front, where they were clearly visible. You had to get along with them because they seemed to have won. And then, with the border fence in place, the fellagha got rarer, and things went back to the way they were before. Fraternity got less noticeable, then disappeared.

On a more general plane, Roy will bear witness to the vision, courage, and determination of his colonizing forbears, but will also raise important questions not normally considered by the descendants of the territory's pioneers. By focusing on the self-interest which motivated their endeavours, he thus produces a telling indictment of the French colonial enterprise. This lucidity regarding the territory's *mise en valeur* [development] puts Roy in an unusually strong position to consider French Algeria's present troubles, enabling him to recognize not only the inevitability of Algerian independence, but also the legitimacy of the FLN's struggle. This is a major departure for a liberal thinker, and one which is made all the more remarkable by Roy's decision to align himself morally with the nationalist revolutionaries, and against his natural allies. Addressing himself to a French army captain whom he met in the course of his researches, the author suggests that he, at least, has come to understand the total nature of a colonial war in which one must, sooner or later, choose between the two sides:

[21] These myths are considered in their own right in Ch. 7.

> Il n'y a plus rien de commun entre vous et moi, capitaine. Je ne serai jamais de votre côté en Algérie et si un jour, dans le collimateur de vos chars ou de vos avions, vous distinguez parmi les ratons en guenilles un grand bâtard de votre race aux cheveux blancs, ce sera moi. N'hésitez pas. Appuyez sur les boutons de feu de vos mitrailleuses. Ce jour-là, vous aurez bien servi la cause de l'Occident. (169–70)

> You and I no longer have anything in common, Captain. I shall never be on your side in Algeria, and if, one day, in the gunsights of your tanks or your planes, you spot a big, white-haired bastard belonging to your own race amongst the ragged wogs, that will be me. Don't hesitate. Pull the trigger of your machine-guns. That day, you will have done the West a great service.

This striking image of inter-ethnic solidarity is probably as near as any *pied-noir* writer can reasonably be expected to get to a position of identification with the killers of his fellow-countrymen. Some might be inclined to argue that such a literary show of support for the nationalist cause costs Roy nothing, particularly as he had already chosen, like Camus, the voluntary exile of the Parisian intellectual establishment. However, to do this would be to underestimate the author's feelings for his native land, former comrades, family, and friends. He makes a point, in fact, of stressing the communal ties which must be put behind him if he is to have a clear conscience in this matter:

> On m'accusera de trahison, je le sais. On me menacera comme on l'a déjà fait. Anonymement. Et puis? Je serai un salaud . . . Acceptons loyalement d'être un salaud. (175–6)

> I know that I shall be accused of treason. I shall be threatened as I have been threatened before now. Anonymously. What else? I shall be a bastard . . . Well, then, let's honestly accept that I am a bastard.

Yet for all this, Roy is unable to appreciate the full implications of his developed critique of the Algerian war and the colonial reality which gave rise to it. Like Pélégri, he continues to express faith in the reformability of French Algeria, explaining its injustice in terms of abuses and errors, rather than as the very foundation of the colonial system. For him, the daily humiliation and chronic poverty of the Algerian population of the territory is an accidental rather than a substantial feature of the French colonial presence; something, in short, that might have been avoided. This is the familiar liberal account of the conflict as a failure of paternalism, as a tale of missed opportunities for the creation of a better *Algérie française*. Such thinking is implicit in several of the foregoing quotations, and is made explicit in passages like the following one, in which Roy explains his personal mission to—who else?—his mother:

> Me voilà, maman. Je suis venu voir notre pays pour essayer de comprendre ce que les autres en ont fait. Nous avons bâti des églises, des banques et des écoles, des routes et des hôpitaux, mais nous avons négligé de nous occuper des Arabes comme il aurait fallu. (26)

> Here I am, Mum. I've come to see our land and to try to make sense of what other people have done to it. We've built churches, banks, and schools, roads, and hospitals, but we've failed to look after the Arabs as we should have done.

Had the colonizers of Algeria paid more attention to the welfare of the colonized population, then, 'none of this need ever have happened', and the economic and political ascendancy of the *pieds-noirs* could have remained unchallenged. For if Roy is prepared to argue for greater social justice in an 'Algerian' Algeria, he is not ready to countenance the end to settler privileges that would be necessary to turn any such dream into political reality. Put bluntly, there could be no safe place in the new Algeria for colonizers: for the European population to have remained would have meant giving up their French citizenship, and, of course, the advantages that went with it. The option of sharing in the nation's independence was open to them, but they would have had to forego their communal 'superiority' in order to avail themselves of it. This they were unable to do, as the scorched-earth policies of the OAS and the subsequent European exodus so dramatically demonstrated.

The fact that Jules Roy should have clung to his belief in the future Algerian role of the *pieds-noirs* is a function of his misunderstanding of the nature of Algerian aspirations at this time. For what the rebels were seeking in 1960 was not limited, as he suggests, to 'leurs droits physiques, civiques et moraux' [their physical, civic, and moral rights], otherwise termed 'justice' or 'dignity' (43; 103). What they now demanded, rather, was that Algerian nation which Roy is able neither to deny, nor yet fully to accept. Such an entity is consequently deemed to have come about only as a result of French mistakes, and to remain in an embryonic form:

> Il n'y en avait pas . . . de patrie algérienne! Les Italiens descendants des Romains, les Juifs, les Turcs, les Grecs ou les Berbères auraient pu autant que les Arabes, derniers occupants de cette terre avant nous, revendiquer

des droits de gouvernement! Et nous avons fait, ou sommes en train de faire la patrie algérienne contre nous, de souder contre nous cette mosaïque de peuples qui se détestaient, se jalousaient et s'égorgeaient les uns les autres. . . . La 'patrie algérienne' n'existe peut-être pas encore dans le sens où le F.L.N. l'emploie, mais elle est en train de se cimenter. (181–2)[22]

The Algerian homeland . . . never existed! The Italians as the descendants of the Romans, the Jews, the Turks, the Greeks, or the Kabyles could all have made as much of a claim to the right to govern this land as the Arabs, who were its last occupiers before us! And yet we have created or are in the process of creating the Algerian nation against us, we are uniting this mosaic of peoples who used to detest and envy one another, and who went around cutting each other's throats. . . . The 'Algerian nation' might not yet exist in the sense in which the FLN uses the term, but it is in the process of coming together.

Two ideological features stand out quite clearly here: the 'natural' potential for the French colonization of Algeria, and the artificiality of the FLN's 'homeland'. Such an approach to nationalist demands brings Roy rather closer to that adopted by the die-hard partisans of *Algérie française* than he might have realized or intended. Indeed, the only conclusion to be drawn from such thinking is that France has every right to assert its sovereignty over the territory and people of Algeria. What is more, it is still not too late for the real integration of the latter into the French national community: 'Tout est possible encore, oui, si nous nous décidons enfin à aimer' [Yes, everything is still possible, if we at last decide to love one another] (201).

Here, Roy appeals overtly to what may conveniently be termed the love-hate problematic: that is to say, a depoliticizing model of colonial society which allows interracial conflict to be read as a failure of fraternity, and which has previously been identified as the root cause of Pélégri's liberal illusions. It was Roy's inability to go beyond this conceptual framework that prevented him from coming to terms with the totality of Algeria's problems, and specifically with the imminent demise of his own community. So, while he may present a most damning indictment of both Algeria's colonial reality and France's colonial war, he is still able to suggest that *fraternité* is a practical alternative to independence:

[22] This theme, most infamously stated by the moderate nationalist Ferhat Abbas before he was converted to the cause of militant nationalism, will be considered further in Ch. 7.

N'arrive-t-il pas qu'on se haïsse et s'entre-tue entre frères, puis qu'on se réconcilie? . . . Ils sont nos ennemis? Sûrement. Pour le moment. Mais aussi nos frères. Pour toujours. (197–8)

Does it not sometimes happen that brothers can hate and even kill one another, and then be reconciled? . . . They are our enemies? Certainly. For the time being. But also our brothers. Forever.

Jules Roy's account of the roots of nationalist rebellion may fruitfully be juxtaposed with the intriguing image of the Algerian war communicated by Albert Camus's short story, 'L'Hôte' [usually translated as 'The Guest']. One of the collection published in 1957 under the particularly evocative title *L'Exil et le royaume* [translated as *Exile and the Kingdom*], this is the only work of fiction by the great *pied-noir* liberal directly to address the issues raised by the FLN's armed challenge to continued French rule in the territory.[23] In consequence, 'L'Hôte' has a privileged position in the writings of this most famous son of *Algérie française*, and will therefore form the subject of the next chapter.

[23] Camus's principal essays on the Algerian war were published together as *Actuelles* iii: *chroniques algériennes* (Gallimard, 1958; also available in Camus, *Essais*, 887–1018).

4

ANTI-COLONIALIST COMMITMENT: CAMUS'S UNINVITED GUEST

Since Camus's premature death in 1960, two tendencies have become apparent in critical studies of his work. Most commentators have tended to concentrate on the 'universal' novelist and philosopher: the popular perception of Camus as what one of his most memorable characters, Tarrou in *La Peste* [published as *The Plague*], describes as 'un saint sans Dieu' [a saint without God].[1] They have consequently played down the properly Algerian dimension of Camus's writing, and especially the *pied-noir* specificity of his fiction. Thus it is that an American critic can argue that: '*The Guest* ['L'Hôte'] has nothing to teach about the Algerian conflict, except insofar as its problems were those of all conflicts, in all ages and in all places, between all sorts of people and for all sorts of reasons'.[2]

In the face of this posthumous critical canonization of the writer, others have sought periodically to 'desanctify' Camus's writing by placing it back into the social context from which it originated, thereby revealing the essentially colonial conditions of its production. This latter approach can actually be traced back to Albert Memmi's 1957 essay 'Camus ou le colonisateur de bonne volonté' [Camus or the Colonizer of Goodwill], an expression of a demythologizing tendency which was amplified in 1961, when the historian Pierre Nora identified *L'Étranger* [published as *The Outsider*] as a precise distillation of the French colonial presence in Algeria.[3] Such

[1] *Théâtre, récits, nouvelles* (Gallimard/NRF, 1962), 1427.

[2] E. Showalter, '*The Guest*: The Reluctant Host, Fate's Hostage', in the same author's *Exiles and Strangers: A Reading of Camus's Exile and the Kingdom* (Columbus, Ohio State Univ. Press, 1984), 76.

[3] 'Camus ou le colonisateur de bonne volonté', *La Nef*, 12 Dec. 1957, 95–6. P. Nora, *Les Français d'Algérie* (Julliard, 1961), 190–1. See also A. Memmi, *Portrait du colonisé précédé du portrait du colonisateur* (Corréa, 1957; refs. are to the Gallimard/NRF edn., 1985), 47–69, and Nora, 'Pour une autre explication de *L'Étranger*', *France Observateur*, 7

thinking has subsequently been developed by Albert Memmi in an essay devoted to 'Une littérature de la séparation' [A Literature of Separation].[4] In this analysis of the European settlers' literary depiction of their relationship with the colonized peoples of North Africa, Memmi argues that a thoroughgoing awareness of the colonized was always precluded by the violence inherent in the colonial system, with the result that the fictional *indigène* [native] remained throughout a shadowy, stereotypical, and insubstantial figure. However, if the *pied-noir* authors proved to be incapable of dealing satisfactorily with the 'contradictory complementarity' of the Franco-Algerian relationship, they were able to communicate, albeit unwittingly, the terminal *malaise* of the settler community. Memmi points to the work of Albert Camus as being of particular importance in this regard, attaching a concrete historical significance to such evocative titles as *L'Étranger*, *Le Malentendu* [published as *The Misunderstanding*], and, perhaps above all, *L'Exil et le royaume* [published as *Exile and the Kingdom*] (1954).

In what follows, I shall argue that both Daru, the European schoolmaster at the centre of events in 'L'Hôte', and the unnamed Arab prisoner with whom he unwillingly finds himself entrusted, are created in the ideological image of Camus himself, and may consequently be regarded as personifications of the *pied-noir* liberal's fundamental alienation from native Algerian society. The narrative testifies to its creator's inescapable estrangement (*étrangeté*) in his homeland, a condition which must ultimately be understood as a dialectical counterpart to that *étrangeté* imposed on the indigenous population of Algeria by a culturally aggressive colonialism. As O'Brien puts it: 'Camus is a stranger on the African shore, and surrounded by people who are strangers in that France of which they are legally supposed to be a part'.[5] It is the tortured liberal's partial awareness of his colonial dilemma that lies behind what Yvonne Guers-Villate terms Daru's 'deliberate refusal to influence others'.[6] The fictional character's predicament is emblematic of Camus's own intellectual quandary: it is a desperately self-justifying representation of his historical unwillingness to take a clear stand on

Jan. 1960, 16–17. For a consciously political reading of Camus, see, among others, C. O'Brien, *Camus* (Glasgow, Collins, 1970), and S. Tarrow, *Exile from the Kingdom: A Political Rereading of Albert Camus* (Alabama, Univ. of Alabama Press, 1985).

[4] *Anthologie des écrivains français du Maghreb* (Présence Africaine, 1969), 11–21.

[5] *Camus*, 14.

[6] 'Rieux and Daru or the Deliberate Refusal to Influence Others', in J. Suther (ed.), *Essays on Camus's Exile and the Kingdom* (Univ. of Mississippi Press, 1980), 143–51.

the Algerian question. Moreover, the text's rhetorical imposition of a tragic reading of Daru's experience may be understood as a mystifying, because depoliticizing, allegory of this authorial 'refusal to intervene'.[7]

Set in the Algerian *hauts-plateaux* [high plains] of the early 1950s, Camus's reworking of the age-old theme of unexpected help from a perceived enemy owes its depth to a double paradox: the European, ordered by the local gendarme to keep an Arab suspect in his school overnight and then to take him to prison, decides instead to give the man food and money before showing him the road to freedom; while the Arab, both surprisingly and significantly, himself takes the road to jail. To make ideological sense of this tale, it is helpful to identify points of tension between the narrative and its diegesis, understood as the sequence of actions and events that the reader construes from the narrative. By so doing, we may demonstrate that the account of Daru's confrontation with the accused native is properly regarded as inadequate from a diegetic point of view, to the precise extent that it fails satisfactorily to account for the latter's actions. The answer to the riddle of the prisoner's failure to escape is, in fact, to be found not so much in the words of the text, as in its failure to say anything about the colonized's political existence: this textual silence is the key to the diegetic mystery of 'L'Hôte'.[8]

In order to justify this claim, it is first necessary to consider the narrative technique of this complex text, and particularly its much-discussed ambiguities. The prime source of this textual ambiguity is undoubtedly the free indirect style, which occurs particularly in the first half of the narrative. Mikhail Bakhtin was one of the first to draw attention to this mode of narration in order to demonstrate that 'narrative discourse can contain a dynamic interaction between two or more voices'.[9] Subsequent critics have usefully developed this initial observation by pointing to the varieties of free indirect discourse which may be in play in a given narrative. So, for

[7] Ibid. 147.

[8] 'L'Hôte', in *L'Exil et le royaume* (1954), in *Théâtre, récits, nouvelles*, 1609–23. Part of the text's enigma derives, of course, from the ambiguity of its title, which can be understood both as 'the guest' and 'the host'. Is the story about Daru, or the Arab? Who is the 'guest': the Arab in the *pied-noir*'s house, or the *pied-noir* in a country which, although his homeland, can be thought of as foreign territory?

[9] D. Forgacs, 'Marxist Literary Theories', in A. Jefferson and D. Robey (eds.), *Modern Literary Theory: A Comparative Introduction* (London, B.T. Batsford, 1982; 1986 edn.), 194.

instance, Seymour Chatman has provided a taxonomic guide to this device, using as his criterion the precise degree of 'dynamic interaction' displayed by the literary text:

. . . free indirect style divides into subclasses, attributable to character or to narrator. In between, there are statements of varying degrees of ambiguity. For language that is clearly the character's, a suitable label . . . is *narrated monologue*. 'Narrated' accounts for the indirect features—third person and prior tense—while 'monologue' conveys the sense of hearing the very words of the character. Narrated monologue is clearly distinguished from narrative report (internal analysis), where the character's thinking or speech is communicated in words that are recognizably the narrator's. Finally, there is the relatively common ambiguous situation . . . where it is difficult to know whose voice speaks.[10]

In what follows, I shall argue that the instances of free indirect discourse to be found in 'L'Hôte' are overwhelmingly examples either of Chatman's 'narrated monologue', or of what the same critic goes on to describe as 'neutralized' indirect free style, in which:

A 'sympathetic' effect arises because there is no reason to assume that [the character's] ideolect differs significantly from the narrator's. Such [narrative] statements imply that character and narrator are so close, in such sympathy, that it does not matter to whom we assign the statement. . . . A feeling is established that the narrator possesses not only access to but an unusual affinity or 'vibration' with the character's mind. There is the suggestion of a kind of 'in'-group psychology . . . [and of a] kind of consensus . . .[11]

This view of the text's mode of narration has important implications for my reading of 'L'Hôte'. Most obviously, it leads me to contest John Erickson's claim that what he, adopting Edward Said's terminology, very aptly describes as Camus's 'discourse of exteriority' in his previous literary depictions of Algeria and the Algerians—a discourse 'of exclusion, superimposition, excision, in short, rewriting of the Maghreb in the language of the Other'[12]—is replaced in 'L'Hôte' by a qualitatively different narrative relationship. So, the Arab may well mirror Daru in his bodily manifested

[10] *Story and Discourse: Narrative Structure in Fiction and Film* (Ithaca, Cornell Univ. Press, 1978), 203.

[11] Ibid. 207; see also Chatman's 'A New Point of View on "Point of View"', in his *Coming to Terms: The Rhetoric of Narrative in Fiction and Film* (Ithaca, Cornell Univ. Press, 1990), 139–60.

[12] 'Albert Camus and North Africa: A Discourse of Exteriority', in B. Knapp (ed.), *Critical Essays on Albert Camus* (Boston, Mass., G. K. Hall, 1988), 74.

obstinacy: the former has 'un front buté' [an obstinate forehead] (1611), while the latter maintains 'son air buté' [his obstinate look] (1612) in dealing with the gendarme.[13] More significantly, as Erickson argues, both men may be seen as victims of their respective situations, and may display a certain parallelism in their reactions to the obligations which are imposed upon them: most notably, both put themselves in jeopardy for reasons which are never fully explained and to no apparent avail. On one, in my opinion, superficial level, the two characters may thus be felt to share a common fate and to 'reflect the same feeling of belonging to a fraternity of the damned'.[14] However, the depiction of the Arab in 'L'Hôte' most certainly does not, as a result of these apparent similarities, constitute 'a moving testimony to the possibility of individuals transcending the differences of culture and overcoming the gulf between their sense of self and other'.[15]

Of course, there can be no denying that the alterity depicted in 'L'Hôte' is, as Jean Sarocchi has suggested, both disrupted and plural: as he points out, the Arab is undoubtedly the Other for Daru, but so—if only to a certain extent—is Balducci, the gendarme, who is a representative of the European's own community.[16] Indeed, when, after being presented with his prisoner by the gendarme, 'une colère subite vint à Daru contre cet homme' (1615) [a wave of anger came over Daru at this man], it is not immediately clear to which of these 'others' the descriptive notation should be referred.[17]

However, if Genette's 'telling' and 'showing'—adopted by Chatman as the basis for his distinction between (narrative voice) 'slant' and (character voice) 'filter'[18]—overlap and even coincide in 'L'Hôte', it is emphatically not the case that the anonymous Arab is a party to this process of sympathetic alignment. On the contrary, if the mode of narration does indeed serve to articulate what Edouard Morot-Sir calls an 'intersubjective complicity' between character, narrator, author, and reader—'the distance realized be-

[13] This point is made by P. Cryle in his 'Bodily Positions and Moral Attitudes in *L'Exil et le royaume*', in A. Rizzuto (ed.), *Albert Camus' L'Exil et le royaume: The Third Decade* (Toronto, Paratexte, 1988), 37.

[14] Erickson, 'Albert Camus and North Africa', 85.

[15] Ibid.

[16] 'L'Autre et les autres', in Rizzuto, *L'Exil et le royaume*, 96.

[17] This point is made by Erickson, 'Albert Camus and North Africa', 84.

[18] *Coming to Terms*, 143–4; Genette's famous distinction was first made in his seminal 'Le discours du récit', *Figures*, iii (Seuil, 1972).

tween hero and author by the effect of the third person . . . is almost paradoxical, almost abolished'[19]—then that complicity is most definitely not extended to the Arab.

In fact, Daru, the European 'host', participates in the processes of the narration in a way that his native 'guest' conspicuously does not: the narrative may be written in the third person, but it is his voice which predominates. Indeed, if it is overstating the case to suggest that Camus's short story might be rewritten in the first person without major disruption or loss of impact, it is nevertheless clear that Daru is the tale's sole plausible homodiegetic narrator. All of which suggests that the European protagonist may be regarded as a partner in the discourse of the text; while in contrast, the Algerian suspect handed over to Daru should properly be thought of as the familiar object of the colonizer's speech.

At the most elementary level, this narrative reproduction of colonial power-relations is revealed in the fact that the native Algerian character is never named: unlike the two *pieds-noirs*—the schoolteacher Daru and the policeman Balducci, who, simply by being identified, are rendered present to the reader, and given a basic autonomy—their prisoner is referred to throughout as 'l'Arabe' ['the Arab']. What is more, as the narrative progresses, this representative of the indigenous population of Algeria will emerge not as a concrete individual, but rather as a type or, more accurately, an archetype. For if the Arab prisoner retains the initial anonymity which the *pied-noir* characters are allowed to shed, it is in order that his lack of specificity should not detract from his value as symbol: although undeniably a more substantial figure than the shadowy *indigènes* who appear elsewhere in Camus's fiction, the unnamed Arab still represents his race as a whole (as, perhaps, does Meursault's anonymous victim in *L'Étranger*). For his part, Daru, in contrast to his Arab 'guest', but in common with the *pied-noir* anti-hero just mentioned, is depicted as a highly individual member of his own racial community, if not actually an 'outsider' in his own right.

Gourdon *et al.* have argued persuasively for a view of the ideological stance adopted by Camus and his fellow writers in the *École d'Alger* as being founded on a rejection of the fundamental colonial distinction between colonizer and colonized. It is this rejection of the core problematic of race which obliges these

[19] 'Humor and Exile', in Rizzuto, *L'Exil et le royaume*, 64.

undoubted men of goodwill to focus their narratives on social and moral themes, as opposed to political ones.[20] Daru's predicament is thus, like that of Meursault before him, presented as being essentially ethical, and even ontological, in nature, rather than as the necessary product of the conflictual politics of the colonial situation.[21] This avoidance of the political as regards characterization is a symptom of a more thoroughgoing failure on the part of Camus and his colleagues to confront the historical reality of *Algérie française*. The roots of this inadequacy are themselves to be found in the difficult position within the European community of the authors concerned: Camus, like Emmanuel Roblès[22] and others in the *École d'Alger*, had his roots in Algeria's urban, poor white community, but was cut off from it by his humanist education, his liberalism, and his taste for travel. Moreover, and specifically in spite of his awareness of Arabo-Berber suffering, he remained profoundly isolated from the world of the native Algerian.[23] It is this intellectual predicament which lies behind the preferred liberal self-image: namely, the torture and tragedy of being caught in the middle between two warring tribes, as 'neither victim nor executioner'. This theme is symbolically appealed to from the opening lines of Camus's short story as the schoolmaster watches the two men, one on horseback, the other on foot, come up the steep path towards his isolated outpost of French civilization (1611).

As a teacher, Daru is at the forefront of the colonizer's attempt to fulfil his nation's *mission civilisatrice*.[24] Indeed, his personal contribution to the enlightenment of the benighted Algerian masses is one which takes for granted the validity of the official myth of the *trois départements*, as the map on his blackboard self-consciously reveals. The gift of French education is not the only thing provided by

[20] H. Gourdon *et al.*, 'Roman colonial et idéologie coloniale en Algérie', *Revue algérienne des sciences juridiques, économiques et politiques*, 11/1 (Mar. 1974), 118.

[21] For a fascinating analysis of the initial composition and rewriting of 'L'Hôte', bringing out the tale's increasingly obvious denial of history and politics, see M. Roelens, 'Un texte, son "histoire" et l'histoire: "L'Hôte" d'Albert Camus', *Revue des sciences humaines*, 42/165 (Jan.-Mar. 1977), 5–22.

[22] Roblès's most obvious contribution to the literature of the Algerian war is his preface to the 1960 edn. of his play *Les Hauteurs de la ville* (Seuil, 1948), which underlined the relevance to the nationalist uprising of a work which, although set during World War II, turns on a young Algerian's murder of his European oppressor.

[23] See Gourdon, 'Roman colonial et idéologie coloniale', 119. Cf. A. Hargreaves, 'Camus and the colonial question in Algeria', *The Muslim World*, 77 (1987), 172.

[24] The primary schoolteacher, both civilian and military, is regularly celebrated in the literature of the Algerian war. See e.g. J. Sutra, *Algérie mon amour: l'histoire d'une institutrice pied-noir* (*Constantine 1920–1962*) (Atlanthrope, 1979).

Daru the schoolmaster, however, as he is also responsible for the distribution of the grain supplied by the colonial authorities to alleviate the effects of the eight months of drought which have directly preceded the present snows. Thus the European educator provides not only intellectual sustenance for the Arab population of Algeria's *hauts-plateaux*, but also its material equivalent. That the author of 'Misère de la Kabylie' (1939)[25] should be aware of the suffering of a large section of the native population of Algeria is as predictable as is his failure to consider the very need for supplementary feeding of this kind as an indictment of the colonial relegation of the indigenous inhabitants of the territory to the most marginal of its constituent lands.

From the outset, the narrative presents Daru as an individual living in splendid isolation from both sides of colonial Algerian society: he is above the common run of humanity, both physically and spiritually, as is underlined by the overtly monastic quality of his spartan existence. However, the seclusion and tranquillity of his world are soon to be shattered by the arrival of Balducci and the Arab: hence the appeal of the image for Camus, the troubled liberal. Daru/Camus is required by each side in the developing colonial conflict to take a positive stand for or against it, with no middle ground being recognized. He attempts, nevertheless, to live in what is a political no-man's-land, and is rejected by both sides in consequence. The two men climbing up the mountain towards him are, in effect, the twin harbingers of his personal fate: unable to align himself wholeheartedly with either the colonizer or the colonized, Daru will be condemned for his failure to obey the Manichaean rules of the colonial game.

Yet this tragic reading of Camus's tale is not easy to uphold in view of the historical relationship obtaining between Europeans and non-Europeans in the Algeria of the 1950s. Daru's apparent rejection of both warring tribes only becomes possible, in fact, through the refusal of colonial logic's own version of the 'law of excluded middle', which denies the possibility of intermediate positions in the Algerian context. For the fact of the matter is that Daru, like Camus himself, can never be anything other than an objective oppressor: willingly or unwillingly, he is condemned by his race to be a colonizer. The very existence of the colonized will therefore be a permanent reminder of precisely that privilege

[25] A. Camus, 'Misère de la Kabylie' (1939), in *Essais*, 903–38.

challenged by the militant nationalism of the FLN and recognized by the European witness to native suffering: 'Devant cette misère, [Daru] . . . s'était senti un seigneur, avec ses murs crépis, son divan étroit, ses étagères de bois blanc, son puits, et son ravitaillement hebdomadaire en eau et en nourriture' [In the face of this extreme poverty, [Daru] . . . had felt like a lord, with his whitewashed walls, his cramped bed, his plain wooden bookshelves, and his weekly delivery of food and water] (1612).

At his post high in the mountains, Camus's *seigneur* bears an uncanny resemblance to the heroes depicted by less-troubled literary defenders of *Algérie française*. This apparent mythological kinship is borne out by the description of the teacher's affinity for the land around him, as the chief characteristic of Daru's *hauts-plateaux* is the absence of its indigenous Algerian inhabitants. The strategy exploited here is the familiar colonialist one of systematically insisting upon the emptiness of the land which the French teacher—the archetypal cultural colonizer—has effectively settled: 'ces terres ingrates, habitées seulement par des pierres' ['this hostile land, peopled only by stones'] (1617).[26] Yet for all its appearance of desolation, this land is, indeed, inhabited by someone other than Daru, and so we read that 'Le pays était ainsi, cruel à vivre, même sans les hommes, qui, pourtant, n'arrangeaient rien' ['The land was like that, cruel to live in, even without men, who, moreover, did not make things any easier'] (1612–3). Here, the presence of the indigenous population of the *hauts-plateaux* is magically transformed into an absence. This prepositional negation of the region's native inhabitants—'sans les hommes'—is symptomatic of a more sinister denial of the colonized's troublesome presence. Where, after all, are the schoolmaster's Arab pupils? Is it really just a coincidence that they, the ostensible reason for his being in the mountains at all, are kept away from the school by heavy snows at the very moment singled out by Camus for our consideration? And why do the starving parents and grandparents of his pupils never come looking for food, as Daru himself expects? We might as well ask why it is that only Europeans seem to die of plague in the Oran of *La Peste*.

In order to deny the existence of the indigenous population of the region even more effectively, it is helpful to demonstrate that Daru himself is an *indigène* in some sense. This is duly done, but not

[26] For a more detailed analysis of the symbolism of this landscape, see P. Fortier, 'Le décor symbolique de "l'Hôte" d'Albert Camus', *French Review*, 46/3 (Feb. 1973), 535–42.

without creating a very revealing tension between the text and its diegesis. Compare the following extracts:

Le pays était ainsi, cruel à vivre, même sans les hommes, qui pourtant, n'arrangeaient rien. Mais Daru y était né. Partout ailleurs il se sentait exilé. (1612–13)

The land was like that, cruel to live in, even without men, who, moreover, did not make things any easier. But Daru had been born there. Everywhere else he felt exiled.

Longtemps, il [Daru] resta étendu sur son divan à regarder le ciel se fermer peu à peu, à écouter le silence. C'était ce silence qui lui avait paru pénible les premiers jours de son arrivée, après la guerre. (1617)

For a long time, he [Daru] remained stretched out on his bed watching the sky close in little by little, and listening to the silence. It was the silence which had seemed hard to bear when he first arrived, after the war.

Was Daru born in the region or was he not? Is he a native of the *hauts-plateaux* or did he move to it after the war? Camus's wish to establish the character's indigenous credentials—underlined by Balducci's observation that 'Tu es d'ici' ['You're from here'] (1616)—is indicative of a profound uncertainty in the *pied-noir* psyche as regards the nature of the settlers' own relationship with the land. Whether born in Algeria or not, the European population could never be of the land in the way that its indigenous inhabitants all too plainly were. They are only there as the result of the use of force, a fact which precludes a normal relationship with either the colonized population or the colonized land. It is this historical truth which must be suppressed at all costs: hence the retreat of the French liberal intelligentsia from practical politics; hence Camus's post-1958 silence;[27] hence the silence at the heart of 'L'Hôte'.

Throughout the narrative, in fact, we are in a silent zone, with Daru himself established from the outset as an essentially uncommunicative figure. Not only Camus's snow-covered *hauts-plateaux*, but also their principal, if not sole, inhabitant, are presented as being 'naturally' silent. So, as the short story opens with the schoolmaster watching Balducci and the Arab climb towards him, he can see the two men, but cannot identify them on account of their distance from him. Moreover, he cannot hear them, or Balducci's horse, until they are very much closer. When one of the men waves to

[27] See Hargreaves, 'Liberal Dilemma', 81, where it is argued that Camus's silence on Algerian politics began in the decade leading up to the 1954 insurrection.

him, Daru does not respond, and even when the distant figures do make themselves heard, he avoids communicating with them:

> A portée de voix, Balducci cria: 'Une heure pour faire les trois kilomètres d'El Ameur ici!' Daru ne répondit pas. (1613)

> When they came within earshot, Balducci shouted out: 'An hour to do the three kilometres from El Ameur to here!' Daru did not reply.

A pattern of non-communication is thus established which will be developed as the narrative unfolds: at key moments, Daru will regularly choose either to refrain from speaking himself or to refuse to listen. This pattern, in fact, is what characterizes the schoolmaster's relationship with the unnamed Algerian, who, moreover, is depicted in wholly negative terms. The treatment begins with the physical description of the prisoner, with attention being drawn to the unhealthy and alien aspects of his appearance: 'Daru ne vit d'abord que ses énormes lèvres, pleines, lisses, presque négroïdes; le nez cependant était droit, les yeux sombres, pleins de fièvre' [All Daru could see at first were his enormous lips, which were full and smooth, almost negroid; his nose, however, was straight, while his eyes were dark and full of fever] (1613). As for the crime which is the primary constituent of the prisoner's identity, Camus is at pains to make clear that it is a common-law offence, and thus neither political nor directed against France:

> 'Enfin,' dit-il [Daru] en se retournant vers Balducci, 'qu'est-ce qu'il a fait?' Et il demanda, avant que le gendarme ait ouvert la bouche: 'Il parle français?'
>
> 'Non, pas un mot. On le recherchait depuis un mois, mais ils le cachaient. Il a tué son cousin.'
>
> 'Il est contre nous?'
>
> 'Je ne crois pas. Mais on ne peut jamais savoir.'
>
> 'Pourquoi a-t-il tué?'
>
> 'Des affaires de famille, je crois. L'un devait du grain à l'autre, paraît-il. Ça n'est pas clair. Enfin, bref, il a tué le cousin d'un coup de serpe. Tu sais, comme au mouton, zic! . . . '
>
> Balducci fit le geste de passer une lame sur sa gorge et l'Arabe, son attention attirée, le regardait avec une sorte d'inquiétude. Une colère subite vint à Daru contre cet homme, contre tous les hommes et leur sale méchanceté, leurs haines inlassables, leur folie du sang. (1615)

> 'Anyway,' he [Daru] asked, turning to face Balducci, 'what has he done?'
>
> And he added, before the gendarme could open his mouth to reply:

'Does he speak French?'

'No, not a word. We have been looking for him for the past month, but they were hiding him. He killed his cousin.'

'Is he against us?'

'I don't think so. But you can never tell.'

'Why did he kill him?'

'A family matter, I think. It seems that one owed the other some grain. It isn't clear. To cut a long story short, he killed his cousin with a billhook. You know, like a sheep . . . '

Balducci mimed the action of cutting his own throat and the Arab, who had noticed this, watched him rather nervously. A wave of anger came over Daru at this man, at all men and their disgusting malice, their tireless hatreds, and their blood lust.

This passage is an extremely dense one in mythic terms, and tells us a great deal about the liberal's troubled perception of the Algerian colonized. To begin with, what stands out here is precisely the 'otherness'[28] of the Arab sitting in front of Daru: the schoolmaster may quickly transform his disgust at 'this man' (which I take to refer to the Arab) and his crime into a generalized diatribe against human wickedness, but the integrated reader will not mistake the primary object of his anger. What sort of man, after all, could kill his cousin with a billhook in a dispute over a few grains of wheat? Who else but the Algerian colonized: the fanatical and bloodthirsty throat-cutter, the *sale et méchant* Arab of French popular myth. It is this profoundly alien figure which Daru is faced with, and will attempt to treat with properly liberal humanity.

Similarly worthy of particular note is the *ils/nous* opposition introduced by Balducci and immediately picked up and put into use by Daru himself: for all his subsequent attempts to place himself in the no man's land between colonizer and colonized, he clearly aligns himself with both the settler community and the French colonial cause. As the gendarme makes clear, this binary opposition is of central importance at a time when open hostilities between the two parties are daily more likely: 'S'ils se soulèvent, personne n'est à l'abri, nous sommes tous dans le même sac' [If there's a rising, none of us will be safe, we're all in the same boat] (1616). The old Corsican's analysis is borne out, as the narrative closes, by the threat made against Daru by the Arab's 'brothers', in spite of his efforts to help the unwanted prisoner to escape.

The gendarme's reply to Daru's enquiry effectively denies the

[28] The dialectic of the Self and the Other forms the subject of Ch. 7.

possibility of a political motive for the murder, while also managing to suggest the existence of a permanent gulf between 'us' and 'them' as regards motivations and affiliations: 'you never can tell' (with them). In Memmi's terms, the stigmatizing, and paradoxically homogenizing, sign of plurality ('la marque du pluriel')[29] is applied without question by both the representative of the coercive forces of the colonial state and Camus's liberal hero. A basic figure of colonialist discourse, this agglomerating denial of the colonized as political agent is a clear hint at the nature of the diegetic hole in Camus's narrative.

Also to be underlined is the Arab's total inability to speak French: not only is the native Algerian deprived of the single most important requirement for integration into colonial society as a whole, he is also put at a major disadvantage in his dealings with any individual European, such as Daru. The schoolmaster, like the gendarme, is able to speak Arabic, and is thus in a position to take charge in all exchanges with the colonized: excluded from the French-speaking community, the colonized must accept the dominance of the colonizer even in the use of his native language.[30]

Finally, particular attention must be drawn to the central figure's judgement of his unwanted prisoner. This is of considerable importance given the generally accepted reluctance of both Camus himself and his literary spokesmen either to judge or to be judged.[31] Here, for once, Camus does judge, and, moreover, he goes so far as to reiterate his judgement of the Arab and his act on two different occasions. In the first of these, the schoolmaster attempts to explain to the gendarme his refusal to turn over the prisoner, whose guilt is never in doubt, to the colonial authorities:

> 'Ecoute, Balducci,' dit Daru soudainement, 'tout ça me dégoûte, et ton gars le premier. Mais je ne le livrerai pas. Me battre, oui, s'il le faut. Mais pas ça.' (1616)
>
> 'Listen, Balducci,' said Daru suddenly, 'all this disgusts me, and your lad here more than anything. But I won't turn him in. I'll fight, yes, if I have to. But not that.'

In the second, the attempt at self-justification is for the schoolmaster's own benefit:

[29] *Portrait du colonisé*, 106. See also A. Hargreaves, 'Personnes grammaticales et relations affectives chez Camus', *Revue Celfan/Celfan Review*, 4/3 (1985), 10–17.

[30] See Memmi, *Portrait du colonisé*, 127. This question is discussed further in Ch. 7.

[31] The characters of Meursault and Tarrou come to mind immediately in this connection.

Le crime imbécile de cet homme le révoltait, mais le livrer était contraire à l'honneur: d'y penser seulement le rendait fou d'humiliation. Et il maudissait à la fois les siens qui lui envoyaient cet Arabe et celui-ci qui avait osé tuer et n'avait pas su s'enfuir. (1621)

This man's idiotic crime appalled him, but handing him over was not an honourable thing to do: just thinking about it was enough to drive him wild with humiliation. He cursed both his own people, who had sent him this Arab, and the man himself, who had dared to kill but had not known how to run away.

The all-inclusive quality of that 'tout ça' is significant. Indeed, the phrase may reasonably be taken to refer to the pressure exerted by the whole situation on Daru, who seems already to be aware of the ethical conflict that is made explicit in the latter quotation. Yet at no stage are we encouraged to believe that Daru, the colonizer of goodwill, will be able to come to terms with his unavoidably profound alienation from the indigenous inhabitants of Algeria. His liberal moralism may make him aware of their suffering, and may even lead to a reluctance to commit himself overtly to supporting the repressive apparatus of the colonial state, but it can never be enough to enable him to bridge the all-consuming colonial divide.

It should be noted here that a case could be made for reading Camus's short story as itself a critique of liberal *pied-noir* universalism. The reference to the map of France is, on this reading, to be regarded as a quite deliberate piece of authorial self-criticism, intended to show the extent of the liberal schoolmaster's failure to appreciate his own role in maintaining the myths of French Algeria. Daru is thus presented as a man tragically blind to a situation that he almost understands. So, left on his own with the prisoner, Daru will experience a real fraternity with his 'guest', but will seek to deny the fact because he is trapped within a scheme of masculine values which does not permit such feelings. Consider Camus's description of the intimacy imposed on the schoolmaster as a result of his having to sleep in the same room as the Arab:

Dans la chambre où, depuis un an, il dormait seul, cette présence le gênait. Mais elle le gênait aussi parce qu'elle lui imposait une sorte de fraternité qu'il refusait dans les circonstances présentes et qu'il connaissait bien: les hommes, qui partagent les mêmes chambres, soldats ou prisonniers, contractent un lien étrange comme si, leurs armures quittées avec les vêtements, ils se rejoignaient chaque soir, par-dessus leurs différences, dans la vieille communauté du songe et de la fatigue. Mais Daru se secouait, il n'aimait pas ces bêtises, il fallait dormir. (1620)

In the room where, for the past year, he had slept alone, this presence bothered him. But it also bothered him because it imposed upon him a kind of fraternity that he refused to accept under the present circumstances and which he knew well: men who share the same sleeping quarters, whether soldiers or prisoners, enter into a strange union, as if, shedding their defences with their clothes, they came together each evening in the ancient community of dreams and fatigue. But Daru shook himself out of it; he did not like that sort of foolishness, and he had to get some sleep.

In fact, what we are faced with here is a characteristic liberal mystification: the history of colonial strife is replaced by the myth of a supra-ethnic fraternity. The fact that Daru chooses to close his eyes, both literally and metaphorically, to the implications of this new relationship with the colonized is, in consequence, less important than the fact that it should be deemed possible at all. Indeed, the passing-up of the occasion fits readily into the liberal perspective of wasted opportunities. What really counts is the author's appeal to the familiar notion of the brotherhood of man, rather than the protagonist's attempted denial of that ethnicity-transcending humanity. Compare the following passage, in which Daru once again finds himself forced, involuntarily, into an awareness of the colonized's existence:

A ce moment, de l'autre côté de l'école, le prisonnier toussa. Daru l'écouta, presque malgré lui, puis, furieux, jeta un caillou qui siffla dans l'air avant de s'enfoncer dans la neige. (1621)

At that moment, on the other side of the school, the prisoner coughed. Daru listened to him, almost in spite of himself, then he furiously threw a pebble, which whistled through the air before embedding itself in the snow.

Daru's violent reaction to the Arab's intrusion on his hilltop isolation—he wishes for nothing so much as to be left alone once again—is symptomatic of his desire to avoid contact with the colonized. When the Arab mysteriously asks the schoolmaster to accompany him and the gendarme the following day, Daru fails to respond either positively or negatively (1619). The Arab's entreaty is itself unexplained—'Pourquoi? . . . Pourquoi? . . . ' asks Daru in vain—and is rendered all the more enigmatic by being left hanging unanswered as the action jumps, without a break, to the middle of the night. The prisoner's appeal 'Viens avec nous . . . ' [Come with us . . .] thus becomes heavy with implied meanings, the most obvious of which is an invitation to the schoolmaster to abandon the side of the colonizers and to throw in his lot with the colonized. The liberal, caught in the contradictions of his revolt against colonial means, while not at the same time condemning colonial ends, seeks solace in silence. Later, he will be led to impose silence on his uninvited guest:

L'Arabe s'était retourné maintenant vers Daru et une sorte de panique se levait sur son visage: 'Ecoute', dit-il. Daru secoua la tête: 'Non, tais-toi. Maintenant, je te laisse.' (1623)

The Arab had now turned to face Daru and something like an expression of panic appeared on his face. 'Listen,' he said. Daru shook his head: 'No, be quiet. I'm going to leave you now.'

Daru's refusal to listen to the Arab at this critical time—the schoolmaster has just told the prisoner to judge for himself between freedom and prison—is, I would argue, indicative of a general refusal on Daru's part to face up to his own need to choose between two mutually exclusive political paths.[32] He longs to be rid of his uninvited guest, after all, in order precisely that he may 'se retrouver seul sans avoir rien à décider' [be on his own again, with no decisions to make] (1618). The panic and indecision of the Arab when forced to choose is thus just one aspect of a broader reluctance to take sides in Camus's narrative; and this in spite of the author's obvious appreciation of the ultimate impossibility of avoiding such a choice in the colonial context. The presence of this fundamental tension undoubtedly makes for a text that is remarkably rich in meanings. However, it is very much open to question how far such a characteristically liberal approach may serve to demystify the role of ethnicity in the Algerian conflict.

In the event, both the Arab and Daru vote with their feet for the colonial status quo. The former prefers European-guided imprisonment to an independent Algerian liberty, symbolized by the desert and its nomadic tribesmen, while the latter returns to his blackboard and its map of France's principal rivers. He may have made an anti-colonialist gesture by providing the Arab with food and money, and by pointing out the direction to freedom, but he has not been able to abandon (*lâcher*) his own kind in the total way necessitated by the colonial context (1616). His earlier reflections on his rather

[32] It will by now be obvious that, specifically as regards 'L'Hôte', I am not persuaded by the argument that 'authentic communication . . . [is achieved in Camus's fictional world] not by making noise, producing superficial and mechanical communication, but in giving silence its full power and its own consciousness'; Morot-Sir, 'Humor and Exile', in Rizzuto, *L'Exil et le royaume*, 56.

brusque treatment of the old Corsican gendarme, Balducci, underline the strength of his ties with his own community—'les siens'—and thus prepare us for this final outcome:

Il pensait à Balducci. Il lui avait fait de la peine, il l'avait renvoyé, d'une certaine manière, comme s'il ne voulait pas être dans le même sac. Il entendait encore l'adieu du gendarme et, sans savoir pourquoi, il se sentait étrangement vide et vulnérable. (1621)

He thought about Balducci. He had upset him, sent him packing, in a way, as if he did not want to be in the same boat. He could still hear the gendarme's farewell, and, without knowing why, he felt strangely empty and vulnerable.

What more appropriate adverb could be applied to Daru's feelings than this 'étrangement', with all its typically Camusian resonances? Like the great *pied-noir* liberal whose mouthpiece he most certainly is, the schoolmaster is an *étranger* in the land of his birth: a foreigner, an outsider, and ultimately an outcast. It is therefore only to be expected that Daru, in the face of the threatened Algerian reprisals against him, should look to the north, and thus towards the Mediterranean and France, as the narrative closes:

Daru regardait le ciel, le plateau et, au-delà, les terres invisibles qui s'étendaient jusqu'à la mer. Dans ce vaste pays qu'il avait tant aimé, il était seul. (1623)

Daru looked at the sky, the plateau, and, beyond, the invisible land which stretched all the way to the sea. In this vast country which he had so loved, he was alone.

Where Daru renounces his beloved Algeria at the end of the story, his Arab 'guest' gives up his freedom. Why? No wholly convincing answer is possible, as Showalter explains:

The prisoner's last gesture . . . is highly ironic, a black parody of Hernani's vow to reconstitute himself prisoner of Don Ruy. It remains, moreover, unexplainable . . . many suggestions have been advanced to justify the prisoner's decision; but with the story narrated rigorously from Daru's perspective, there can be no fully persuasive explanation.[33]

Even more revealingly, the critic notes that 'we cannot hope to solve the problem through understanding the Arab because Camus does not tell us enough about him'[34]. For the real answer to the enigma of the Arab's choice of prison over liberty is to be found in

[33] Showalter, *Exiles and Strangers*, 74.
[34] Ibid. 79.

Camus's failure to describe the figure in sufficient depth and detail. The anonymous victim of a European's gratuitous violence in the Algiers of *L'Étranger*, ignored in the Oran of *La Peste*, the colonized is mysterious and unconvincing in the mountains of 'L'Hôte'. As depicted by Albert Camus, the native Algerian is essentially unknowable: a permanent puzzle for author, narrator, protagonist, and reader alike. Deprived of a political dimension from the moment he and his crime are introduced, in this, the only one of Camus's literary texts to refer directly to the violent challenge of the Algerian nationalists to continued French rule in the territory, the colonized finds himself denied what is perhaps the most fundamental constituent of his, and our, humanity. In the process, the specifically political violence which rocked Algeria in the 1950s gives way to the evil done by all humankind. The history of France's principal North African colony is thus replaced in 'L'Hôte' by an altogether less troublesome universalism, common to Camus and his fellow liberals in the *École d'Alger*. If the author's imaging of the colonized suffers in consequence, then at least this failing serves to draw attention to the very real heights attained by the same writer in his depiction of the terminal psychic *malaise* of French Algeria.

Part 2

Remembering the War Without a Name, 1962–1992

5

'LA QUILLE, BORDEL!': RECALLING *LE RAPPEL*

It was the French Revolution itself which gave rise to the concept of 'the nation in arms', and thus to the practice of conscription. However, ever since its introduction under the Directory in 1798—specifically to provide the necessary manpower for Napoleon Bonaparte's attempt to turn Egypt into France's first North African colony—compulsory military service, though attractive in theory, has given rise to numerous difficulties in practice. In the modern era, this discrepancy has led French governments to continue to voice their faith in the benefits of non-vocational military service, while at the same time presiding over the emergence of a genuinely professional military apparatus. The end result of this dual approach has been an undeclared division of the French army into two effectively separate forces: an army in which those civilians called upon to serve the Republic might fulfil their patriotic obligations; and a very different army, the one which was relied upon to do the real fighting as France sought to re-establish her grip on an overseas empire profoundly affected by the Second World War. It was this 'real' army which had fought, and lost, in Indo-China; and it was the shattered remnants of this same army which set about avenging that defeat in Algeria.

The great difference, as far as successive Paris administrations were concerned, between the army's disastrous Indo-Chinese campaign and its operations in Algeria, was the quite distinct juridical status of the two territories: Indo-China may have been a French colony, but Algeria was an integral part of France itself. This belief, enshrined in law since 1848, is none other than the myth of the three *départements*, or the foundation myth of *Algérie française*. It was this fundamental ideological given which was appealed to by the authorities to justify the use of conscripted military manpower in Algeria, in direct contrast to Indo-China. So in spite of the official wisdom that the army was not fighting a war in Algeria, but was merely involved in operations designed to restore public order, the better part of half a million national servicemen found themselves committed to the struggle against the nationalists at its peak, with some three million in all being deployed over the eight years that the conflict lasted.[1]

It was therefore a second Revolutionary theme, that of the 'one and indivisible' French Republic, now stretching from Dunkirk to Tamanrasset, which provided the rationale for a significant hardening in the Mendès-France government's attitude towards the maintenance of its overseas empire: French citizens were being sent to Algeria to fight for the integrity of the nation. Or rather, they were not being sent to fight exactly, but to guard European farms and strategic installations; a role which owed almost as much to the wish of the terminally fragile ministries of the Fourth Republic to avoid upsetting public opinion as it did to the military's new enthusiasm for the pacification of Algeria on the basis of a territory-wide system of military surveillance (known as *quadrillage* or partitioning). In the event, the issue of conscription would not only awaken French public opinion to the full extent of the regime's troubles in Algeria, but would become a source of disharmony in its own right. A measure justified in terms of national unity in Algeria would thus contribute directly to increasing disunity in France itself.

At the height of the Algerian conflict, conscript-centred literature had been remarkable primarily as adversary *témoignage* [testimony]: a wave of criticism of the conduct and continuation of the war—especially the use of torture and other abhorrent 'pacification' methods—based upon the first-person accounts of *appelé* and *rappelé* eyewitnesses.[2] However, a few veterans of Algeria looked beyond these intense and urgent testimonies to more consciously literary forms of expression in an attempt to communicate the essence of

[1] It fell to the then Interior Minister, François Mitterrand, to defend the introduction of this unpopular measure before the National Assembly on 11 Dec. 1954.

[2] Representative egs. of this output are the collective *Des rappelés témoignent* (Minuit, 1957) and *Ceux d'Algérie: lettres de rappelés* (Plon, 1957). The term *rappelés* refers specifically to those conscripts 'recalled' to serve in Algeria after having completed their statutory period of military service in France. Older and generally more settled than the mass of first-time conscripts, their resentment was, not surprisingly, particularly intense.

their recent 'éducation algérienne'.[3] Through novels and short stories, ex-conscripts like Jacques Malori, Georges Mattéi, Robert Deligny, and Daniel Zimmermann sought to explain the abiding legacy of their average twenty-seven months of service in Algeria, as did a smaller number of committed metropolitan writers, like the communists Vladimir Pozner and André Stil. This twin perspective reflected two complementary readings of the *rappel* itself: as the characterizing trauma of what one such veteran has called 'the third war generation [*génération du feu*], the one called the *djebel* generation, the one which has remained silent, which is ashamed';[4] and as an indictment of the apparently uncaring nation responsible for making it so painful to have been male, twenty years old, and French between 1954 and 1962.

Even at this early stage in the long-drawn-out and still only partially accomplished process of mourning necessitated by the Algerian war, the two themes which would come to dominate the literature of conscripted service in Algeria could already be identified as the vain attempt to forget the unforgettable, and the tension between solitude and solidarity in the face of the Algerian experience. Both of these themes have been developed as the war itself has retreated further into the French collective memory, with the ex-conscripts' proclaimed will to forgetfulness giving way to what is, in fact, the other side of the same psychological coin, namely the fervent wish for the French nation as a whole to assume its responsibility for committing some three million young Frenchmen—the overwhelming majority of their generation—to a futile colonial war.[5] Thus it is that the individual and collective memories of *le rappel* have become established as both the *raison d'être* and the principal theme of the very many more or less autobiographical novels, novellas, and short stories produced by veterans of the Algerian campaign since 1962.

In this context, to talk glibly of 'le silence du contingent', as many commentators do, can be profoundly misleading. Successive French administrations may have sought to deny the reality of 'the war without a name' throughout its duration, and subsequently,

[3] This term is suggested by a comic book representation of the conscripts' experiences: G. Vidal and A. Bignon, *Une éducation algérienne* (Dargaud, 1982).

[4] D. Zimmermann, preface to B. Sigg, *Le Silence et la honte : névroses de la guerre d'Algérie* (Messidor/Éditions Sociales, 1989), 12.

[5] This preoccupation mirrors the continuing attempt made by the Fédération Nationale des Anciens Combattants d'Algérie (FNACA), the principal veterans' organization, to obtain official recognition of its members' status as genuine former combatants.

but those called upon to fight in Algeria have since kept up a steady barrage of literary reminders of precisely that lived historicity, very many of them published at their own expense. The problem, of course, is that the great majority of the texts which make up what is undoubtedly the largest category of metropolitan French fiction about the Algerian conflict remain unread, or, even more cruelly, unremembered. It is this fact which meant that Bertrand Tavernier's montage of filmed interviews with ex-conscripts from the Grenoble region, *La Guerre sans nom* (1992), could, with justice, be hailed as doing for the Algerian war what *Le Chagrin et la Pitié* [The Sorrow and the Pity] (Marcel Ophuls, 1970) did for the Occupation period.

In the discussion which follows, I shall chart the course of the *contingent*'s attempts to articulate the Algerian experience through literature, and will suggest why the narratives produced to date have generally failed to achieve this objective. To this end, I shall pay particular attention to the pair of thematic oppositions which, I believe, both inform and structure the majority of the texts in question: namely, the twin dialectics of memory–forgetfulness and solitude–solidarity. More specifically, I shall seek to show how this doubly binary narrative framework has permitted the implementation of a number of frequently elaborate textual and ideological strategies which serve either to reinforce or, less frequently, to challenge a broader process of *récupération* (understood as a takeover or harnessing of radical dissent by established interest groups). In this way, the constitutive experiences of 'la génération algérienne' are brought into line with predetermined political positions and objectives, and are thus deprived of their troublesome specificity.

The key function which I attach to the disjunction of homogeneity and heterogeneity in literary accounts of conscripted service reflects the conspicuous desire of military apologists to integrate the metropolitan conscript into the community of the *Armée d'Algérie*: a rhetorical figure which combines the suppression of a historical difference with the assertion of a mythical sameness. Clearly, no conscripted man could have long remained an island in the Algeria of the war years. Moreover, the transformation of disparate individuals into a unitary fighting force is very much a stock theme of military literature. However, what I shall seek to show is the way in which this basic plot element was manipulated to particular sectional advantage in the Algerian context.

Xavier Grall, whose 1962 novel *Africa Blues* will itself be considered in Chapter 6, was responsible that same year for the publication of one of the first, and still most important, surveys of *appelé* opinion. Himself a veteran of Algeria, Grall concluded that the traumatic experience of war *là-bas* [over there] actually set French youth apart from an increasingly homogeneous post-war Europe.[6] This trauma had been graphically depicted by Vladimir Pozner as early as 1959, in a seminal collection of short stories with the general title *Le Lieu du supplice* [The Place of Execution].

Recounted much as in the detective genre, 'Les Étangs de Fontargente' [The Fontargente Pools] is the tale of an Ariège peasant who commits suicide shortly after returning from his military service in Algeria. It is only in the wake of the young protagonist's seemingly inexplicable death that his friends and relatives attempt to piece together the evidence of his short life and thus come to a partial awareness of his Algerian suffering. The reader of Pozner's narrative thus enters the story-world via the perceptions and conceptions of the supporting actors in the central drama. So whereas the omniscient third-person narration provides us with what is apparently direct access to their (peasant) consciousness and (village-centred) world-view, it is only through their words and thoughts, that is to say their character-mediation, that we can come to a knowledge of Louis himself. For the protagonist is definitively excluded from the narrative present, and thus permanently distanced from the reader, by the text's opening statement that: 'Tous ceux qui avaient connu Louis Salvaing s'accordaient pour dire qu'ils n'avaient jamais rencontré de garçon plus serviable et mieux équilibré' [All those who had known Louis Salvaing agreed that they had never met a more obliging or well-balanced boy] (67). The calamitous recent event provides the rationale for an inherently limited, because second-hand, and inevitably anachronous account of Louis's Algerian experiences. This takes the form of an extended flashback or *analepsis*[7], as the sympathetically depicted Ariège peasants struggle to re-read the young man's troubled return from North Africa in the awful light cast by his self-immolation.

The single exception to the pattern of character-mediation, and thus distancing, just described is the brief third-person account of Louis's arrival and first months in North Africa. In spite of both his inexperience and the military's strenuous propaganda efforts, Louis

[6] *La Génération du djebel* (Desclée de Brouwer, 1962), 7–8. See also E. Bergot, *La Guerre des appelés en Algérie, 1956–1962* (Presses de la Cité, 1980), and J.-P. Vittori, *Nous, les appelés d'Algérie* (Stock, 1977; Messidor/Temps Actuels, 1983).

[7] See Ch. 2, n. 13.

Salvaing is conscious, as soon as he steps off the troop-ship in Bône, of the manifestly foreign nature of 'French' Algeria. As he is drawn ever deeper into the conflict, his experience of its brutality will lead to an even more troublesome awareness of the dubiousness of the French cause, particularly in view of the clear parallel between the war so recently waged against the Nazi occupier by the FFI in his native Ariège, and the FLN's present campaign against the French in the mountains of Kabylia.[8] On his return, relatives and friends in the close-knit community will find the young man outwardly unscathed, but inwardly scarred. So for all his reluctance to discuss his time in Algeria—he goes so far as to deny his extensive experience of combat—Louis's head remains very much *là-bas*. Increasingly tortured by his recollection of his personal participation in atrocities, he will eventually disappear before killing himself with his uncle's shotgun. As his shocked parents struggle to make sense of their son's apparently senseless death, an old exercise book is discovered in which the troubled young man has put down the otherwise unavowable memories of his Algerian war in poems and prose. The essential message of this tragically inadequate attempt at a literary catharsis of psychological trauma is a simple one, and one which we will regularly see repeated in the literature of *le rappel*:

> Jamais de ma mémoire ne s'effacera
> Le souvenir de mon service militaire
> J'ai eu trop de misères . . . (136)
>
> Never will I be able to forget
> The memory of my military service
> I experienced too much misery . . .

Yet as the tale comes to a close, it is the French nation's collective will to forgetfulness which is evoked, rather than that recognition of guilt which is an essential prerequisite for true forgiveness. As Louis's father turns for advice to a trusted family friend before burning the photographic evidence of the dead conscript's involvement in the murder of innocent Algerian men, women, and children, it is the sins neither of the son nor of the father which are the focus of the narrative's attention, but those of *la mère patrie* [the

[8] The conscripts' recognition of colonial injustice on the one hand and the parallel with the Occupation period on the other is, Bernard Sigg argues, the root cause of the sense of shame which characterizes their experience of Algeria: *Le Silence et la honte*, 59–101.

motherland]. In this sparely written and tightly constructed short story, Pozner powerfully evokes the overlapping trauma constitutive of the veteran experience: the unforgettable memory of horror, and a profound individual and generational alienation from a national community only too ready to lower the curtain of forgetfulness on its Algerian drama. Moreover, he persuasively depicts both the attractions and the limitations of literature as a means of coping with and conveying the Algerian experience.

The period after 1962 saw an immediate departure from the established pattern of conscript-centred chronicles with the publication of Pierre Bois's *La Friche* [The Fallow Land] (1963). Like many other treatments of the *rappel* theme, this novel turns on the alternation of images of boredom and brutality in Algeria. Where it breaks with convention is in its hallucinatory quality and the quasi-automatism of its protagonist-narrator, features which contrast strikingly with the testamentary realism and narratorial soul-searching of earlier texts. Indeed, this novel points the way forward to commentators like Pierre Guyotat (1967) and Claude Bonjean (1977) in its exploitation of the motifs of drunkenness, debauchery, and sexually inspired violence as symptoms of the thoroughgoing *mal algérien* not only of the conscript, but also of the French nation. However, for all the obvious originality of its narrative strategy, this work conforms to a pattern of literary resistance to the Algerian conflict which makes it more of a contemporaneous product than a mature postwar reassessment of the experience of conscription. That would come, or at least begin, around 1966–7, with a series of variously challenging reappraisals of the role played by metropolitan conscripts in France's final colonial war.

The first of these significant texts is, on the face of it, one of the most flippant contributions to the whole literature of the Algerian war. Yet Georges Perec's *Quel petit vélo à guidon chromé au fond de la cour?* [*What Little Bike with Chrome Handlebars at the Back of the Yard?*] (1966) is, in fact, not only one of the most innovative and entertaining treatments of the *rappel* theme, but also one of the most historically persuasive, as the pathos of the conscript's predicament becomes bathos in the hands of this renowned formal innovator. Having satirized Parisian demonstrations of anti-war militancy in a few densely-packed pages of his 1965 Prix Renaudot winner, *Les Choses*, Perec turned his attention the following year to the related issue of conscription in a typically dazzling display of verbal pyrotechnics.[9] This mock-heroic tale of an archetypal *deuxième classe* [private] and his vain attempt to avoid posting to Algeria in the final days of the war provides the author with the perfect vehicle for a humorous examination of the competing myth-systems of Left and Right, and thus permits a remarkably subtle and sympathetic debunking of some, at least, of the French nation's Algerian fantasies, which thereby stand revealed as a tissue of romantic misconceptions and 'war-is-hell' truisms. The broader historicity of Algeria—a real war fought by real people on both sides, rather than by the traditional Right's 'glorieuse armée française (la meilleure parce que la plus vendue)' [glorious French army (the best because it's the best selling)] (82) and the radical Left's 'braves moujahids' [brave freedom fighters] (84)—effectively defeats the collective imagination of Perec's characters, as does the specific experience of conscripted service in that war. Ending with a disabused image of metropolitan passivity as the hapless conscript sets off for Algeria, Georges Perec sets the French Left's historical campaign against conscription into a literary frame which is at once entertaining and illuminating. The same could be said, *a fortiori*, of the major contribution made to the literature of the *rappel* by the journalist, novelist, and film-maker Philippe Labro.[10]

In his self-consciously autobiographical novel *Des feux mal éteints* [Poorly Extinguished Fires] (1967), Labro looks to the typical conscript's humble kit in order to assert the specificity of his own Algerian experience. In particular, it is the *calot* [forage cap], despised by those few soldiers entitled to wear the famous red, green, or blue berets of the parachute regiments, which is seized upon by the highly authorial first-person narrator as a means of communicating his generation's inevitably complex and problematic historicity. By setting the motif in its historical context, the narrative is able to make an appropriately myth-critical affirmation of what we might describe as the multiple individuality of the Algerian *bidasse* [squaddy]. Taking as his starting point the decision, taken in the wake of de Gaulle's victory over the military's seditious elements, to reintegrate the parachute regiments by equipping all French troops with headgear very like their famous coloured berets, Labro's narrator comments on his own experience of Algeria:

[9] G. Perec, *Les Choses: une histoire des années soixante* (Julliard, 1965); *Quel petit vélo à guidon chromé au fond de la cour?* (Denoël, 1966; refs. are to the 'Folio' edn.).

[10] *Des feux mal éteints* (Gallimard, 1967; refs. are to the 'Folio' edn.).

> . . . de fait, cette décision eut l'effet psychologique prévu. Les paras perdirent leur singularité, leur mythe, leur prestige. Entre-temps, l'Algérie était devenue indépendante. Cette histoire de calots et de bérets n'avait rien à voir à l'affaire mais elle marqua, pour le bidasse moyen, le passage d'une ère à une autre.
>
> S'il fallait donc définir ma génération, ou plutôt les garçons dont j'ai envie de parler et que j'ai connus, je dirais que ce fut la dernière de celles qui portèrent un calot—et je ne m'aventurerais pas plus loin. (39)

> . . . in fact, this decision had the anticipated psychological effect. The paras lost their singularity, their myth, their prestige. In the meantime, Algeria had become independent. This tale of berets and forage caps had nothing to do with it, but, for the average squaddy, it marked the passage from one era to another.
>
> So if I had to define my generation, or rather the boys that I knew and want to talk about, I would say that it was the last of those which wore a forage cap—and I would go no further than that.

Wholly persuasive from a historical point of view, Labro's comments on the differences between the uniforms worn by the representatives of 'the nation in arms' and the military élite serve to cast new light on the roles played by both the *armée de métier* [regular army] and the *contingent* in Algeria. His examination of the experience of conscription—which, he has suggested, caused him personally to age ten years[11]—insists throughout on its specificity, both with regard to that of other elements of the French military, and to that of other members of the *contingent*. The forage cap worn by Labro and his comrades not only distinguishes them from the paratroopers, after all, but also from later cohorts of *appelés*. This is an important point, serving to highlight the peculiarly disparate character of the conscripts' experiences in Algeria.

For the author of *Des feux mal éteints*, it is precisely this lack of homogeneity which distinguishes the veteran of the Algerian campaign from his counterparts in two world wars; it also explains the ease with which the bulk of the returning conscripts were reintegrated into metropolitan society:

> Paris et la France les gobèrent comme des boeufs font des mouches: par paquets de dix. Ils furent avalés, absorbés, car ils n'avaient pas d'identité. Une génération ne peut se définir sous le prétexte que trois millions d'enfants perdus ont vécu trois millions d'expériences solitaires, singulières et contradictoires . . . On peut avancer que 1914 et 1940 furent des

[11] See J. Planchais, 'Les Vétérans de la guerre d'Algérie', *Le Monde*, 6 July 1985, 8.

expériences quasi unanimes. Mais l'Algérie, non: une multitude de solitudes. Aucune universalité, chacun pour soi. (354)

Paris and France swallowed them up just like cattle swallow flies: by the score. They were swallowed, and absorbed, because they had no identity. A generation cannot define itself on the pretext that three million lost boys had three million solitary, singular, and contradictory experiences . . . It can be argued that 1914 and 1940 were virtually universal experiences. But not Algeria: it was a multitude of solitudes. There was nothing universal about it: it was every man for himself.

The principal contribution made by Labro's novel to the literature of the Algerian war is precisely its attempt to give a voice to this lost generation of French youth; that of Labro himself, of those aged between twenty and thirty in the period 1954 to 1962. Opening with a detailed evocation of daily life in a France in the full throes of postwar modernization, the text subsequently follows the progress of the author–narrator as he undergoes not the whole of the Algerian 'experience', but merely 'une petite portion, un segment, la fin, les derniers sursauts' [a little portion, a segment, the end, the last throes] (38). Having contrived to delay his posting to North Africa, the narrator eventually arrives there just as the European terrorism of the OAS is beginning to dominate the life of Algiers. From the outset he is alone, having lost touch with the rest of his cohort as a result of his attempts to avoid service in Algeria. His civilian background in journalism will exacerbate this marginality by causing him to be separated from the mass of conscripts in order to work on an army newspaper. His involvement in what he calls 'cette fausse guerre et ce faux pays' [this false war and this false country] (39) is thus rendered even more artificial as he joins 'cette hétéroclite phalange de faux soldats, les *détachés*' [that motley crew of false soldiers, who had been 'detached' from their units] (59).

By focusing on the inadequacies of such estranged individuals, Labro will seek to bring the reader of *Des feux mal éteints* to an awareness of the specificity of an entire generation, and its characterizing *multitude de solitudes*. For Labro's conscripts, a radical loss of innocence in Algeria will shatter the comfortable illusion of solidarity generated by superficial similarities in origins, tastes, and interests. Indeed, the whole thrust of the narrative is conditioned by this properly dialectical tension between the group and the individual, solidarity and solitude. Of particular interest in this regard are the linguistic codes employed both by the professional military and by Labro's fellow conscripts in an attempt to establish a communal identity. In the case of the former, this integrating tactic will achieve its desired end, but only imperfectly and temporarily, as the self-conscious narrator reflects:

> *Terminé*: adjectif typique du militaire—je m'aperçois que je l'ai utilisé trois fois en quelques paragraphes. Mais cela devait disparaître facilement, de même que vous alliez vite réapprendre à répondre oui ou non, plutôt qu'*affirmatif* ou *négatif*. (348–9)

> *Terminated*: a typically military adjective—I see that I have used it three times in just a few paragraphs. But that would easily disappear, just as you would soon get used to saying yes or no again, rather than *affirmative* or *negative*.

Labro picks up on this linguistic homogenization precisely in order to deny its power to integrate the military's conscripted element in anything other than a superficial and short-lived way. His description of the draftees' own attempts to achieve unity through linguistic conventions is to be regarded in this same demystified light. So a familiarity with the strange language of the *Armée d'Algérie* does not imply a profound relationship with one's fellow *appelés*, still less anything approaching a common experience of the Algerian conflict. By the same token, the narrator's parting reference to the returning conscripts' collective ignorance of the very latest linguistic conventions may serve to draw attention to a common alienation from metropolitan society, but it cannot hope to define the group's particular Algerian experience. The collective yearning for *la quille* [demobilization] thus gives way to a complex reality of problematic individual reintegrations, maintaining to the last the historically persuasive obligation of each member of the *contingent* to come to terms with his enforced presence in Algeria as an essentially isolated individual.

Having been sent to an 'ersatz' war (91) by a largely indifferent metropolitan France, Labro's conscripts meet with varying degrees of success in their individual quests for some compensatory form of personal authenticity. A prime case in point is Seb, a close friend of the narrator and the only *appelé* in *Des feux mal éteints* with first-hand experience of the 'hot' war being waged against the FLN in their mountain strongholds. Like Lartéguy's 'mutins de Versailles', Seb owes his incorporation into an operational unit to a disciplinary measure; unlike them, however, he can hope for no mythical transformation into a military demi-god. Typically, the severe trauma which Seb will suffer is not represented as a standard feature of the metropolitan conscript's *éducation algérienne*, with the narrator at pains to point out the exceptional nature of the character's intensive exposure to the sharp end of the Franco-Algerian conflict. A rare individual in a dangerous situation, Seb is potentially a romantic figure, but this dimension is to a large extent offset by the regular emphasis placed both on the criminal pointlessness and brutalizing monotony of his combat experiences, summed up as 'la même routine avilissante' [the same degrading routine] (188). As Seb bitterly and ineloquently tells his tale, a determinedly anti-romantic image of pacification emerges which will be familiar enough to any reader of the conscript-centred testimonies of the war years.

What the reader of *Des feux mal éteints* is encouraged to reflect upon most systematically, however, is not so much the war itself, as its catastrophic impact on Seb's personality. In particular, it is the psychological retreat of the conscript in the face of an unacceptably awful Algerian reality that is insisted upon. Unable to cope with the memory of his part in the war's incomprehensible horror, the troubled conscript commits suicide upon his return to France, thus ending his very existence as the only real escape from the trauma of the Algerian experience. Though exceptional in itself, this extreme fictional response is represented as symbolic of a general historical predicament: all those touched by the war will discover that the characterizing feature of this particular load of suffering and guilt is its radical incommunicability, which is the very opposite of the traditionally vaunted brotherhood of arms.

Inevitably, this failure of communication is exacerbated as the narrator, together with the rest of the *contingent*, returns home, 'magistralement dépaysé' [magnificently disorientated] (360), to a booming France which will make not the slightest attempt to understand the experience which it has imposed on its young men:

> ... la France n'était pas au rendez-vous de son contingent. Le contingent, comme son nom l'indique, n'intéressait plus grand monde. Je jetai un coup d'œil sur mon petit dictionnaire illustré, un vieux modèle dont je m'étais servi très longtemps pour faire mes *rédactions*. Je pus lire: *Contingent: qui peut arriver, qui peut échoir, qui peut être ou n'être pas. Part que chacun doit fournir ou recevoir.*
>
> D'ailleurs, à votre retour d'Algérie, vous aviez comme une grande fringale de Larousse. Fallait-il y chercher ce que personne n'avait pris la peine de vous définir: responsabilité, dignité, générosité, liberté? *Qui peut être ou n'être pas* ... Considérez que vous aviez une marge de choix assez

large: être ou n'être pas, c'était la question. Arrivés en France, vous n'étiez pas, et voilà tout! (348)

. . . France did not turn out to welcome back her conscripts. The *contingent*, as its name suggests, was no longer of any interest to most people. I had a glance at my little illustrated dictionary, an old one that I used for a very long time when I had to do my 'compositions'. It said: '*Contingent*: that which may occur, which may come about through fate or chance, which may or may not be. The part or share that each individual must give or receive.'

For that matter, when you got back from Algeria, it was as if you had a raging hunger for the dictionary. Was it that you felt the need to look up what no one had ever taken the trouble to define for you: responsibility, dignity, generosity, liberty? 'What may or may not be . . .'. As a matter of fact, you had a pretty big decision to make: to be or not to be, that was the question. When you arrived back in France, you ceased to be, and that was the end of it!

It is singularly appropriate that the task of repoliticizing both an army and a war which had become shrouded in linguistic mystification—the syndrome of 'the war without a name'—should have fallen so often to the *contingent*. For as Roland Barthes has pointed out, it is precisely the ability of myth to deprive the world of its contingent quality that characterizes it as a depoliticized *parole* ['speech' or act of communication].[12] What could counter myth's eternalized and essentialized image of the world more directly, then, than the *contingent*, a body of men whose collective identity is characterized by their being called up for a predetermined period, and whose condition inevitably connotes changeability and an absence of necessity?

As for the humorous allusion to *Hamlet*, this belies the importance of the theme of suicide in *Des feux mal éteints*. Like Pozner's Louis Salvaing, Labro's Seb blows his brains out not because suicide was particularly prevalent amongst returning conscripts, but rather as an image of French society's failure to face up to its responsibilities as regards the *contingent*. So, having been marked for life by its period of service in North Africa, the generation of the Algerian war is condemned to collective and individual oblivion by a guilty nation:

. . . quelque expérience qu'il ait eue, à peine en était-il sorti que chaque bidasse se voyait enveloppé dans le silence et dans l'oubli, car aucun adulte ne voulait franchement assumer la responsabilité de l'avoir envoyé là-bas,

[12] *Mythologies* (Seuil, 1957), 230.

n'acceptait de préciser au nom de quoi cet enfant avait vécu ce qu'il avait vécu. (354)

. . . whatever experience he may have had, hardly had each squaddy emerged from it than he found himself shrouded in silence and forgetfulness, for no grown-up was prepared honestly to accept responsibility for having sent him over there, nor was anyone prepared to spell out the exact reasons for making this child live through what he had lived through.

The *appelés* returned home not so much pariahs as an unfortunate reminder of colonial ambitions which had been discarded in favour of a new, 'hexagonal', vision of France and its future role in the world.[13] Much like the million or so 'repatriated' European settlers—and even more obviously those few exiled *harkis* fortunate enough to escape the retribution which awaited them in their homeland[14]—the approximately three million members of the *contingent* became a source of embarrassment to the nation that had encouraged them to believe that Algeria was an inalienable part of a Greater France. As consumerism replaced colonialism in the France of the *Trente Glorieuses*[15]—the boom years, 1945–75—the full employment of the day would facilitate their social and economic reintegration, just as it would ease the mass immigration of the *pieds-noirs*. Nevertheless, it was left to the conscripts themselves to come to terms with the psychic implications of the nation's erstwhile Algerian obsession, in order to understand, and thus to assume, their own contradictory experiences of a war which was as much a fantasy of the Left as it was of the Right. For many veterans of the Algerian conflict, literature was to offer a privileged mode of access to the memories denied by an indifferent mother country.

Labro's highly individual approach to metropolitan conscription may very usefully be compared with the treatment of the theme found in an even more idiosyncratic novel, also published in 1967. Pierre Guyotat's *Tombeau pour cinq cent mille soldats* [Tomb For Five Hundred Thousand Soldiers] is, beyond any doubt, the most formally ambitious attempt by an ex-conscript—and, arguably, by anyone—to capture the Algerian experience in literature. Indeed,

[13] This distinction helps to explain the difference between the French experience in Algeria and the American experience in Vietnam.

[14] The fate of these native Algerians, who fought on the French side in the war with the FLN, will be discussed in Ch. 7.

[15] See J. Fourastié, *Les Trente glorieuses* (Fayard, 1979).

his text's treatment of the war raises a number of the pivotal theoretical questions addressed in our general introduction in an unusually dramatic fashion: questions bearing upon the relationship between fiction and reality, and more specifically, between formal innovation and socio-political defamiliarization. For in marked contrast to the limpid realism of *Des feux mal éteints*, published the same year, Guyotat's narrative obliges the reader to search for the collective memories of *la génération du djebel* in a peculiarly dense thicket of words. Indeed, the author of *Tombeau pour cinq cent mille soldats* is clearly of the opinion that for literature to talk usefully about the world, it must consciously and constantly stress its own fictionality.

Such thinking has resulted in some 500 packed pages, sub-divided into seven 'songs': a solid block of text in its manuscript form, paragraphs were only inserted later by a copy typist, at the insistence of the publishers[16]. Small wonder, then, that *Tombeau pour cinq cent mille soldats* should have an 'unfinished' quality. In Barthes's terms, it eschews the comforting closure of the (traditional) *lisible* narrative, in favour of a radical openness or *scriptibilité*.[17] So enigma is not generated in Guyotat's text in order that it may be divertingly resolved, but rather so that it can be foregrounded by the torrential narration. The end product is a peculiarly nightmarish vision of the Algerian war, in which the stream of an omniscient narratorial consciousness typically combines a bludgeoning scatology and a minute attention to sensationally detailed sexual violence, especially of a homosexual kind and frequently involving children, to produce a fictive universe lit only by 'la pénombre excrémentielle' [the excremental half-light] (213). Familiar military jargon thus appears alongside allegorical elements and brutally graphic descriptions of perverted sexuality as 'les soldats de l'armée d'occupation et de maintien de l'ordre' [the soldiers of the army of occupation and the maintenance of order] are sent from 'Ecbatane' to suppress the rising in 'le profond de l'île' [the depths of the island] (55).[18] While reference may occasionally be made to identifiable persons or events, the reader is not permitted to maintain his/her bearings for

[16] P. Guyotat, *Tombeau pour cinq cent mille soldats* (Gallimard, 1967).

[17] See the discussion in the Introduction of Barthes's famous distinction between the *lisible* (readerly) work which is passively consumed and the *scriptible* (writerly) text which must actively be produced by the reader.

[18] The term 'the island' is a reference to 'Al-Djazaïr', the original Arabic name for both Algiers and Algeria. It is appealed to in titles like that of Alain Cavalier's film *Le Combat dans l'île* (1962).

too long, much as in the writing of Jean Genet[19] and William Burroughs; and the overall impression produced is one of unrelenting turmoil and confusion.

Quite how such an approach is meant to further our understanding of either the communal or the individual experience of Algeria remains unclear, and indeed it is far from obvious that this is the text's basic project. As a hallucinatory vision of the brutalizing—and especially the sexually perverting—impact of the war on the youth of France, Guyotat's treatment might be said to possess a certain critical force, but the extreme opacity of his narrative is not readily compatible with the goal of communicating the specificity of the Algerian experience; or, at least, not on any large scale. To come to this conclusion is necessarily to take issue with Barthes's argument that radical formal innovation is essential for the production of a truly revolutionary literary discourse.[20] More specifically, it is seriously to question the belief that there is a necessary connection between practical politics and the modernist—and, a *fortiori*, post-modernist—preoccupation with 'the permanent revolution in poetic language, and in literary forms in general'.[21] This is not to deny that formal innovation possesses the capacity to defamiliarize, and thus demystify, colonial ideology by bringing literature's own specificity as an ideological practice into a dissonant conjunction with the discourse of colonialism. On the contrary, I shall argue in Chapter 6 that just such a demystifying relationship between form and ideology is to be found in the writing of Jean-Pierre Millecam. However, it is to suggest that the reader implied (in Iser's sense) by Guyotat's text is very much a 'super-reader': intensely dedicated to the generation of meaning(s), and hugely resourceful in coping with the permanent challenge of the narrative's polyphony; an implied reader, in short, with few plausible counterparts in the French reading public.

Aimed at a very restricted audience, *Tombeau pour cinq cent mille soldats* is primarily intended for consumption as high art, and only secondarily, if at all, as socio-political commentary. A literary evolution of this kind is doubtless only to be expected as the Algerian conflict recedes further into the depths of the past and the

[19] Genet's own contribution to the literature of the Algerian war, his play *Les Paravents* (1961), is itself an exercise in hallucinatory violence in this mould.

[20] Barthes's argument is discussed in the Introduction.

[21] D. Robey, 'Modern Linguistics and the Language of Literature', in A. Jefferson and D. Robey (eds.), *Modern Literary Theory: A Comparative Introduction* (London, B.T. Batsford, 1982; 1986 edn.), 55.

collective memory. Nevertheless, a great number of novels have been published since 1967 which, for all their changes of perspective, continue to keep the issue of military service in Algeria high on the literary, if not the political, agenda.

The highly individual and innovative treatments of conscription put forward in the years 1966–7 may very usefully be compared with those presented in two novels published rather more recently; because Guy Croussy's *Ne pleure pas, la guerre est bonne* [Don't Cry, It's a Good War] (1975) and Claude Klotz's *Les Appelés* (1982) may be shown, in spite of a variety of essentially superficial differences of scope and style, to be operating within the same ideological framework, and thus to come to very similar conclusions about the nature of the conscripts' Algerian experiences. A common problematic, in short, may be seen to produce fundamentally similar images of military service in Algeria.

As its title suggests, *Ne pleure pas, la guerre est bonne* relies to a great extent on irony to make its critical points about the French use of conscription in the Franco-Algerian conflict. In this very oppressive narrative, attention is focused exclusively, and, indeed, obsessively, on the hunt for a single FLN guerrilla by a specially selected unit. As the central figure and narrator, Pierre Rose, puts it: 'Nous étions quatre hommes réunis pour capturer Amirouche mort ou vif' [There were four of us, and we had been brought together to capture Amirouche dead or alive] (47). It is this classic commando mission which will dominate the action of Croussy's novel, with the four principals only giving up their vain manhunt when they are killed, a denouement which is structurally prepared and philosophically situated from the outset, thanks to a remarkable prefatory quotation from Albert Camus's friend and mentor, Jean Grenier:

> Il me semble que la suprême félicité pour certains êtres ne se sépare pas du tragique, elle en est le sommet . . . à ce moment même il se fait dans l'âme un grand silence. (7)
>
> It seems to me that, for certain human beings, supreme happiness cannot be separated from tragedy; rather it constitutes its peak . . . at that precise moment a great silence occurs in the soul.

This properly Cornelian notion of a peak of human experience at which joy becomes indistinguishable from tragedy is not an uncommon one in the literature of the Algerian war (or, indeed, in the wider discourse of French militarism and anti-militarism). However, it is appealed to in a particularly striking fashion in the two novels presently under discussion, in both of which it is presented in anticipation of the main body of the text, thereby serving to establish a conceptual framework for the narrative itself. Through this presentation of the role played by conscripts in a brutal colonial conflict in terms of 'supreme happiness' or, in the case of Klotz's Prologue, 'le plus beau jour' [the perfect day] (7–8), the unpalatable historicity of the *contingent*'s Algerian war is mythically subsumed into an altogether more reassuring tradition of military comradeship.

Croussy's intense concentration on a very small group of soldiers does not preclude some, attractively disabused, early comments on the heterogeneity and multiple frailty of the *contingent* as a whole. However, such an emphasis on difference and weakness is only the starting-point for an account of the emergence of something very like the brotherhood of arms so beloved of the military's defenders. Indeed, it is this soldierly transcendence of civilian relations between individuals which is the key to an understanding of Croussy's particular version of the tragedy-as-joy theme. So, as the 'Commando Pivoine' sets out on its mission, its members will exchange the company of the mass of men for an ever more intense awareness of themselves and each other. The narrator, Pierre Rose, focuses the integrated reader's attention on the miraculous nature of this process:

> Quel miracle pourrait unir, un jour, un comptable devenu accordéoniste dans un orchestre musette avant de s'engager, un médecin pressé de rentrer dans sa famille et qui accepte l'épreuve du commando pour accélérer sa libération, un prêtre—venu d'où?—et le jeune homme que je suis encore? (47)

> What miracle could, one day, bring together an accountant who worked as an accordionist in a dance band before joining up, a doctor in a rush to get back to his family and who has only agreed to become a commando in order to get out of the army more quickly, a priest—where can he have come from?—and the young man that I still am?

The four make up a strange and, indeed, a rather implausible group. The narrator, for his part, and as is so often the case, is a *muté disciplinaire* [the subject of a disciplinary posting].[22] Rose's

[22] This is notably the case for the conscripted heroes of such stridently anti-war films of the period as René Vautier's *Avoir vingt ans dans les Aurès* (1972) and Yves Boisset's *R.A.S.* (1973), both discussed in Ch. 7. For a useful introduction to the tradition of writing about such punishment battalions (known collectively as *le biribi*), see the

'crime', we discover, was to have refused to 'finish off' an Algerian, a stand which is itself readily understandable as an expression of his belief that it is the war itself that is the crime (54). However, this conscientious objection to the war does not prevent the character from participating very effectively in it: a fact which is, perhaps, the key to this figure's appeal for self-proclaimed opponents of military romanticism. Taciturn in the extreme, with neither friends nor family ties, Rose is very much an enigma. He is as apparently contradictory in himself as he is in his attitude to the war; a fact which leads Grenier, the unfrocked priest, to describe him as 'toujours triste et toujours heureux' [always sad and always happy] (55). By the same token, Rose is both voluble and reticent. As the narrator, he undoubtedly possesses the narrative's most privileged voice; however, as a character in the story which he himself tells, he makes it a point of honour to avoid speaking any more than is absolutely essential. This attitude will, together with the silence of the mountain setting, contribute to the silence which is both an important part of the novel's atmosphere and one of its principal motifs. Most mysterious of all, however, is the strange injury which Rose has in the palm of his left hand. This is frequently referred to as the action progresses, but will only be 'explained' at the very end of the novel: it is a tattoo of the word *Non*, and thus a patent symbol of the conscript's abiding opposition to the war in which he has been made to fight (189).

The point here is that these variously remarkable characters will, thanks to their mission, come to know that 'miraculous' unity longed for by the narrator. The tragedy is that they must die in order to come to this new awareness of one another, symbolized by their refusal to surrender the bodies of their dead, even to their own side. The process of isolation which begins with the selection of the group for the 'Commando Pivoine', and is intensified as the team moves higher into the mountains and loses touch with the outside world, is shown in death to effect a marvellous unification of the four men. As they are picked off in turn, their bodies are recovered by those who survive, to prevent them falling into the hands either of the enemy or of an army from which the group has grown hopelessly estranged. Their continued progress towards Amirouche becomes steadily more absurd, with its value as a token of the war's senselessness becoming ever more apparent. It will fall to Rose

discussion of Georges Darien's *Biribi* in W. Redfern, *Georges Darien: Robbery and Private Enterprise* (Amsterdam, Rodopi, 1985), esp. Ch. 2.

himself to be the last survivor, and thus to take responsibility for his three comrades. This is a role which he valiantly assumes, with the assistance of a captured mule, until he too dies. The four men, mere *bidasses*, are thus united eternally in a life-transcending death; like the four buzzards which now soar effortlessly above both their dead bodies and the other signs of human suffering in Algeria, they have sprouted wings.

As a depiction of the absurdity of colonial war, Guy Croussy's formally ambitious narrative is of considerable merit. However, as an image of conscripted service in Algeria it must be reckoned profoundly misleading; not on the grounds of its historical implausibility, but rather because its insistence on the growth of a mystical communion between fellow combatants conforms to a pattern of mystification which, although far older than the Algerian war, has continued to inform literary treatments of that conflict.

Even more obviously than Croussy's novel, Claude Klotz's *Les Appelés* makes a point of displaying its credentials as a conscript-centred testimony. Here too, the action focuses on just four *appelés*, a fact which might be dismissed as a coincidence were it not for the romantic connotations of an arrangement of characters which moved *Le Monde*'s reviewer to compare Klotz with Dumas *père*, and his novel with *Les Trois Mousquetaires* [The Three Musketeers].[23] The ease with which Klotz's novel is assimilated to an earlier tradition of military romanticism is an accurate indicator of the text's mystification of the conscripts' experiences. Naturally, we do not expect to find an old-style romance complete with happy ending in a contemporary chronicle of war; *Les Appelés* closes rather with the absurd deaths of its four principals, accidentally killed by their own side. However, this is no more than is to be expected in a novel of the 1980s, given 'the general demythologizing tendencies which the Vietnam War precipitated in western intellectual circles in the late 1960s and early 1970s'.[24] What we have in Klotz's novel, as in Croussy's, is a minimal demystification of conscripted service in Algeria: the very least that can reasonably be expected in a post-Vietnam account of service in a colonial war. The fiction's closing nod at the horrors of war is revealed in this light to be a recuperative device intended to steer the disabused consciousness of the contemporary reader away from its profoundly romantic treatment of the central theme. For even if we take the

[23] B. Alliot, 'Avoir vingt ans dans les djebels', *Le Monde*, 4 June 1982, 19.

[24] A. Foulkes, *Literature and Propaganda* (London, Methuen, 1983), 64.

narrative's tragic finale into account, the image of the Algerian experience which emerges from *Les Appelés* is a wholly positive one. Indeed, the tragedy is really the apogee of the joy experienced by Klotz's four heroes, just as it is in Croussy's novel. Algeria, for all its horrors—and we are shown the full range of military errors and atrocities—remains the site of a higher existence, a privileged space where the barriers variously imposed by metropolitan society can be transcended.

In Klotz's fictive Algeria, even more obviously than in Croussy's, individuals who would normally be mutually hostile or indifferent are brought by their common lot to an experience of their shared humanity. A Parisian philosophy teacher rubs shoulders with a second-hand dealer from the capital's working-class suburbs, an aristocratic doctor from Bordeaux, and a country priest from the Vendée coast, with the end result that all four come to a new awareness both of self and others. Whatever the varied origins of its conscripted participants, whatever their personal failings and private obsessions, the Algerian adventure brings about a qualitative improvement in their respective conditions. Labelled and pigeon-holed by themselves as much as by the metropolitan society from which they originate, Klotz's *appelés* come, through their common experience of Algeria, to attain a mythical homogeneity. Their simultaneous demise, which brings the novel to a close, thus sees them transformed from individual conscripts into the Algerian incarnation of the universal soldier. This mythical distortion of lived experience is particularly apparent at the level of form, as we shall see when we come to examine the narrative's containment of the characters' apparently disparate voices within a single, pro-military and pro-colonial, discourse. The mode of narration thus structurally reinforces the text's overtly stated claim that the conflictual politics of metropolitan France cannot long survive exposure to the elemental realities of conflict in the country's North African territory (32), as an Algerian 'substance' and a conscripted 'essence' replace the 'accidents' of metropolitan existence and allegiance (19).

Klotz's characterization is of clear importance in this regard, for if the four principals are archetypal, it is for the simple reason that such characters fit most easily into the novel's symmetrically ordered universe and accede most readily to the demands of its mythifying project. Berlier, Gino, Debard, and Barret—this is the order in which they are repeatedly presented in the novel—are not so much concrete individuals as representatives of the modern nation's constituent estates. Klotz's characterization conforms to an essentially feudal model, in fact: Debard, the hereditary ruler, and as such the only officer; Barret, for the clergy; Berlier, representing the Republican tradition of the lay educators; Gino, who incarnates the vital wit of the lower orders. Alternatively, the protagonists can be set against a preferred map of France: the capital with its intellectual pretensions and commercial realities, its *grands boulevards* and its *banlieue*; the traditions and solidity of the provinces; the peace of the rural heartland. Other, equally valid, taxonomies—spiritual, philosophical, political, even physical—could be provided. The real point is that the four principals are chosen for their radical disparity, according to the standard terms of reference of mainland France. This is in order that their metropolitan differences may be all the more dramatically reconciled in Algeria, a reconciliation which will be perceived by the parties to it as paradoxical, and rationalized for the reader via the myth of an essential Algerian camaraderie. Prompted by his wife, Debard reflects, like Berlier before him, on his surprising choice of friends:

> C'est vrai, elle a mis le doigt sur quelque chose qui aurait dû m'étonner: pourquoi Barret et ses simplicités, ses origines paysannes, Gino et ses cafés de banlieue, Berlier et ses opinions si contraires aux miennes? (152–3)

> That's right, she has put her finger on something that should have surprised me: why Barret with his simple ways and peasant origins, Gino and his seedy suburban cafés, Berlier and his ideas so unlike my own?

Having now been transmuted into a military *toubib* [the slang term for medical officer], the erstwhile *châtelain* is in a position to voice the preferred answer to his own question, thereby resolving the enigma upon which the text as a whole is grounded: 'Nous sommes tous des soldats' [We are all soldiers] (153). The four men's military identity is again presented as their essential, indeed their only, characterizing feature just a few pages later: 'Nous ne sommes que quatre soldats trop débraillés au cœur de cette nuit imprévue' [We are just four very scruffy soldiers caught in the middle of this unexpected darkness] (159). It would not be difficult to imagine Croussy's Rose uttering these words; nor is it coincidental that we may so readily link the two texts in this way. There, as here, what we are faced with is the mythical glossing-over of objective social disparities. How much more aesthetically pleasing to have four such different representatives of 'the nation in arms' brought together by the Algerian adventure than a less heteroclite group; and how much more appropriate to the articulation of the myth of the conscripts' homogeneity.

In fact, *Les Appelés* formally denies the disparity insisted upon by Labro, while seeming all the while to foreground it through its systematic use of interior monologue. That the historical fragmentation of the Algerian experience should be susceptible to such usurpation by a mythical universality is a function of the narration's homogenizing structure. More specifically, the introduction of the notion of 'le plus beau jour' by means of an authoritative third-person prologue serves to establish an appropriately pro-military diegetic framework for subsequent narrative developments. It is here that the four principals, as yet unidentified, are themselves first described. Out on patrol in the Ouarsenis, they decide to halt at a village well, where a suitably venerable native introduces them to the local myth of the single, perfect day divinely preordained for each of them, as for every human being:

> Une légende peut-être, une tradition ou le résultat d'une sagesse propre à ces pays où les roches sont nues . . .
>
> À partir de cet instant et sans que jamais ils ne se le soient avoué l'un à l'autre, aucun des quatre soldats n'oublia l'histoire du vieillard des plaines, et chacun se demanda, dans les longs mois qui suivirent, si, parmi les jours qu'ils allaient vivre, se trouverait celui qui leur était destiné, celui-là même qui serait leur plus beau jour. (7–8)

> A legend perhaps, a tradition or the result of a wisdom peculiar to these lands where the rocks are bare . . .
>
> From that moment on and without ever confiding in one another, none of the four soldiers would forget the tale which the old man of the plains had told them, and each of them would wonder, in the long months which lay ahead, whether, among the days that they were destined to live, the one that had been reserved for them would come along, the very one which would be their perfect day.

The prologue's transparent appeal to a tradition of orientalist romanticism in the literary depiction of North Africa is less remarkable than its emphasis on the role of predestination in Klotz's fictive Algeria, for a common military destiny will ultimately be revealed by the group's collective demise. The narrative introduced in this fashion displays a rigid structural parallelism throughout. First, the departure of each of the four central figures is recounted with equal brevity. Though depicted in the particular styles appropriate to the characters and their milieux, each one of these *tableaux vivants* culminates in an essentially similar expression of a single Algerian future (9–16). The four 'books' which follow are, in turn, each dominated by one of the principals, in the order established in the prologue: Berlier, Gino, Debard, Barret. This format serves both to develop the characters and to forward the action, resulting in a narrative which respects an age-old formula, as the teacher's tale is followed by those of the second-hand dealer, the doctor, and the priest. Having from the outset established the principals as a military unit—thanks to the episode of 'le plus beau jour'—the text's subsequent concentration on them as individuals serves only to emphasize the process of coming-together in Algeria: its homogenizing narrative symmetry makes for the integrated reader's perception of apparently foregrounded individuality as essentially secondary to a common military identity. It is, we realize, very much a case of 'One for all, and all for one'.

It is only with the epilogue that Klotz's conscripted pilgrims, having told their stories on the way, finally complete their Algerian journey. In so doing, they both fulfil the mythic promise of the prologue, and reveal just how close their own odyssey comes to that of Croussy's heroes. For Klotz's *appelés* are destined to die absurdly just as their own finest day dawns, a joint demise which may be read on at least two levels. On the more obvious of these, the denouement is to be regarded as straightforwardly ironic, with its political message being an equally uncomplicated statement of the senselessness of war. On a rather deeper level, however, the conscripts' deaths conform to the tragedy-as-joy ethos of *Ne pleure pas, la guerre est bonne*. What is of importance here is the second-level depiction of this common fate as the culmination, and, indeed, the consummation, of a genuinely communal destiny. The textual signal for this reading is the increasingly rapid oscillation of narrative points of view which occurs in the minutes leading up to and in the very moment of the principals' deaths (249–59). This formal device has the mythical effect of unifying the individual conscripts, and thus transforming their individual experiences into a transcendent *appelé* consciousness: an eternalized expression of the text's foundation myth of the conscripts' homogeneity. The fact that the Algerian war was, historically, singularly lacking in danger for the vast majority of its drafted participants only serves to underline the mystification effected by the tragic finales of both this novel and Croussy's variation on the theme. And what more typically Romantic climax could be imagined, in fact? Here, after all, we are confronted with a particularly familiar literary commonplace: the achievement by socially disparate individuals of a transcendent and everlasting harmony in death.

The Algerian novels of Croussy and Klotz are, at least in their preoccupation with the mental processes of their central figures, very much products of their time. In the decade from the mid-1970s to the mid-1980s, literary treatments of the *rappel* were characterized most obviously by a shift away from overt socio-political commentary and towards psychoanalytical representations of the Algerian experience. This shift in preoccupations is accompanied, in the case of Franck Venaille's *La Guerre d'Algérie* (1978), by a geographical transposition of the eponymous war to the Flemish coast, where the traumatized narrator remembers his violently sexual relationship with one 'Algéria de Vanantwerpen', recounting it in a hallucinatory style which may be likened to that of Pierre Guyotat.[25] A similar atmosphere pervades Claude Bonjean's *Lucien chez les barbares* [Lucien in the Land of the Barbarians] (1977), a grim account of one twenty-year-old's brutalizing exposure to the horrors of the war, which at no point mentions the disputed territory by name.[26]

Jean Yvane's *L'Arme au bleu* [With Guns Pointing Skyward] (1978) is of particular interest, in that it combines a persuasive critique of the Algerian war's violent absurdity with a sustained enquiry into its impact on the minds—and particularly the conscious and unconscious memories—of individual conscripts. Although the group of soldiers involved are all wiped out as the novel closes, *à la* Croussy and Klotz, there is no suggestion of their having attained any transcendent state of soldierly enlightenment in the process. Hopelessly trapped in a cave, the conscripts attempt to save their lives by surrendering to the FLN with their rifles pointing in the air—'l'arme au bleu', as in the title. In the eyes of the more mature and perceptive *sursitaire* [deferred conscript], Coulonges, this attempt is doomed from the outset. Nevertheless, he is unable to refrain from participation in the suicidal break-out, for reasons,

[25] Cf. the exiled *pied-noir* Albert Bensoussan's narrative confusion of a passionately remembered Algeria and his adopted home in Brittany in *La Bréhaigne* (Denoël, 1973).

[26] This work is discussed in detail in Ch. 7. Rather less typical of the prevailing literary mood are such reworkings of previously published material as André Stil's *Trois pas dans une guerre* (Grasset, 1978), a compilation of the 3 novels published between 1956 and 1962, and ex-*rappelé* paratrooper Noël Favrelière's *Le Déserteur* (Lattès, 1973), the barely fictionalized account of his desertion and aid to the FLN, a rare adventure already recounted to greater effect as *témoignage* under the title *Le Désert à l'aube* (Minuit, 1960). A similarly celebrated testimony, *Le Déserteur* (Minuit, 1960; Manya, 1991) by Jean-Louis Hurst or 'Maurienne', was published originally as a 'novel' in a vain attempt to avoid seizure and prosecution.

presented as the narrative closes, which transform a rather familiar image of absurdity into an altogether more potent commentary on the radical solitude of the Algerian *bidasse*:

> Finalement Coulonges a décidé de suivre le mouvement. Ou pour ne pas rester seul. Ou pour être solidaire. On ne saura jamais . . .
>
> . . . quand on a été dehors, très vite, ça a pété de tous les côtés. Est mort qui a dû. A fait la mort qui a pu. (221)

> At last, Coulonges decided to follow the movement. Either to avoid being left on his own. Or to stand by the others. We shall never know. . . .
>
> . . . as soon as they got outside, there was firing from all over the place. The ones who had to, died. The ones who could, killed.

Coulonges dies as he and those like him have lived in Algeria: vainly attempting to discover a deeper truth in the absurdity of their individual Algerian experiences. Memory is crucially important in this regard, in that the collective experiences which might, in any other situation, serve to found a communal or, more broadly, generational culture and identity are systematically denied by the conscripts. Here, as so often in the literature of the Algerian war, the case of torture is of particular importance.

Much as in Roger Ikor's evocatively titled *Les Murmures de la guerre* [The Whispers of War][27], Yvane's conscripts are presented as inhabiting the conflict's anteroom: they only become aware of torture at one remove, learning of its existence without ever witnessing or participating in it. The tell-tale signs of the practice are nevertheless fully recognized, and its psychic impact is no less traumatic for not being overtly perceived. Thus it is that the seemingly innocuous hosepipe used, at a distance, to torture an FLN suspect as the narrative opens should continue to appear as a leitmotif through a series of imperfectly suppressed flashbacks to the relevant events. Memory itself, both collective and individual, is thus integrated into the narrative's structure in time-honoured fashion, as is the silence which pervades the novel's fictive space, much as it does in Camus's 'L'Hôte'.

Recounted through the eyes and in the words of a typical *deuxième classe*, the tale makes much use of orality, obscenity, military slang, and rough barrack-room humour to depict its Algerian *scènes de la vie de caserne*. Yet in the face of the undeniable reality of the war's horrors—torture, massacre, mutilation, and other atrocities, on both sides—its narrator has nothing to say: 'La

[27] *Les Murmures de la guerre* (Albin Michel, 1961); see Ch. 2.

seule arme était bien le silence' [Silence was certainly our only weapon] (139). Indeed, it is this collective will to deny the events responsible for causing individual trauma which constitutes the *génération du djebel*'s only real solidarity: 'question silence, on était tous au même point' [as far as keeping quiet was concerned, we were all in the same position] (204). Necessarily implicated in the repression of the colonized population, the conscripts may well feel 'qu'on n'y était pour rien . . . dans tout ça' [that we had nothing to do with any of that] (214); but they will never be able wholly to prove their innocence. Plenty of scope would thus remain for the writers of the 1980s to attempt to pierce both the silence of the *contingent* and the wilful forgetfulness of the French nation.

Many of these commentators would turn to psychoanalytical representations of the Algerian experience in an attempt to communicate the specificity of their own or their generation's *rappel*. With the exception of the occasional atavism[28], there is general agreement as regards the Algerian conflict's largely suppressed legacy of individual and generational trauma; so a novel like Guy Lagorce's *Le Train du soir* [The Evening Train] (1983) is able to compare the Algerian experience with the multiple traumas of the Occupation period, as memories of both conflicts are painfully prised out of the three central characters.[29] Similarly, in Richard Liscia's *Le Conscrit et le Général* (1980), the eponymous *bidasse* provides the reader with a blow-by-blow account of his infatuation with a seditious senior officer and consequent unwitting involvement in the shadowy underworld of military plot and counterplot.

As for Robert Pépin's *Pavillon 114* [Ward 114] (1981) and Pierre Bourgeade's *Les Serpents* [The Snakes] (1983), both seek insights into the war in the neuroses of a single conscripted participant. Moreover, both end with the suicide of their respective central figures following their unwilling implication in the torture of Algerian suspects. For Léon Mercadier and Albin Leblanc, then, Algeria becomes their tomb—*à la* Guyotat—and it is no coincidence that the final part of Bourgeade's narrative should bear this title. In *Pavillon 114*, again just as in Guyotat's work, Algeria is never referred to by name, becoming instead 'le Territoire National et Démocratique et Colonial', while the conflict there is deemed

[28] Such as Alain Dubos's *L'Embuscade* (Presses de la Cité, 1983), a remarkably unreconstructed paean to the French military's selfless provision of medical care for the *indigènes*.

[29] G. Lagorce, *Le Train du soir* (Grasset, 1983). See Ch. 8 for a discussion of the use of a similar technique in Alain Resnais's film *Muriel* (1963).

responsible for infecting the protagonist and many of his fellow conscripts with a strange, and apparently incurable, disease: 'certaine atteinte au physique, à l'intellectuel et au moral dénommée '*gangrena major*' à laquelle aucun remède n'avait été trouvé' [a physical, intellectual, and moral illness called 'gangrena major', for which no cure had been discovered] (37). A commonplace of the Algerian war, the gangrene metaphor is given a new potency by being made concrete: in Pépin's work it really is a disease, as well as a symbol of the Algerian war's corruption of French youth.

Similar use is made of images of clinical neurosis in Pierre Bourgeade's variation on the theme of conscription. To a certain extent, *Les Serpents* exploits the Algerian conflict as a backdrop to its principal interest in the œdipal relationship between a virginal country teacher and his widowed mother, with the phallic symbolism of the work's title constituting an accurate indicator of its real preoccupations. However, Bourgeade's Algeria is rather more than a convenient setting for this exercise in Freudian psychoanalysis. In particular, the work's insistence throughout on the youth, immaturity, and, above all, innocence of Albin Leblanc—doubly emphasized by his name—serves to make points about conscription which are of broader interest. The most important of these is its indictment of metropolitan public opinion, characterized in turn by belligerence and indifference. Albin, his rural idyll forever shattered by the delivery of his *rappel*, will, like Louis Salvaing, like Labro's Seb, have to suffer and die to expiate the unavowed guilt of a French nation which may be only too ready to give the *contingent* the traditional heroes' send-off (129), but will prove to be incapable of the sustained effort of national consciousness needed to appreciate the Algerian conflict's potential for inflicting psychological damage on those young Frenchmen obliged to take part in it.

As Albin first takes a stand against the military's use of torture for intelligence gathering, and then, in a dramatic reversal, is led by the evidence of rebel atrocities to offer to interrogate FLN suspects himself, he comes to incarnate the multiple contradictions of conscripted service in Algeria. Like those numerous literary suicides already discussed, his consequent decision to take his own life serves to focus attention on an unavowed national neurosis by presenting the reader with a stark image of one individual's mental collapse in Algeria (247). In short, it is the failure of the French people as a whole to assimilate the largely unacknowledged experiences of the millions who served there, and who now form the middle-aged backbone of the nation, which is brought to the fore by such psychoanalytical treatments of the theme of conscription.

In marked contrast to both Pépin and Bourgeade, Georges Mattéi has not limited his struggle against the French nation's role in the Algerian conflict to the literary domain. Indeed, *La Guerre des gusses* [The Lads' War] (1982) is the product of his own experiences of both the conflict itself and active metropolitan resistance to it.[30] But do Mattéi's biographical credentials make his novel the 'true story' that some critics have claimed? Is the work really capable of filling in the 'black hole' allegedly left in the French collective consciousness? Our reading of the text suggests not, in both cases, and for reasons which have to do precisely with Mattéi's membership of the 'Sartrean' Left, the Left of *Les Temps modernes* and the Jeanson network.

Although its title suggests a general applicability, Mattéi's account of the Algerian odyssey of 'Nonosse'—a *rappelé* who demonstrates against being sent to Algeria, witnesses the brutal repression of the Muslim population, deserts, joins the FLN, and is finally captured, tortured, and murdered by the *paras*—has very much more to do with the author's own exceptionally active response to service in Algeria than it does with the daily life of the *contingent*.[31] This background of profound personal commitment helps to explain Mattéi's counter-productive tendency to demonize every supporter of the French colonial cause. More particularly, it is in the discussion of the Algerian conflict in terms appropriated from the lexicon of the 1939–45 hostilities that the writer most clearly lays himself open to the charge of far-left mystification. Of course, appeals to this common mythical stockpile are a basic given of the literature of a conflict which began only a decade after the Occupation ended. However, while the Right's appeals to the mythology of World War II may be steadfastly exposed by Mattéi, his own left-wing exploitation of its powerfully affective sign-system is presented as accurate reportage.

A readily apparent mythical thread, for instance, links the *ancien combattant* who launches himself at the demonstrating conscript—and narrator—growling 'Mort aux Juifs!' [Death to the Jews!] (16), and the 'trois Mousquetaires' who torture Nonosse in the wake of his desertion to the FLN, one of whom is described as

[30] See H. Hamon, and P. Rotman, *Les Porteurs de valises: la résistance française à la guerre d'Algérie* (Albin Michel, 1979), *passim*, for an account of Mattéi's own anti-war militancy.

[31] The name 'Nonosse' suggests that the figure is modelled on Noël Favrelière, as does René Vautier's 'Nono'; see notes 19 and 22 above.

wearing the Iron Cross on his 'leopard' camouflage (162). Nonosse's reasons for deciding to go over to the enemy are repeatedly voiced in a similarly loaded fashion, with the FLN unequivocally equated with the *Résistants* and the French military with 'les Boches' (111, 172). This Nazi theme is reiterated when the protagonist is eventually led away by his paratrooper tormentors towards the inevitable *corvée de bois* [summary execution]. As the French conscript goes to meet his fate, his Algerian fellow prisoners loudly proclaim their solidarity and fraternity, prompting the *paras*' own, mythically articulated, expression of faith:

> Pour couvrir les cris des compagnons de Nonosse, les militaires entonnèrent lentement un chant aux accents germaniques.
> *Ce monde vétuste et sans joie*
> *Croulera demain devant notre foi*
> *Nous luttons pour notre idéal*
> *Pour un ordre nouveau*
> *Pour un* ORDRE *idéal . . .* (175)
>
> To cover the cries of Nonosses's fellow prisoners, the soldiers slowly struck up a song with Germanic tones.
> *This worn-out and joyless world*
> *Will tomorrow collapse in the face of our faith*
> *We are fighting for our ideal*
> *For a new order*
> *For an ideal* ORDER *. . .*

This inability to resist the clichés associated with the myth of the *para démoniaque* detracts from Mattéi's discussion of the Algerian conflict to the precise extent that it replaces the relativity of politics with a spurious, absolute evil. Moreover, the implications of the narrative's tendency to demonize the author's real-life adversaries—the military, the police, and other repressive apparatuses of the French state; the traditional Left (including especially the PCF); the essentially passive and conservative mass of the metropolitan population—are clear: its caricatural presentation of historical actors necessarily implies a similar distortion of the relevant events. In particular, Mattéi's mythical equation of the Vichy regime and de Gaulle's Fifth Republic (214) is seriously misleading, and reflects the radical Left's historical inability to come to terms with de Gaulle's unexpected determination to rid France of its colonial burden. The same could be said both of the comic-book goodness of Nonosse—a far cry from the messy historical reality of desertion and direct action in the Algerian nationalist cause, as epitomized by the cases of *l'aspirant* [officer cadet] Maillot and Fernand Yveton—and the unrelenting badness of his enemies. In fact, our reading of *La Guerre des gusses*, while not denying the text's ability to make a contribution to the historical awareness of a younger generation of French readers, suggests that some thought must be given by such consumers to the narrative's own 'ignorance', the convenient omissions and simplifications necessitated by the far-left stance of its author.

Perhaps the most intriguing variation on the theme of conscription produced in this particularly rich period of the early 1980s is that presented by Antoine Le Carvennec in his *La Mémoire chacale* [Scavenging Memories] (1983). As its title suggests, this characteristically autobiographical first novel by an ex-*rappelé* places the accent very firmly on the problematic of memory in its telling of a series of interlocking tales prompted by the experience of service in Algeria.[32] The reader thus initially enters the Algerian story-world, as so often, through a narrative present which has been irrevocably shattered: in this case by the recent death in action of Karl, the novel's central figure. The close friend of Emmanuel, the first-person narrator, and, like him, a conscript, Karl's story is told by means of a series of non-chronologically presented summaries of conversations between the two men, evoking both their recent experiences in Algeria, and Karl's early years in Paris. The narration's combination of (past) confessional and (present) stream-of-consciousness modes enables it to dovetail childhood memories of the Occupation and adult impressions of the war *là-bas* in an unusually productive fashion.

Despite the rather tired exoticism of the brothel setting for Karl's extended confession to the author-narrator, the theme of male sexuality is as persuasively presented as the proper basis for an informed understanding of 'the lads' war' as it probably can be. For Le Carvennec, indeed, it is the adolescent desire to be seen to 'avoir des couilles' [to have balls], together with the permanent terror of having them cut off, either psychologically, by the impotence-inducing horror of the conflict, or, more often, literally, by the FLN, which characterizes the conscript's predicament (53–5). The military's knowing exploitation of these sexually rooted emotions ensures the *appelés*' obedient participation in the war effort, with the result that they become 'les couillons de l'histoire' [the idiots—lit-

[32] A similar preoccupation with memory is reflected in J.-P. Bardery, *La Longue Mémoire* (La Table Ronde, 1984).

erally, 'the balls'—of the (hi)story] (70). Moreover, such thinking explains the French army's provision of delights like the famous mobile brothels (*bordels militaires de campagne* or BMC) to enliven the warrior's rest. In this light, the little Mostaganem brothel where Karl and Léon talk can itself be seen to fit into an imaginatively conceived pattern of failed attempts to escape the Algerian dungheap (*merdier*), thus adding a bitter twist to the *contingent*'s preferred slogan: 'la quille, bordel!' [roll on my demob, damn it!]. These attempts to break free, albeit temporarily, from the personal turmoil which Algeria brings are generally solitary, often sordid, and always futile. They include not only the brothel, but also masturbation, drinking, indiscipline, and the temptation of suicide, as well as, importantly, the whole process of social interaction, including especially writing about the war and its horrors. In short, and in the absence of a more thoroughgoing amnesia, the best the traumatized conscript can hope for in the face of injustice, incomprehensible cruelty, and the regular death of others is temporary relief through a self-imposed silence. This is a stance which will be encouraged, as in Labro's novel, by the silent condemnation of an effectively uncaring *métropole*. Yet, in the long run, only death will offer a durable escape route for those who, like Karl, remain traumatized by their complicity in a self-evidently unjustifiable conflict:

> Je ne suis pas du genre triste; ni rivé aux principes; mais il y a des trucs qu'on ne peut pas supporter! Et que je n'oublierai jamais! Avoir vingt ans et être ici, c'est une foutue saloperie! (269)

> I'm not the miserable type; nor am I particularly attached to principles; but there are some things that no one can bear! And that I shall never forget! To be twenty years old and here is a bloody mess!

The high priest of the impossibility of escape from the Algerian war is without doubt Daniel Zimmermann. As so often, it is his personal determination to come to terms with his own participation in the long-denied conflict which explains his repeated attempts to write his way out of trouble, first in a harrowing series of harshly illuminated snapshots of the daily life of the *contingent* in Algeria, *80 exercices en zone interdite* [Eighty Exercises in the Forbidden (i.e. free-fire) Zone] (1961), and, three decades later, in the substantially extended reworking of this collection of short stories as *Nouvelles de*

[33] D. Zimmermann, *Nouvelles de la zone interdite* (L'Instant, 1988; Manya, 1992); refs. are to the Manya edn. This reworking, he explains in a preface to the 1988 edn. (p.10) was carried out in response to abiding personal trauma.

la zone interdite [Tales of the Forbidden Zone] (1988).[33] In the fifty short prose pieces which make up this mature version of the work, Zimmermann subtly switches the focus away from the horrors of the war as lived in the killing grounds along Algeria's heavily fortified frontiers, and towards its psychological after-effects for the three million members of the *contingent*. The work's abiding message is encapsulated in its concluding *tableau*, the subject of which is precisely *la quille*, that liberation longed for so regularly and so volubly by the members of each cohort of conscripts:

> Les quillards font leurs adieux. Dans quatre jours chez soi. . . . On sera mal à l'aise. On sera abruti par la traversée, dépaysé par la France. On retrouvera, on se taira à jamais. Mais cela ne servira à rien. . . . Personne n'a jamais pu quitter la zone interdite. (97)

> The demobbed conscripts are saying goodbye. In four days they will be back home. . . . They will feel ill at ease. They will be worn out by the crossing, and will feel disorientated by France itself. They will get their bearings again, and they will keep quiet for ever. But it will all be to no avail. . . . No one has ever been able to leave the forbidden zone.

Demobilization can never constitute a genuine liberation, any more than can the other false escapes presented in Zimmermann's work. The tone is effectively set by the similarly brief opening story, which is called precisely 'La Fausse Évasion':

> Le cuirassier Morgani se masturbe toutes les trois nuits. Quand il est de garde. Il engage un chargeur dans le fusil-mitrailleur, le dresse sur ses béquilles, le pointe vers le djebel Debbarth. Il s'assoit sur des sacs de terre. Les gerboises sautillent dans les barbelés et les chacals glapissent dans le dépôt d'ordures. Le ciel est pur. Le cuirassier Morgani est seul. Mais personne n'a jamais pu quitter la zone interdite. (11)

> Trooper Morgani masturbates once every three nights. When he is on guard duty. He inserts a clip into the machine-gun, sets it up on its stand, and points it towards the Debbarth mountains. He sits on sandbags full of earth. The jerboas hop about amongst the barbed wire, and the jackals yap around the rubbish dump. The sky is clear. Trooper Morgani is alone. But noone has ever been able to leave the forbidden zone.

Lifted intact from the 1961 version, which it also introduced, this *tableau* skilfully exploits the not uncommon military theme of *la veuve poignet* to highlight the solitude, secrecy, shame, and sordidness of the conscript's condition, together, of course, with its definitive inescapability. Onanism thus becomes an appropriate symbol for the *contingent's* participation in a war in which, as Bernard Sigg has powerfully argued, the sexualization of authority, exacerbated by the cultural clash of a monogamous European colonialism and a traditionally polygamous Islamic society, encouraged an unprecedented explosion of sexual—and especially homosexual—violence.[34] Of particular interest in this regard is the tale entitled 'œil pour œil' [An Eye for an Eye], which tells of a conscript so traumatized by a nightmare vision of falling into the hands of the FLN, and thus becoming the victim of repeated homosexual rape, amongst other horrors, that he loses control and castrates the corpses of a number of dead *fellagha* (91–2).

An uncompromising catalogue of atrocity, absurdity, and ever present death, Zimmermann's snapshots of the war are undoubtedly at their most original and most forceful in the regular evocation of the violent, neurotic, or otherwise perverted sexuality of the *contingent*. Altogether more sparely and realistically presented than in Guyotat, this theme is as powerful in its detailing of the pitiful 'Statistiques' of *appelé* self-abuse (28) as in its revelation of the system of 'Hygiène' in use at a military brothel (34). By alternating boredom and brutality, *Nouvelles de la zone interdite* convincingly evokes 'l'ordinaire' [the daily round] of the average *gus*:

> Tout est pareil et on attend. . . . Barbelés du matin, barbelés du soir. . . . Le soleil ou la boue. . . . Engueulades pour un oui, bagarres pour un non, branlages, les discussions ne servent à rien, les copains c'est de la merde. On attend. (54)

> Everything is the same and we wait. . . . Barbed wire in the morning, barbed wire in the evening. . . . Sun or mud. . . . Rows for a yes, fights for a no, jerking off, discussions which never go anywhere, your mates are all shits. We wait.

With this unflinchingly stark image of futility, complicity, solitude, and self-loathing, we have come up to date in our survey of conventionally literary methods of recalling *le rappel*. However, this is by no means to say that we have exhausted the possibilities for discussion. In particular, we might usefully consider the attempt made to communicate the Algerian 'experience' through theoretically marginal, but genuinely mass-market, literary forms such as comic books and detective fiction (*polars*). While Vidal's and Bignon's *Une éducation algérienne* (1982)—a *bande dessinée* combina-

[34] *Le Silence et la honte*, 37. Sigg draws on arguments developed by Armand Frémont in his *Algérie-El Djazaïr* (Maspero, 1982).

tion of plausible barrack-room scenes and rather less persuasive anti-OAS action—remains very much a one-off, several writers have looked to the equally wide appeal of detective fiction to tell the still imperfectly assimilated story of the *contingent*.[35] In the case of former infantryman Gérard Delteil, the adventures of a reluctant conscript lucky enough to do his military service in France are used to demonstrate the Algerian war's ability to impinge on metropolitan life, at least during its latter stages. Against the background of the secret war being fought out on the streets of the capital by the FLN, the OAS, and a variety of parallel security forces (*barbouzes*), *N'oubliez pas l'artiste!* [Don't Forget the Artist!] (1985) shows how no-one is immune from this colonial war, least of all its profoundly indifferent conscripted protagonist.

Although not ultimately able to escape the war's reality, Delteil's hero fares rather better than the traumatized conscript focused on at the close of Jacques Syreigeol's *Une mort dans la djebel* [A Death in the Mountains] (1990). Accurately described by Breton and Gérard as the blackest of the *romans noirs* inspired by the Algerian war[36], this hymn to amnesia leaves the veteran to be pursued by Algerian ghosts as he wanders around the psychiatric ward of a military hospital in Rennes, perhaps for ever. A more thoroughgoing analysis of the troubled memory of the *contingent* is provided by François Joly in *L'Homme au mégot* [The Man with the Dog-End] (1990). Like *Meurtres pour mémoire* [Murders for the Record] (1984), Didier Daeninckx's masterly application of the methods of detective fiction to the historical cover-up of the crimes of 17 October 1961[37], Joly's novel combines form and content to particularly persuasive effect.

The work centres on a durably traumatized conscript's transformation into an avenging angel who is determined to rid French society of its most nefarious elements, very much in the style of Robert de Niro's Vietnam veteran in Martin Scorsese's *Taxi Driver* (1976). However, it is not so much this tale which captures the imagination, as the more modest attempt made by the protagonist,

[35] G. Delteil, *N'oubliez pas l'artiste!* (Fleuve Noir, 1985); J. Syreigeol, *Une mort dans le djebel* (Gallimard, 1990); F. Joly, *L'Homme au mégot* (Gallimard, 1990); D. Daeninckx, *Meurtres pour mémoire* (Gallimard 1984). See P. Lebedel, 'Polar: dix livres après', in L. Gervereau, J.-P. Rioux and B. Stora (eds.), *La France en guerre d'Algérie* (MHC-BDIC, 1992), 240–1.

[36] 'La Guerre d'Algérie au miroir de la fiction française', in the collective, *Trente ans après: nouvelles de la guerre d'Algérie* (Le Monde Éditions/Nouvelles-Nouvelles, 1992), 182.

[37] This work will be discussed in more detail in Ch. 7.

a former comrade in Algeria, to track the deranged killer down. In the process, he makes contact for the first time since his return to France with the surviving members of his *section*, thus reawakening imperfectly suppressed memories and reopening superficially healed psychic wounds, his own as well as theirs, some thirty years after the relevant events. It is no exaggeration to say that there is something of the feel of Patrick Rotman's painstaking research for Bertrand Tavernier's *Guerre sans nom*, as Pierre Curveillé—now significantly remembered by his old army nickname of 'Pedro'—quietly tracks down his former comrades, with the towns and villages of the Rhône replacing Rotman's and Tavernier's Isère.[38] Indeed, there is something, too, of the emotional charge so movingly conveyed by this epoch-making film in Curveillé's own interviews with his variously ageing contemporaries, all of which serve to underline the still-traumatic nature of the *contingent*'s Algerian war experiences. Although Joly provides us with a selection of these imperfectly suppressed memories of horror, the narrative could arguably do without them. For it is emphatically not the well-documented brutality of the Algerian war itself which remains to be conveyed, but rather the psychological mechanisms by which individual conscripts, *la génération du djebel*, and the French nation as a whole have long sought to deny its historicity. It is worth noting, by way of a conclusion to this chapter, that one of the most recent examples of mainstream literature devoted to the Algerian conflict has similarly resorted to the *polar* mode to tell this still-painful tale of memory and forgetting, an initiative which effectively brings the theme of conscription full circle.

The collective *Trente ans après: nouvelles de la guerre d'Algérie* [Thirty Years On: Tales of the Algerian War] (1992) is everything that *L'Homme au mégot* is not: self-consciously 'literary', self-consciously 'new', self-consciously 'balanced'—eight French writers, eight Algerian ones—and altogether more cynically aimed at the substantial market generated by, and no doubt for, the thirtieth anniversary of the Évian Agreements which brought the war to an end in 1962. Yet, not so paradoxically, this collection of new fiction is far from entirely original and, in its French component, clearly draws upon the tradition of oppositional testimony by former conscripts, together with what has become its common stock of clichés. It is thus symptomatic of the work's dearth of inspiration

[38] This important film is discussed in Ch. 8.

that the most persuasive of its constituent elements should make use of the *polar* format to justify its retelling of Vladimir Pozner's seminal 'Les Étangs de Fontargente'. 'L'Homonyme' [The Namesake], by François Salvaing, is a well-crafted account of the author-narrator's attempt to track down the family and friends of his namesake, Pozner's Lucien Salvaing.[39]

For those unfamiliar with the original story, this *nouvelle* may well constitute a useful introduction to Pozner's writing, itself justly praised for its rare sobriety (94–5). However, for more informed readers, the original account of the mysterious demise of a likeable, biddable, and deeply ordinary young Frenchman, the first conscript-centred *polar*, must remain one of the privileged sites for the communication of the troubled and troublesome memory of the *contingent*'s role in Algeria. Thus regarded, the narrative stands out against the range of variously elaborate forms of coping with the trauma of conscripted service which have consistently suggested themselves to its literary chroniclers, as do the very varied contributions made by Labro, Yvane, Pépin, Bourgeade, Zimmermann, and Joly. Yet even here, it is possible that we are still in the midst of literary obfuscation, for no less than six of these narratives turn on the real or effective suicides of their protagonists, while the seventh tells of his transformation into a homicidal maniac. What we appear very close to, in fact, is an adversary myth—doubtless informed by American research, carried out in the wake of the Vietnam war, into post-traumatic stress disorder—of the *appelé déboussolé* [the conscript who has lost his bearings]. Designed primarily for a television-conscious contemporary audience, rather than, as for so long, the ex-conscripts' own interest group, this literary imaging of the returned French soldier as what American commentators have termed the 'tripwire veteran' is a subject to which I shall return in Chapter 7.

[39] Collective, *Trente ans après*, 94–102.

6

THE WILL TO BELONG: THE MYTHS OF THE *PIEDS-NOIRS*

It was Pierre Mendès-France who, having only a few months earlier wound up the French army's catastrophic Indo-Chinese campaign, first committed his country's forces to the defence of *Algérie française*. This seemingly illogical reaction to the Algerian insurrection could, in fact, hardly be avoided, given the presence in the territory of some one million well-established settlers. Without the *pieds-noirs* there would have been no Algerian war: it was they who constituted 'French Algeria', and it was their entrenchment which made the 1954–62 conflict both so inevitable and so intractable.

In this chapter, I shall outline the system of myths developed by the settler community, and repeated by its metropolitan defenders, in an attempt to legitimize European minority control of the colony. These myths may have served to reassure the *pieds-noirs* when their ascendancy was challenged by the FLN, but they also prevented them from comprehending the political roots of Algerian nationalist violence. For the purposes of analysis, the relevant themes may be formally divided into four types, myths of origin, place, identity, and mastery; but these will often be found to overlap in practice, as a result of their common political motivation.[1] To say that the colonist was courageous and hard-working was, from an ideological point of view, the same thing as saying that he had been a valiant defender of France in two world wars: both themes established the settler community's 'right' to a privileged position in Algeria. In the event, the various settler myths would be

[1] This taxonomy is derived from that suggested in A. Chennells, 'Settler Myths and the Southern Rhodesian Novel', unpubl. D. Phil. thesis (Univ. of Zimbabwe, 1982), 242–57.

rendered similarly ineffectual by historical developments: generated both to justify European dominance and to eternalize it, they first contributed to the demise of *Algérie française* and then, in the wake of the settlers' political defeat, primed the desperate violence which was to make impossible their continued presence in an independent Algeria. In this way, the myths of the *pieds-noirs*, designed for their self-assertion and self-preservation, served in the long run to compound their downfall and to hasten their final evacuation.

By setting the relevant mythical themes against the background of the colonization of Algeria, it will become possible to see how the European settlers responded to the basic questions posed by their presence in a manifestly foreign land: 'Who are we? How do we prove that this country belongs to us and that we are at home here?'.[2] Such properly ideological considerations obviously predated the 1954–62 conflict, but would take on a fresh immediacy as the FLN's challenge to French rule intensified. Some commentators would respond to this test with new mystifications; others, less numerous, would attempt honestly to come to terms with the new Algerian reality.

The most fruitful way of approaching the complex of myths which, over the years, became attached to the settler presence in Algeria is to look, in the first instance, at their development in the literature of the French colony. Jean Déjeux has identified three main phases in the emergence of this 'Algerian' literature, which may straightforwardly be related to changes in colonial demography.[3] To begin with, in the early years of military occupation and small-scale civilian settlement, Algeria was seized upon by metropolitan writers as the perfect setting for the literary expression of their variously imperialistic and/or romantic preconceptions: military adventures thus vied for attention with the exotic charms of a new Orient. So while the likes of Barrès and Maurras lauded the triumphs of the *Armée d'Afrique*, such celebrated literary tourists as Fromentin and Maupassant made the trip to North Africa in search of highly personal forms of spiritual exaltation and earthly delight.

However, the 'littérature d'escale' [port-of-call literature] produced by these and other metropolitan travellers was not without a

[2] J. Déjeux, 'De l'éternel méditerranéen à l'éternel Jugurtha', *Revue algérienne des sciences juridiques, économiques et politiques*, 14/4 (Dec. 1977), 725.

[3] *La Littérature algérienne contemporaine* (PUF, 1975), 13–53. See also J. Hureau, *La Mémoire des pieds-noirs de 1830 à nos jours* (Olivier Orban, 1987).

significant critical dimension. So, for instance, the young Gide would undoubtedly discover in the extreme vitality and undisguised sensuality of his existence in North Africa both a means of liberation from the puritan morality of his Protestant upbringing, and a release from the pressures of his repressed homosexuality. Yet this insight into the conditions of his own liberation was to go hand-in-hand with an awareness of the racial exploitation upon which the colonial system itself was predicated: his early stays in Algeria would notably be followed by visits to the French sub-Saharan territories, and would thus lead, in the 1920s, to a series of attacks on his country's treatment of the colonized peoples.

As colonization spread, French Algeria became both more economically independent and more politically assertive. A corresponding attempt was made by the colony's artists to establish its aesthetic autonomy. The moving spirit behind this challenge to metropolitan cultural hegemony was Louis Bertrand, who, in novels like *Le Sang des races* [The Blood of the Races] (1899),[4] presented the territory as a *terroir* or agricultural land for the first time, thereby promoting its European cultivator to a new and leading role in French colonial mythology. Bertrand was convinced that a *peuple neuf* had come into being in Algeria, and that it should begin to voice its own values in a 'national' literature, drawing on its past experiences and its future aspirations.

This thesis was taken up and developed by the *Algérianistes* in the first three decades of the twentieth century. Robert Randau's 1905 novel, *Les Colons*, for instance, was intended as a celebration of the new Algerian homeland.[5] The work's title accurately reflects this home-grown literary movement's characterizing preoccupation with, and glorification of, the European settlers of Algeria. *Algérianisme* remained in the ascendant until well into the 1930s, when a combination of domestic pressures (such as the stagnation of the wine industry and the growth of Algerian nationalism) and international developments (most notably global economic depression and the rise of Fascism) contributed to its decline. As for the

[4] An excellent analysis of Bertrand's place among the early currents of French writing in and about Algeria, and one couched in terms directly relevant to my own project, is given by P. Siblot, 'Pères spirituels et mythes fondateurs de l'Algérianisme', in M. Mathieu (ed.), *Le Roman colonial* (L'Harmattan, 'Itinéraires et contacts de cultures', 7, 1987), 29–59.

[5] See Siblot, 'Pères spirituels et mythes fondateurs' 32–4, on the ideological importance of contemporary prefaces to novels such as this (together with that of an intrusive authorial 'meta-discourse' within the relevant texts).

movement's mythical thrust, this may best be summed up as an insistence on the Latin heritage of the French colonial presence in North Africa.[6]

With the progressive shift of the European population away from the farms of the hinterland and into the urban centres of the littoral, the colony's mythical preoccupations underwent a second major change. New literary themes emerged from about 1935 onwards to reflect this reorientation of the settler imagination, as the 'Mediterranean' sensibility of Albert Camus and the lesser lights of the *École d'Alger* replaced the paeans to *Algérianité* of Bertrand, Randau, and their followers.

To these three distinct phases of European myth-making must be added a fourth: the period of violent conflict, 1954–62. The liberation war would lead the settlers' literary spokesmen to appeal to all of these myth-systems in an ever more desperate attempt to defend the colonizers' ideological hegemony. To use an appropriately military metaphor, these were the broad strategic options open to the colonialist psyche once the threat of militant nationalism had been revealed by the November 1954 rising. The small number of myths developed in response to specific political and military developments, such as those which centre on the notions of missed opportunities, fraternization, and abandonment, appear in this light to be basically tactical in character: holding-operations, intended to stave off the inevitable defeat just a little longer. As Jean Déjeux rightly points out, such behaviour is very much a characteristic of societies in crisis: every attempt is made to keep up mythical appearances and thus preserve the threatened symbolic order, right up to the moment when the masquerade (*le jeu des masques*) comes to an end and the historical actors are brought face to face for the denouement.[7]

In the particular case of French Algeria, we might go even further and suggest that, for some actors in the drama at least, the masks never fell away. Indeed, even in the treatment accorded to the seemingly naked racial violence of the OAS, we can find evidence of an uninterrupted process of settler self-mystification. Our concentration on works produced after 1962 will, in addition,

[6] Although the colonial literary myth of *latinité* is generally associated with Louis Bertrand, it has been traced back at least as far as Eugène Sue: see E. Weber, *My France: Politics, Culture, Myth* (Cambridge, Mass., Belknap/Harvard Univ. Press, 1991), 32.

[7] Déjeux, 'De l'éternel méditerranéen', 725. Cf. A.-G. Slama, 'La Guerre d'Algérie en littérature ou la comédie des masques', in J.-P. Rioux (ed.), *La Guerre d'Algérie et les Français* (Fayard, 1990), 582–602, 676–82.

reveal examples both of what Montherlant referred to in his anti-colonialist masterpiece, *La Rose de sable* [The Sand Rose] (1967), as *nostalgérie*[8]—the exile's veneration of a mythified past—and of various *post facto* attempts to uphold, or excuse, the historically discredited world-view of *Algérie française*.

Before considering the major mythical themes of this very particular *Weltanschauung*, it is useful to underline the nature of the relationship obtaining between all such myths and the historical events upon which they draw. For not only colonial Algeria, but every society, makes ideological myths out of its history, both to provide justifications for its world-view, and to confer legitimacy upon its adopted system of economic, social, and political relations. Moreover, this continuous process of myth-formation is conducted with scant regard for historical evidence. Myths may thus live on long after the particular reading of history which gave rise to them has been refuted: they are not designed passively to describe history, in short, but actively to make it.

The essential autonomy of ideological myths is particularly evident in the case of the French Algerian theme of settler dispossession. So while historians may explain that immigrants of crisis were not responsible for the large-scale settlement of Algeria,[9] the literary defenders of *Algérie française* regularly appeal to a communal foundation myth which states exactly the opposite. According to the myth, the characterizing feature of the lot of the first colonizers of Algeria was its injustice: dispossessed by the old continent, through no fault of their own, the early colonists were obliged to seek their salvation in a hostile Africa. It was this background of extreme poverty (*la misère*), rather than a desire for profit, which explained the European presence in Algeria: suffering at home was the motive force behind the colonization of the territory. So, for instance, in Jeanne Montupet's *La Traversée de Fiora Valencourt* [Fiora Valencourt's Crossing] (1961), the heroine's impoverished parents are obliged to flee their native Corsica by the spectre of imminent starvation. They are thus united in the mythical pantheon of French Algeria with such disparate groups as the political exiles of the Second Empire, destitute Spanish peasants, Southern wine-

[8] H. de Montherlant, *Romans et œuvres de fiction non-théâtrales* (Gallimard, 1982), 179. Although originally written in the period 1930–2, this work was only published after the process of French decolonization had been completed. See also P. Azoulay, *La Nostalgérie française* (Baschet, 1980).

[9] See J. Talbott, *The War Without a Name: France in Algeria, 1954–1962* (London, Faber & Faber, 1981), 10.

growers ruined by the phylloxera, and the victims of the Prussian annexation of Alsace-Lorraine.[10] By the same token, in a more recent contribution to this tradition, *Le Jardin de Juan* [Juan's Garden] (1976), Guy Franco may concentrate on Spanish immigrants of crisis, but also manages to include references to other powerfully affective tales of dispossession:

> Ce Français faisait partie de ces nombreux Alsaciens et Lorrains qui, après la guerre de 1870 et l'annexion de leur province à l'Allemagne, avaient décidé de partir pour rester français et de s'installer sur une nouvelle terre française: l'Algérie. Ils ne se doutaient pas qu'un siècle plus tard leurs descendants auraient de nouveau des problèmes et seraient obligés de quitter leur nouvelle province, toujours pour rester français. (27–8)

> This Frenchman was one of those numerous inhabitants of Alsace and Lorraine who, after the annexation of their provinces by Germany, had decided to leave in order to remain French, and so had set up shop in a new French land: Algeria. They had no inkling that a century later their descendants would themselves encounter difficulties and would, once again, be obliged to leave their new province in order to remain French.

The myth of dispossession is an inherently attractive one: by suggesting injustice and the victimization of people who have in no way deserved their fate, it encourages the maximum sympathy on the part of the integrated reader for the minimum outlay as regards characterization and plot-development. Moreover, the myth actually denies the historical importance of the colonial profit motive, both as regards the original colonizers of Algeria and their mythical descendants: these Europeans are not in North Africa to make their fortunes, but to 'survive'; 'they have nowhere else to go'. However, its real potential for the legitimization of the French colonial enterprise only becomes fully apparent when the personal advancement achieved in Algeria by these dispossessed Europeans is taken into account. Here again, the approach adopted by Montupet's novel is exemplary: the contemporary prosperity of the *pieds-noirs* is presented as the product of the boundless energy and unstinting hard work of earlier generations of colonists, such as Fiora's parents.

If the colonizers started out with nothing, and have built up their prosperity and power thanks only to their own enterprise and effort, then who can reasonably deny their right to their present

[10] The regular literary reference to Alsace-Lorraine makes Slama's observation that it is generally absent from the fiction of the Algerian war a somewhat surprising one: 'La Guerre d'Algérie en littérature', 677, n.31.

privileged position? In characteristically entreating fashion, colonial injustice is legitimated by means of the complementary myths of dispossession and pioneering creation. So deeply ingrained in the colonial psyche is the myth of dispossession, in fact, that even Jules Roy, that most clear-sighted and self-critical of *pieds-noirs*, continues to cling to it in his epic treatment of the French presence in Algeria, *Les Chevaux du soleil* [The Horses of the Sun] (1967–75).[11] In addition to the unity inherent in an extended treatment of a single historical theme, very considerable continuity is achieved in this novel cycle by focusing on the development of various military and colonial dynasties. One such settler clan is the Paris family, whose name is taken from a branch of the author's own family. The grim circumstances of their arrival in Algeria are contemptuously described by another immigrant, Antoine Bouychou, who is himself an ex-lumberjack from the Ariège and a veteran of the 1830 Algiers Expedition:

> Ces Francs-Comtois avec qui il s'était lié au camp de Birmandreis, les Paris, avaient souri quand il leur avait . . . laissé entendre qu'il n'était pas venu comme eux sans vert, attiré par le miroir aux alouettes du gouvernement qui offrait des primes pour défricher les terres d'Algérie et se débarrasser des têtes brûlées, des républicains. Les yeux du père Paris s'étaient emplis de vinaigre et peu à peu les yeux des fils étaient devenus comme ceux du père. Ils avaient raison, ces misérables que le sergent Hugon avait poussés vers l'Afrique . . . (1:34)

> Those people from the Franche-Comté whom he had made friends with at the Birmandreis camp, the Paris family, had smiled when he had . . . given them to understand that, unlike them, he had not come unprepared, drawn by the lure of the grants that were offered by the government to those prepared to clear the Algerian scrub, and which were intended to rid it of the Republicans and other hotheads. The eyes of old man Paris had filled with sorrow, and little by little the sons' eyes had done the same. They were right, these poor wretches whom Sergeant Hugon had pushed towards Africa . . .

[11] 6 vols. (Grasset); numbered refs. to individual vols. are given with the page-extents. Roy's novel cycle may not have met with universal critical acclaim, but it is certainly preferable to the recent hackneyed variation on the theme produced by J. Roseau and J. Fauque, *Le 13e convoi: chronique romanesque (1848–1871)* and *Le 113e été: chronique romanesque (1903–1962)* (Robert Laffont, 1987; 1991). In one of the more bizarre twists of the Algerian drama, Jacques Roseau, co-author of these novels and president of the leading organization for 'repatriated' French Algerians, 'Recours-France', was assassinated by rival *pied-noir* militants in Montpellier on 5 Mar. 1993. This murder was extensively reported in the French press.

It is only to be expected that this background of *la misère* should be evoked by later generations of Roy's settlers once the seriousness of the Algerian nationalist challenge to the colonial ascendancy has become apparent. Thus, in the concluding volume of *Les Chevaux du soleil*, the direct descendants of 'ces misérables', Dr Paris and his widowed mother, look back through the pages of the family photograph album to the coming of their forbears to Algeria in 1854 (6: 41–3). With the outbreak of war in the colony exactly a century after their ancestors' landing in North Africa, the myth of dispossession acquires a new poignancy for the Paris family and their fellow *pieds-noirs*: it is they themselves who now face the threat of expropriation and eviction. The injustice of the situation is plain to the doctor as he drives along the country roads on his rounds in May 1958, in the midst of the seemingly omnipresent Arabs:

> Rien ne serait plus comme avant. On avait protégé les fourmis, donné ses droits aux fourmis et les fourmis finissaient par vous boulotter. (6: 27)

> Nothing would be as it was before. You protected the ants, gave the ants rights, and the ants ended up devouring you.

The spectre of this new dispossession—'Paradise Lost', as Roy's rather hackneyed image has it—brings the myth full circle. The predisposition of the European population and its metropolitan allies to image past generations of colonists in terms of *la misère* led them almost inevitably to look on their own difficulties in a similar manner. Rather than accept their communal responsibility for the collapse of *Algérie française*, the settlers preferred to appeal to the final version of the myth of dispossession: abandonment (*l'abandon*).

As we have seen, Jules Roy would, in his non-fiction, be one of the very few Europeans to oppose this sort of mystification. Nevertheless, he does not seem to be totally immune to its spell in his fictional production. Other, and lesser, literary representatives of the *pieds-noirs* would have no such redeeming side to their work, and de Gaulle and his supporters would thus come to replace such long-established villains as Louis-Napoléon and Bismarck in the settlers' catalogue of infamy. Hence the proliferation, in the wake of the community's defeat, of what Jean-Claude Vatin has memorably termed 'les plaidoyers ou "larmoyers" français' [the French speeches for the defence or 'tear-jerkers'].[12] With such patently lachrymose products as José Castano's *Les Larmes de la passion* [The

[12] *L'Algérie politique: histoire et société* (Armand Colin and Fondation Nationale des Sciences Politiques, 1974), 309.

Tears of Passion] and Micheline Susini's *De soleil et de larmes* [Of Sunshine and Tears] (both 1982), the same resonances that first made the theme of dispossession attractive come to exercise a masochistic appeal for the definitively exiled settler.[13]

One of the more readable of these *pied-noir* 'tear-jerkers' is Gabriel Conesa's *Bab-El-Oued* (1970), which is typically subtitled 'notre paradis perdu'. Like much of the settlers' creative writing, this is a consciously literary essay, rather than a novel, and its abiding interest lies not so much in its 'literariness' as in its retrospective distillation of the myth-systems of *Algérie française*. Here again, great play is made of the widowed mother, a stock figure in settler mythology whose archetype is no doubt Dr Rieux's mother in *La Peste* (1947) and thus Camus's own, Catherine Sintès. The opening lines of Conesa's autobiographical narrative provide a particularly clear illustration of the ultimate double-stranded form taken by the myth of dispossession in the imagination of the European inhabitants of colonial Algeria:

> Ma mère et l'Algérie ne sont qu'une seule et même personne.
>
> L'une et l'autre ont commencé à vivre vers 1885. Ensemble elles ont grandi et ont servi la France: ensemble elles sont passées du néant à l'épanouissement. Aujourd'hui à quatre-vingt-quatre ans, elles retournent ensemble au néant.
>
> L'une et l'autre ont ouvert les yeux au moment où on commençait à traverser la Mitidja à pied sec et sans se faire égorger. L'Algérie manquait d'hommes. Personne n'y venant, elle se peuplait des fils des Quarante-Huitards que les Français y avaient déportés et des Alsaciens et Lorrains que les Prussiens avaient chassés de chez eux. Elle se décidait à peine à entrebâiller ses portes que sa maison s'emplissait déjà de tous les fils de la Méditerranée.
>
> Ma mère qui est née près d'Alicante arriva à Alger parmi ses frères et ses soeurs. Son père était, je crois, carrier, et la misère l'avait poussé à l'exil. Pour les gens ruinés, l'Algérie était une terre fertile où enfouir leur passé et où semer le grain de leur faim et de leur courage. Sa famille s'installa à Bab-El-Oued qui n'était qu'un rassemblement de baraques que les maisons en dur remplaçaient lentement. Mais c'était déjà un village, un univers, une patrie. (9–10)

My mother and Algeria are one and the same.

Both of them started out on life around 1885. Together they grew up

[13] See V. Cabridens, '"Algérie perdue": analyse de titres—Écrits de Français sur l'Algérie publiés après 1962', in J.-R. Henry *et al.*, *Le Maghreb dans l'imaginaire français* (Aix-en-Provence, Édisud, 1985), 175–89; and P. Siblot, 'Retours à "l'Algérie heureuse" ou les mille et un détours de la nostalgie', ibid. 151–64.

and served France: together they started as nothing and went on to bloom. Today, at eighty-four, they are returning to nothingness together.

They first opened their eyes at a time when it was just becoming possible to cross the Mitidja without getting your feet wet or your throat cut. Algeria lacked men. As no one came forward, she populated herself with the sons of the 1848 revolutionaries whom the French had deported, and with people from Alsace and Lorraine that the Prussians had driven out of their homes. Hardly had she decided to half-open her door than her house began to fill up with all the sons of the Mediterranean.

My mother, who was born near Alicante, arrived in Algiers together with her brothers and sisters. Her father was a quarryman, I believe, and poverty had forced them into exile. For those who had been ruined, Algeria was a fertile land where they could bury their past and sow the seeds of their hunger and their courage. Her family set up shop in Bab-El-Oued, which was only a collection of shacks that permanent houses would slowly replace. But it was already a village, a universe, a homeland.

This introductory passage is remarkably rich in mythical significations. Not only are dispossession and the theme of the widowed mother appealed to, but also the myths of pioneering creation and the eternal Mediterranean, as well as two distinct brands of *pied-noir* patriotism, not forgetting Conesa's central preoccupation with his personal version of the myth of Bab-El-Oued. Dispossession itself is here perceived to be a return to an original, and, indeed, constitutive state: an ultimate and immutable destiny, from which the settlers' years of relative plenty, though paid for in blood, sweat, and tears, could only ever be a temporary respite. Both *Algérie française* and the *pieds-noirs* grew from nothing, flowered briefly, and now return to nothing.

For Henri Martinez, the author of the pseudo-Camusian confession *Et qu'ils m'accueillent avec des cris de haine* [Let Them Greet Me with Cries of Hatred] (1982), it was precisely the spectre of 'nothingness'—the supposedly total loss of identity habitually associated with the end of French Algeria—that gave rise to the European terrorism of the Organisation Armée Secrète, or OAS:

Que pouvions-nous faire d'autre? Choisir la mort des moutons dans les égorgeoirs? Partir dès cette époque vers une métropole qui nous repousse? Mais comment déménager les meubles de presque 2500 familles tous les mois? Et les biens intransportables? Toute une vie, tout l'héritage d'un passé délibérément abandonnés? Et pour s'installer où? Quel métier? Quel avenir? En quelle ville ou village? Rien! Rien! Le néant . . .

Nous étions seulement pieds-noirs; c'était comme une corporation. Et nombre d'entre nous eurent, dès le début, le réflexe malheureux de vouloir défendre jusqu'au bout, et contre le simple bon sens, les avantages acquis par la vieille misère, et leur courage récent. (44–5)

What else could we do? Choose to die like sheep in a slaughterhouse? Leave straight away for a metropolitan France which rejects us?. . . But how do you move the belongings of nearly 2500 families each month? And what about the things that cannot be transported? A whole life, the entire heritage of a deliberately abandoned past? And in order to set yourself up where exactly? What job are you going to do? What future are you going to have? Which town or village will you live in? Nothing! Nothing! Nothingness . . .

We were just *pieds-noirs*; it was like a corporation. And many of us had, from the outset, the unfortunate and instinctive reaction of wishing to defend, to the very end, and in defiance of all common sense, the advantages paid for with our community's past misery and recent courage.

Communal dispossession was to lead, via the OAS, to individual 'perdition' in a final mythical development: the last-ditch defence of the settlers' *patrie* would result, in the relevant literature at least, in the loss not only of *pied-noir* lives, but also of the sanity and even the 'souls' of the defenders. This terminal twist might conveniently be thought of as a loss of personal identity with the collapse of the community: when the colonial edifice crumbles, so does the psychic and even the spiritual integrity of the individual colonizer. This is the central theme of *Dernières nouvelles de l'enfer* [Latest News from Hell] (1984), a tale of an Oran OAS fighter's metropolitan life after death, which may reasonably be regarded as Henri Martinez's fictional follow-up to his *apologia pro vita sua*:

Où suis-je seulement? Je vais avoir vingt ans, et je ne sais plus ce qui en moi est mort, et ce qui reste de vivant. Une seule certitude, j'aborde chez l'ennemi. L'autre ennemi, celui que j'ai quitté là-bas, ne l'était que par erreur. Celui-là est le seul véritable, qui, déjà, exilait mes ancêtres il y a plus d'un siècle vers ces rivages fiévreux du continent africain, pour, le plus souvent, déjà, les crimes de pauvreté et de sale gueule. (15)

Where am I anyway? I'm nearly twenty, and I'm no longer sure what part of me is dead and what is still alive. . . . One thing I do know, is that I'm landing on enemy shores. The other enemy, the one that I left behind over there, was only my enemy by mistake. This is the only real one, the one who, over a century ago, was already sending my ancestors into exile on the fever-infested shores of the African continent, more often than not for the crime of being poor or because their faces didn't fit.

Yet the theme of dispossession is only one aspect of the European population's quest for a mythical origin. Another constantly recurring feature of the literature of the Algerian conflict is the appeal to the ancient history of the territory in an attempt to legitimize the contemporary colonial presence; that is to say, the 'heritage' of the Roman conquerors of North Africa is looked to by the settlers—*à la* Louis Bertrand—to provide them with a communal origin, and thus both an identity and a rationale for their privileged position in Algeria.

Gabriel Conesa's *Bab-El-Oued* is a case in point. Time and again, Rome is presented as a fundamental point of reference for *pied-noir* Algeria. So, for instance, Conesa's native *quartier* is likened to a Roman forum (22), while the 1930 Centenary of the Algiers Expedition becomes the Roman triumph of France in Algeria (47–8). At opposite poles of peace and war, a child's street game is attributed to the Romans (54), and the besieged European stronghold of Bab-El-Oued becomes, *in extremis*, 'un théâtre romain déserté, mangé de soleil et parcouru par des lézards et où, à la place de la voix des acteurs, ne résonne plus que celle des cigales' [a deserted Roman theatre, devoured by the sun and a home to lizards, and where the booming tones of the actors have given way to those of the cicadas] (215–16).

At no stage does Conesa need to make explicit the significance of these regular allusions to the Roman occupation of the Maghreb, for their mythical import will be readily apparent to any reader familiar with the symbolic order of French Algeria. Indeed, these textual references to classical antiquity—so obviously inspired by Camus's 'Noces à Tipasa' [Nuptials at Tipasa] (1939)—conjure up the standard images of the colony's *héritage latin*: namely, the ruins found at Tipasa, Timgard, and the lesser Roman sites. More importantly, such images inevitably communicate the French colonialist propaganda historically attached to these archaelogical remains. This turns on what Déjeux has identified as the myth of the eternal Mediterranean, the timeless incarnation of Bertrand's *latinité*, which has never ceased to be present in North Africa. The region's Arabic and Islamic dimension is thus reduced to a historical parenthesis, an inessential phase during which the conquering Arab hordes did little more that camp amid the remains of Roman Africa.[14] With the 1830 invasion, the parenthesis is deemed to be closed, as France takes on the civilizing mantle of Rome. The theme of the eternal

[14] Francine Dessaigne memorably utters this article of colonialist faith in her *Journal d'une mère de famille pied-noir* (1962), likening the pillaging nomads to locusts destroying all in their path (71).

Mediterranean serves to unite the disparate settler community by providing it with a common mythical origin.[15] However, the figure is inherently self-contradictory, for Algeria's classical sites not only bear witness to the Romans' historical presence, but also to the passing of their minority colonial rule. As for the country's systematically denied Arabo-Islamic inheritance, this was to prove only too obviously resistant to French attempts to consign it to the dustbin of history.

Louis Bertrand, at least, was clear in his aims: what he sought was a 'Roman' Algeria, to be ruled forever by the colony's European minority. Subsequent defenders of the *pied-noir* cause would fight shy of such honest racism, coming to prefer such illusions as *intégration* to Bertrand's thoroughgoing supremacism. Nevertheless, these later partisans of *Algérie française* would continue to play the Latin card to the fullest mythical advantage. The theme's most obvious attraction, simply stated, was that it transformed a conquered land into a French legacy: Algeria was not so much being taken from the Arabs as restored to the heirs of classical Rome. This type of thinking is the first of the two related, but ideologically distinct, brands of Mediterraneanism which we shall encounter in the present chapter.

The political thrust of this particular formulation of the myth of *pied-noir* Latinity is clear: as the rightful heirs to the glory that was Roman, the European settlers of Algeria cannot reasonably be considered to be invaders or usurpers. Indeed, on this mythical plane, their presence magically predates that of the Arab conquerors of North Africa. Even more dramatically, as a Mediterranean region, the Maghreb ceases to be a part of Africa and becomes a natural European colony. Geographically divided from Black Africa by the Sahara, North Africa is, in contrast, linked to Europe by a sea which unites more than it separates. Enshrined in their own language's debt to that of ancient Rome[16], the modern colonizers' *latinité* serves to transform a historical expropriation into a mythical

[15] The defenders of French Algeria would not only incorporate this foundation myth into their fiction, but also into their political writings, and even into the academic history of the colony. See Vatin, *L'Algérie politique*, 8–56; cf. A. Calmes, *Le Roman colonial en Algérie avant 1914* (L'Harmattan, 1984), 13–18.

[16] In the literature, French and its speakers are often referred to by Algerians as *le roumi* and *les Roumis* respectively (i.e. Latin and the Romans). See e.g. G. Franco, *Le Jardin de Juan* (Fayard, 1976), 25; cf. Saint-Laurent, *Les Passagers pour Alger* (Presses de la Cité, 1960), I, 86.

inheritance, and thus to legitimize and eternalize the contemporary injustice of *Algérie française*.

Such thinking has clear links with the militant Catholicism and anti-Semitic ultra-nationalism of the *Action française* movement. Of the greatest importance in this regard is Charles Maurras's concept of the Latin West, the proto-fascist associations of which are entirely appropriate given Mussolini's historical attempt to impose Italian hegemony over the Mediterranean, and thus to re-establish its status as *mare nostrum*. Yet, paradoxically, those literary commentators who consciously rejected this far-right version of Mediterraneanism in favour of its later, Camusian, form would not thereby avoid the position's inherent contradictions.

It is difficult to overstate the primacy of the land in the settlers' quest for legitimacy. What is the myth of Latinity, after all, but a means of establishing ownership of the Algerian soil? The pre-colonial Algeria of 1830 came to be depicted as a wilderness for precisely the same reason. Of course, there can be little doubting the hardships encountered by the early settlers of Algeria, nor the frontier grit needed to overcome them. What is open to dispute, however, is the extent to which later generations of *pieds-noirs*—living predominantly in the urban centres of the littoral, and variously employed in the manufacturing or service sectors, or as public employees—were entitled to image themselves as the heirs to those glorified North African voortrekkers in an attempt to legitimate their own increasingly contested presence.

The theme of creation *ex nihilo* is the real essence of the European claim to the land; indeed, it constitutes the most obviously self-justificatory aspect of the settlers' insistence on their development (*mise en valeur*) of the territory. As such, its dubious historical validity is of less importance than the use made of it by the literary defenders of *Algérie française*. Of particular symbolic interest in this context is the Mitidja, which is taken to epitomize the achievements of the early pioneers. This is clearly true, for instance, of Conesa's introductory reference to the much-vaunted draining and cultivation of the malarial swamps of the region. For him, as for the majority of French commentators, the Mitidja is to be regarded as the masterpiece of colonial enterprise in Algeria. There is thus no question of the European settlers' having seized the most productive lands from the indigenous population of the territory in the way suggested by historians and recognized by Jules Roy:

Du côté de Boufarik une fumée montait, que le ciel aspirait et couchait vers l'ouest, devant les montagnes où d'autres fumées s'étiraient, car les montagnes, où les colons n'allaient jamais, étaient habitées. Là s'étaient réfugiés les Arabes qu'on avait chassés de leurs terres en occupant la Mitidja. (II: 25)

In the direction of Boufarik a column of smoke was rising, which the sky sucked up and spread out towards the west, in front of the mountains where other columns were stretching up, for these mountains, which the settlers never visited, were inhabited. That was where the Arabs had taken refuge when they had been driven off their land as a result of the occupation of the Mitidja.

On the contrary, for Gabriel Conesa, the chronicler of Bab-El-Oued, this objective expropriation never took place, and pre-colonial Algeria may therefore be straightforwardly summed up as a land where everything was lacking (52). A wholly negative entity, the uncultivated Arabo-Berber Algeria of 1830 was clearly destined to attract a force for positive change, and is thus to be contrasted with the fertile and developed French Algeria of 1954. The proprietorial implications of this preferred view of the colonial *mise en valeur* are clear, and turn on a *pied-noir* reworking of the biblical myth of Cain, who was not only the first murderer, but also the first tiller of the soil. Similarly, the French conquest of Algeria may have involved an element of evil (*le mal*), but the subsequent fertilization of the land can only be perceived as good (*le bien*).[17] The colonist is thus seen to be the legitimate owner of the land which his forbears created from the pre-colonial chaos, and which he continues to make productive. The Muslims, meanwhile, may possess something like an original innocence, but, like the nomadic shepherd, Abel, have done nothing to make the earth bear fruit. That they should now threaten the property and lives of the land's European cultivators is therefore as unjust as it is backward-looking. As an Alsatian farmer puts it in *L'Embuscade* [The Ambush] (1983),[18] Alain Dubos's remarkably unreconstucted paean to settler values:

Mes ancêtres n'ont pas eu les moyens, ou le temps, d'irriguer plus au sud.

[17] Cf. the views expressed by a small-scale European farmer in the Sersou region in Cécil Saint-Laurent's *L'Algérie quand on y est* (Le Livre Contemporain, 1958): '"Qu'ont fait mon père et mon grand-père, dans ce pays? se demande Batteur. Du bien ou du mal? Ils ont créé. Ils ont sorti des choses durables du néant."' ["What did my father and grandfather do in this land?" wonders Batteur. "Good or evil? They created. They made something that would last out of nothing."] (114). Note that Batteur's own name has connotations both of combativity and construction (*battre* and *bâtir*).

[18] A. Dubos, *L'Embuscade* (Presses de la Cité, 1983).

Peut-être un jour, si cette guerre finit, pourrons-nous fertiliser un bout de ces rocailles désolées . . . (32)

My forebears never had the resources, or the time, to irrigate the land further to the south. Perhaps one day, if this war ends, we might be able to fertilize a part of this stony wasteland.

For the myth-makers of French Algeria, it is the perceived failure of the Arabs to cultivate the land over which they nomadically roamed that disqualifies them from ownership of it. Moreover, in a reversal of historical truth, the early colonizers are deemed to have settled not on the richest farming land, but on the most marginal. If the Algeria of 1954 is to be regarded as a colonial garden of Eden, then this is a paradise which is emphatically not to be regarded as God-given. As Guy Franco openly declares in *Le Jardin de Juan*, a *pied-noir* pastoral which concentrates precisely on the creation of one particular 'garden':

Emigrants espagnols, misérables va-nu-pieds de la colonisation de l'Afrique du Nord, je chante ici, solennellement, votre courage et votre misère, votre aveuglement et votre déraison, votre insouciance et votre modestie, l'amour de votre famille et votre soif de vie. . . . Je voudrais dire comment vous avez souffert et supporté la maladie, quel a été votre tribut à la mort dans ce grand œuvre qu'a été la colonisation de l'Afrique du Nord . . . (36)[19]

Spanish emigrants, barefoot wretches of North African colonization, I now solemnly sing the praises of your courage and your poverty, your blindess and your folly, your devil-may-care attitude and your modesty, the love of your family and your thirst for life. . . . I would like to say how much you suffered and coped with illness, and what tribute you were required to pay as a contribution to this great task of colonizing North Africa . . .

In fact, the literary descendants of those first *défricheurs* [tillers of the land] face as much of a struggle against bankruptcy as they do against the FLN. That they should remain in Algeria at all, in fact, is to be understood in terms not of profit, but rather of the *pieds-noirs*' love of their native land: a passionate sense of belonging which transcends every other consideration, and which continues to be appealed to in titles such as Josette Sutra's *Algérie mon amour* [Algeria My Love] (1979), and Alain Vircondelet's *Maman la Blanche*

[19] For all its self-consciously modernist *cassure du récit*, Alain Ferry's *El-Kous* (Seuil, 1978), hailed by some as a new insight into the colonial universe, is remarkably familiar in its nostalgic insistence upon the childhood idyll lived out by the author-narrator on a wine-estate in pre-1954 Algeria.

[(Algiers) My White Mother] (1981) and *Alger l'amour* [Algiers (My) Love] (1982). It is this love of the soil which leads Marie Cardinal, in *Écoutez la mer* [Listen to the Sea] (1962), her own variation on the theme of the pastoral idyll, to relate her childhood memory of rolling on and in the wet Algerian earth when the rains finally come after a period of intense heat (108). The child is thus at one with the very soil of Algeria, a land which the exiled adult would describe in a later work as her real mother.[20] Here, Conesa's maternal metaphor is taken to its logical conclusion.

Heirs to the Romans, creators of Algeria *ex nihilo*, the European settlers are, on this reading of colonial history, great humanitarians into the bargain, and are thus regularly depicted extending paternalistic care to their Muslim employees and the wider Algerian community. So, for instance, we learn that Dubos's Gertall has effectively adopted a young Berber as his son (31). Moreover, if the slightest guilt does attach to the colonial enterprise, it is emphatically not to such courageous small-scale farmers as Gertall, but rather to those anonymous *gros colons* who have prospered during the colony's good times. It is these agribusinessmen, the argument runs, who are responsible for those few colonial abuses which have occurred: they alone are opposed to change, and they will be the first to quit the country when the going gets tough. History might suggest that agricultural production was dominated in the Algeria of 1954 by a cartel of industrial growers and that, under pressure, the small farmers would prove to be at least as reactionary as the major producers, but as far as the myth-makers are concerned it is the *petit blanc* who incarnates the vital spirit of the European community.[21] Henri Martinez is therefore repeating a familiar *pied-noir* refrain when he puts forward an outraged defence of the 'Petits agriculteurs riches en cailloux et en poussière, tout fiers de se nommer eux-mêmes colons' [Little farmers rich in rocks and dust, who were so proud to be able to call themselves colonists] (*Et qu'ils m'accueillent*, 27).

[20] M. Cardinal, *Les Mots pour le dire* (Julliard, 1975), 112. Cf. Martinez, *Dernières nouvelles*, 30. In what is perhaps her best-known work on the theme of exile (and temporary return), *Au pays de mes racines* (Grasset, 1980), Marie Cardinal remembers the Algeria of her childhood and compares it with her impressions of the modern independent state. Her account of life in the country both before and after independence is a highly selective one, which contrives to evoke a 'natural' continuity, rather than acknowledging the radical cultural cleavage that gave rise to the events of 1954–62.

[21] See H. Gourdon *et al.*, 'Roman colonial et idéologie coloniale en Algérie', *Revue algérienne des sciences juridiques, économiques et politiques*, 11/1 (Mar. 1974), 144.

The myth of the *petit colon* is clearly a more palatable version of the colonial exploitation of Algeria's agricultural potential than the oligopolistic reality represented by wine barons like Henri Borgeaud. By the same token, the underlying paradox of this legitimizing strategy—its invocation of pioneer virtues in support of a process of (ultimately unsuccessful) stabilization[22]—was never apparent to the mass of the *pied-noir* community, nor to their literary spokesmen. Indeed, the myth would, true to form, survive both the eviction of the European population of Algeria from the land which they had supposedly created, and their relocation in new, and still less plausible, wildernesses: proof, if it were needed, of the durability of the myth-systems of *Algérie française*.

As heirs to the twin traditions of dispossession and pioneering creation, the Europeans of Algeria are able to see themselves as the possessors of what Chennells, working in the Southern Rhodesian context, has called 'an identity forged from hardship'.[23] This mythical theme draws its material from both the heroic past of Algerian colonization—as celebrated in novels like Marcel Moussy's *Arcole ou la terre promise* [Arcole or the Promised Land] (1953)—and more recent French and world history. In particular, a debt of gratitude is deemed to be owed by the mother country to the *pieds-noirs*, on account of their blood sacrifices in two world wars. The appeal made to the theme by Gabriel Conesa is thus properly regarded as exemplary. In the following extract from his *Bab-El-Oued*, we find what is a typical blend of self-glorifying patriotism and smug intransigence:

> L'histoire de ma famille n'est pas intéressante. Elle n'a que la valeur d'un exemple répandu chez nous à des dizaines de milliers d'exemplaires.
>
> La première fois que mon père a mis les pieds en France, c'était pour faire la guerre; la première fois que j'ai mis les pieds en France, c'était aussi pour faire la guerre. Pendant qu'il se battait, sa mère est morte; pendant que je me battais, il est mort. Il avait choisi la France et cela nous a coûté à tous les deux dix ans de nos vies dont sept de guerre.
>
> Qui prétend nous enseigner la France? (17)

> My family history is not an interesting one. It is only worth noting as one of the tens of thousands of similar examples that you could find among our community.
>
> The first time that my father set foot in France, it was to fight in a war; the first time that I set foot in France, it was also to fight in a war. While

[22] J. Berque, *Le Maghreb entre deux guerres* (Seuil, 1962), 29.

[23] A. Chennells, 'Settler Myths and the Southern Rhodesian Novel, 242–57.

he was fighting, his mother died; while I was fighting, he died. He had chosen France, and that cost us both ten years of our lives, including seven years of war.

Who can claim to teach us about France?

Military service holds pride of place in Conesa's scheme of values as the supreme test of patriotic sentiment, with combat itself perceived as the high point of the *pieds-noirs*' love affair with France (51). However, the historical contribution made by *Algérie française* to the French cause in World War II must be sanitized if it is to be mythically exploited, and Conesa is at pains to excuse the settler community's general support for Pétain and Vichy in the period 1940–42 (134–5). Nevertheless, the settlers' war service may still plausibly be appealed to in order to justify their privileged position in Algeria.[24] It need hardly be added that the historically denied rights of those Algerians who fought and died for France in two world wars are not a subject for Conesa's outspoken protest.

Conesa's insistence on the Frenchness of the European population prompts some basic questions about the nature of the settlers' attachment to a 'mother country' which, in many cases, had never been their ancestral home. How precisely did the *pieds-noirs* feel themselves to be 'French'? In what ways did their communal self-image resemble that of the inhabitants of metropolitan France? And, most importantly, in what respects did they consider themselves to differ from their mainland counterparts? Central to the settlers' sense of self is the legal fiction that Algeria is not a colony at all, but rather an integral part of *la plus grande France*. The literary assertion of this primary mythical concept has a long pedigree, as anyone familiar with Daudet's comic masterpiece *Tartarin de Tarascon* (1872) will be aware:

Aux premiers pas qu'il fit dans Alger, Tartarin de Tarascon ouvrit de grands yeux. D'avance, il s'était figuré une ville orientale, féerique, mythologique, quelque chose tenant le milieu entre Constantinople et Zanzibar . . . Il tombait en plein Tarascon . . . [25]

On taking his first steps in Algiers, Tartarin de Tarascon opened his eyes wide. Before he arrived he had imagined an oriental, magical, mythological

[24] In a particularly intriguing combination of ideas, F. Valmain, in *Les Chacals* (Fayard, 1960) pp.28–9, links this theme with the Latin myth when he describes the local *monument aux morts* as being shaped like a Roman column and surrounded by stones recuperated from Roman sites in the vicinity.

[25] p. 74.

city, something like a cross between Constantinople and Zanzibar . . . And here he was slap in the middle of Tarascon . . .

Unhappily, the debunking of metropolitan exoticism is no guarantee against colonial mystification.[26] Indeed, this image of the Southerner 'coming home' to Algeria is one which exemplifies the literary obfuscation of the colony's status; for the precise nature of the territory's Frenchness is far from obvious, and if the *pieds-noirs* are to be regarded as provincial Frenchmen, then it is as profoundly troubled and ambivalent ones.

In her essay 'Les livres comme patrie', Janine de la Hogue has argued that those Europeans who left Algeria when the war for the territory had been lost have subsequently attempted to regain their 'lost province' through its literary evocation.[27] This is certainly a plausible explanation of the exiles' abundant literature of nostalgia. However, we might reasonably go a step further and suggest that the European population of Algeria was always searching for that mythical province in its literature: the real site of *Algérie française*, after all, was never the objective reality of the colony, but always the colonial imagination. Indeed, the inherently problematic nature of the *pieds-noirs*' communal identity is revealed by their very insistence on the Frenchness of both the land and themselves. Like the threatened settler populations of other colonies—most notably the Rhodesians and the Ulster British—they loudly proclaim their national allegiance to a metropolitan audience whose own identity is beyond question. Conesa's distillation of the mythology of French Algeria, *post mortem*, is typically revealing in this regard. So while the young author and his contemporaries may appear strange and shocking to the metropolitan French, their war service under the Republic's colours will put their common nationality beyond doubt (78).

The belief that Algeria was just another French province, albeit a very special one, underpins the writing of *pied-noir* and metropolitan authors alike. Where Henri Martinez likens rural Algeria to Alsace, Champagne, and the Aisne (*Et qu'ils m'accueillent*, 27), the generally sympathetic 'francaoui' Alain Dubos likens the Gertall's besieged farm to the agricultural 'fortresses' of the Beauce (32). The settler preoccupation with being French and loving France also explains the

[26] See Gourdon *et al.*, 'Roman colonial', 133.

[27] J. de la Hogue, 'Les Livres comme patrie', in L. Elia, and M. Elia (eds.), *Les Pieds-Noirs* (Philippe Lebaud, 1982), 112–13.

regular literary depiction of love affairs between metropolitan French characters and *pieds-noirs*. A typical example of these symbolic relationships would be the one, set at an unspecified point in the pre-1954 golden age, which constitutes the main action of *Le 'Bar à Campora'* [Campora's Bar] (1969) by Max Guedj. The name chosen for the couple's baby, 'France' (180) surely betrays a profound uncertainty as to the wider community's identity.[28] Moreover, this communal preoccupation may readily be made to reveal the essentially conditional nature of European allegiance to the French nation. Thus, Henri Martinez revealingly insists upon the settlers' love of France on the occasion of the historic events of 13 May 1958; that is to say, at a moment when their ascendancy seemed once more to be assured (*Et qu'ils m'accueillent*, 32).

In fact, the settlers' much-vaunted patriotism was only ever offered on their own, permanently preferential, terms. A mythical France could thus be invoked to legitimize the European population's systematic refusal to accept the authority of the elected administrations of the historical France whenever colonial privilege was threatened. This was the real message of *le 13 mai*, an occasion which, more than any other, revealed the determination of Algiers to resist the decolonizing will of Paris, come what may. Like the allegiance to the Crown but not to Her Majesty's Government of the Ulster Unionists, the Europeans' devotion to France was patently self-serving, and thus in constant need of reassurance. For this reason, it was the historic refusal of de Gaulle to continue to meet the settlers' conditions which provoked their final, and most dramatic, identity crisis.

De Gaulle's return to power meant that unconditional French support for the European population had ceased to be a given of the Algerian political equation. A new response now suggested itself, *in extremis*, to the beleaguered settler community, in the form of a separatist assertion of *pied-noir* 'national' independence. Though confined to a radical minority, such as Martinez, this position is the logical outcome of the communal difference so loudly proclaimed by mainstream loyalists like Gabriel Conesa and Roland Bacri, the latter a representative of a younger generation of exiles still eager to assert the reality of 'notre piénoiritude à nous' [our very own *pied-noir*-ness].[29] Indeed, the tendency of *pied-noir* and metropolitan

[28] The case of French Jews in the 1930s would be an obvious point of comparison in this regard.

[29] *Le Beau Temps perdu: Bab-el-Oued retrouvé* (Lanzmann/Seghers, 1978), 11.

commentators alike for long to ascribe an 'Algerian' national consciousness and identity to the (European) *Français d'Algérie*—as opposed to the (indigenous) *Français de souche nord-africaine*—is the real root of this particular confusion.

This leads us naturally to consider the Europeans' assertion of their individuality and independence as a race. Young, energetic, and virile, the *peuple neuf* is to be contrasted with both the Arabo-Berber population—perceived as the representatives of a 'dead' Algeria—and the inhabitants of a supposedly decadent *métropole*. So, writing half a century after Louis Bertrand, Gabriel Conesa emphasizes the physical and moral health of his community (102). The robust well-being 'de ceux qui ont trop de problèmes à résoudre pour prendre le temps de les penser' [of people who have too many problems to solve to waste time thinking about them] (176–7) is deemed to derive from the European population's mixed Mediterranean ancestry, which is itself a major theme of the settler imagination. Take, for instance, the account provided by Henri Martinez of his own ancestry:

> A ma naissance, les fées qui se penchèrent sur mon berceau y déposèrent . . . une grosse tranche d'Espagne, pimentée peut-être d'une pincée mauresque de Grenade, une part d'Europe centrale légèrement saupoudrée de juifs réchappés des pogroms polonais et une lichée alsacienne pour justifier ma carte d'identité française. Si le pavillon de Breteuil recherche un jour un modèle typique de la race pied-noir, je crois qu'il ne ferait pas une mauvaise affaire avec mon cas. (*Et qu'ils m'accueillent*, 25)[30]

> When I was born, the fairies looking over my cradle dropped in . . . a big slice of Spain, perhaps spiced up with a pinch of Moorish Granada, a portion of central Europe lightly sprinkled with Jews who had escaped from the Polish pogroms, and a hint of Alsace to justify my French passport. If the Pavillon de Breteuil is ever looking for a typical example of the *pied-noir* race, I do not think it would go too far wrong with me.

While other, self-justifying, racial elements are clearly present here, it is nevertheless the Mediterranean one which predominates. The fact that this aspect of the author's ancestry should be specifically Spanish is only to be expected of a native of French Algeria's second city, Oran. The Spanish reference would be equally appropriate to the working-class districts of Algiers, such as the Belcourt of Camus and his mother. Above all, it could be applied to the Bab-El-Oued of Musette's picaresque hero Cagayous and his literary

[30] Cf. R. Bacri, *Et alors? et oilà!* (Balland, 1971), 17.

descendants, the 'Hernandez et Perez' of popular lore and literature.[31] As for the quarter's principal literary chronicler, Conesa recalls that 'quoi que je dise, j'étais toujours l'Espagnol' [whatever I said, I was always the Spaniard] (169).

However, the *pied-noir* society depicted by such writers is neither an entirely Spanish entity, nor yet a Franco-Iberian hybrid.[32] Rather, it is a properly Mediterranean amalgam, in which the French and Spanish stock combines with elements from every shore washed by *mare nostrum*. So the Algeria described by Conesa is peopled by a generous and spontaneous Latin mix, whose racial memory goes back to 'Valence, Alicante, Majorque, Ischia, Malte, Naples ou Palerme' (77). This is the well-documented brand of Mediterraneanism first inspired by the work of Gabriel Audisio, and most famously associated with the writing of Albert Camus as the leading light of a young and dynamic *École d'Alger*.

It is no coincidence that this new variation on the Mediterranean theme should have made its first appearance in the 1930s, at a time when modern Algerian nationalism emerged to challenge both the political and ideological assumptions of the colony's minority rulers, a historical context which serves to define the mythic potential of the new Mediterraneanism. For if the Mediterranean is the real homeland of the settlers and the Arabo-Berber population alike, then nationalism is based on an enormous fallacy: that of Algerian nationhood itself. Indeed, the proposition that an Algerian nation did not exist and had never existed was to become a basic premise of French colonial thinking.[33] There is, according to the myth, no essentially French, nor even European, community in Algeria; still less an essentially Arabo-Berber one. On the contrary, both ethnic groups belong, on a deeper level, to a single *peuple méditerranéen*. The specific forms taken by this mythical integration of the indigenous population thus share a common ideological function: to dissolve a nascent national political consciousness in a Mediterranean sea of liberal humanism.

The profound irony of the Mediterraneanist insistence on a common humanity is made apparent when we consider the historical indifference of the *pieds-noirs* to the indigenous Algerian community. The relevant mystification may be understood in terms of the

[31] See G. Audisio (ed.), *Cagayous de Musette* (Balland, 1972).

[32] The Oran of writers like Emmanuel Roblès might properly be considered as Franco-Iberian. See especially *Saison violente* (Seuil, 1974).

[33] See Ch. 3, n. 23.

humanist universalism of the *École d'Alger*, as a single illustration of Camus's primordial influence on the subsequent literary imaging of *Algérie française* will show. In his essay 'Le Minotaure ou la halte d'Oran' [The Minotaur or the Stop in Oran] (originally written in 1939, but only published in *L'Été* [Summertime] in 1954), Camus describes the twin local delights (*voluptés*) of having one's shoes cleaned, and then showing them off in a stroll along the city's boulevards. As for the Arab boot-blacks who actually do the necessary work, 'great-hearted Camus'[34] has this to say:

> Juché sur de hauts fauteuils, on pourra goûter alors cette satisfaction particulière que donne, même à un profane, le spectacle d'hommes amoureux de leur métier comme le sont visiblement les cireurs oranais.[35]

> Perched up on high chairs, it is possible to savour the particular satisfaction that is to be gained, even by the uninitiated, from the spectacle of men who are visibly in love with their work, as are the Oran boot-blacks.

For all his reputation for humanity and intellectual integrity, the great *pied-noir* liberal once again emerges as the archetype of Memmi's 'colonizer of good will' or 'colonizer who refuses himself'.[36] Yet it is Camus the Nobel prizewinner that is regularly appealed to by Gabriel Conesa to lend his own literary production a spurious weight. In particular, his treatment of the shoeshine theme reveals his indebtedness to Camus's version of the Mediterranean myth:

> Monter sur une estrade et s'asseoir dans un fauteuil pour faire cirer ses souliers est un plaisir qu'on ne comprend pas hors de la Méditerranée où, tout de suite, on parle de dignité, ce qui n'a rien à voir à l'affaire. (193)

> To climb up onto a platform and sit in a chair while you have your shoes polished is a pleasure which is not appreciated outside the Mediterranean, where, immediately, it is a question of dignity, which has nothing to do with it.

Where Camus's indifference was unconscious—and only ever partial, for it must be set against the background both of his public pronouncements and private efforts on behalf of the indigenous population of Algeria—that of Conesa is genuinely self-assertive: the literary apologist of a defunct *Algérie française*, he chooses attack as the best form of defence for the exiled European community's

[34] A. Horne, *A Savage War of Peace: Algeria, 1954–1962*, (London, Macmillan, 1977), 55.

[35] *Essais* (Gallimard/Calmann-Lévy, 1965), 816.

[36] See Ch. 4, n. 3.

blinkered vision. Thanks to the myth of the eternal Mediterranean, historical conflict is replaced by a magical identity: the shoeshine boy and his customer, the Algerian and the European, the colonizer and the colonized, are deemed to be incarnations of the same apolitical essence. The nature of this mythical integration of the Arabo-Berber majority into the European minority's world-view is most evident in Conesa's depiction of the Mediterranean world of Bab-El-Oued.

The reader of Conesa's paean to this most celebrated *quartier* of colonial Algeria is immediately struck by the regular insistence on the ethnic blend that is deemed to have existed in the Algiers suburb in the golden age before the onset of racial hostilities. For this is a world, it is claimed, where 'nationalité ou race n'avaient pas plus d'importance que la couleur d'un maillot de bain, chacun se sentant avant tout Méditerranéen et membre d'une même et vaste famille' [nationality or race had no more importance than the colour of your swimming trunks, because everyone felt themselves to be Mediterranean, first and foremost, and thus members of a single huge family] (196).[37]

This rosy image of a genuinely integrated community was tested to destruction between 1954 and 1962; in this period, when the settler ascendancy was challenged, ethnicity prevailed, and the much-vaunted Mediterranean amalgam was thus revealed to have been no more than a temporarily peaceful coexistence. Moreover, it becomes clear on closer inspection that those 'Mediterranean' aspects of Bab-El-Oued so regularly celebrated by Conesa are wholly European in origin. Indeed, the essential character of the district derives exclusively from the national particularities of its constituent European populations; the Arabs of Bab-El-Oued—and, for that matter, the Jews—are only admitted to its community occasionally, and always to make a clearly defined mythical point. The supposedly all-encompassing Mediterraneanism of Bab-El-Oued is consequently manifested in a remarkably ethnocentric fashion: Christian festivals, French national celebrations, private cars, and European picnic food are the very particular signs of *l'éternelle Méditerranée* (152). Indeed, the spirit of Mediterraneanism is, on occasion, to be straightforwardly equated with a liking for *anisette*, the *pieds-noirs*' beloved aniseed-flavoured aperitif (156).

However, Conesa attaches rather greater importance to the contri-

[37] Cf. M. Guedj, *Le 'Bar à Campora'* (Albin Michel, 1969) 133.

bution made by those indigenous Algerians to the dialect spoken by *le peuple neuf*, the famous *pataouète* of Bab-El-Oued: 'Il se dégage naturellement du français, du provençal, de l'espagnol castillan, du valencien, de l'italien, du napolitain et du sicilien, du maltais et aussi de l'arabe' [It's a natural blend of French, Provencal, Castilian Spanish, Valencian, Italian, Neapolitan and Sicilian, and Maltese, as well as Arabic] (119).[38] The great importance attached to the 'miracle' of *pataouète* from Louis Bertand on suggests that the dialect's historical function as the *lingua franca* of Algeria's poor whites is by no means the end of the story. Conesa likens the *patois* to Bab-El-Oued's favourite sport—the supposedly Mediterranean civilization of football (65)—as well as to the stream which gives the district its name, in an attempt to capture its feel and to make clear its leading role in the life of his community (120–1). More specifically, he contends that the speech of *le peuple neuf* is adequate to the communicative needs of 'tout le monde' or 'tout Bab-el-Oued'. Yet despite the presence of a few words of Arabic origin, *pataouète* is plainly a brand of French, and one influenced essentially by other Romance languages. The linguistic specificities of the Arabo-Berber 90 per cent of the Algerian population are thus effectively denied by Conesa, just as their religious, national, and cultural affiliations have been suppressed throughout.[39]

In the event, the myth of inter-communal harmony was to be dramatically overtaken by historical developments. When this happened, the *pieds-noirs*' literary defenders would try to produce new variations on old mythic themes in a last-ditch attempt to rationalize the European community's loss of its long-established privilege. The demonization of de Gaulle was one such response. Consider Martinez's account of the innocent settlers' betrayal at the hands of the duplicitous French leader:

> Mais le peuple pied-noir n'a que cent vingt ans, c'est un peuple enfant, il aime encore ses hochets bleu, blanc, rouge. . . . Poussé par ses tontons, il choisit—peut-on en vouloir à un enfant?—d'appeler son papa pour l'aider à comprendre. Et le papa arrive; il le comprend, ce garnement de peuple, ça comprend tout, un papa. Il jure de tout arranger. Il nous fait promettre

[38] See also R. Bacri, 'Le Pataouète', in Elia, *Les Pieds-Noirs*, 89–96, and the same author's *Trésors des racines pataouètes* (Belin, 1983). This *patois* was celebrated by Audisio in his 1972 edition of Musette's *Cagayous* (1931), and was traditionally put to literary use by *pied-noir* writers like Edmond Brua, whose *Parodie du Cid* (1941) is particularly renowned.

[39] See Camus, *Essais*, 1325, and C. O'Brien, *Camus* (Glasgow, Collins, 1970), 12.

de lui obéir toujours. C'est normal, pour un papa; tous les papas aiment ça; et il s'en va.

Et l'enfant ne s'est pas rendu compte que son papa ne l'aime pas, ne l'a jamais aimé. Peut-être même qu'il n'est pas son vrai papa. Alors, pour sa punition, il va se retrouver tout seul sans y croire . . . (*Et qu'ils m'accueillent*: 33–4)

But the *pied-noir* people is only a hundred and twenty years old: it is still a childish people, and likes its red, white, and blue toys. . . . Encouraged by its uncles, it decides—can you blame a child?—to ask its daddy to help it to understand. And daddy arrives; and he understands this young tearaway of a people, because dads understand everything. He promises to sort everything out. He makes us promise always to obey him. Nothing unusual about that; all dads like that; and off he goes.

And the child hasn't realized that his daddy doesn't love him, and has never loved him. Perhaps he's not even his real daddy. So, as a punishment, he is going to find himself all alone, and will not be able to believe it . . .

What we are faced with here is the myth of the *peuple maudit* [the damned people], to adopt the terminology of the *pied-noir* author and activist Jean Brune.[40] According to this myth, the French population of Algeria, simple and loyal, were betrayed by de Gaulle—*la grande Zohra*—whom they, together with the French army, had foolishly entrusted with the future of *Algérie française*. Central to this reading of events is de Gaulle's celebrated declaration to the huge crowds assembled on the Algiers 'Forum' on 6 June 1958—'Je vous ai compris!' [I have understood you!]—the precise significance of which has long been debated.[41] In restrospect, it would seem that a basically vacuous statement was filled with whatever meaning best corresponded to the aspirations of the individual listener or group of listeners. For the *pieds-noirs*, this meant that the words of the new head of state were taken to indicate unconditional support for the cause of *Algérie française*, a term which de Gaulle himself would very significantly refuse to employ. When the old man's determination to be rid of the Algerian problem became clear—most obviously, after his epoch-making 'self-determination' speech of 16 September 1959—the settlers knew that their communal demise was only a matter of time. It was the theme of *l'abandon*, the mother country's desertion of its colonial sons and daughters, which best captured the settlers' feelings

[40] J. Brune, *Cette haine*, 536.

[41] De Gaulle's 'abandonment' of the *pieds-noirs* forms one of the reasons for the establishment of a rebel 'Cathar' state, based in Toulouse, in Gaston Bonheur's very unusual and highly entertaining *La Croix de ma mère* (Julliard, 1976), 273.

at this time and subsequently. Compounded of fear, frustration, and, above all, righteous indignation, it was this which enabled the European population of Algeria to cling onto the belief that they were in no way responsible for their eventual fate. A final version of the foundation myth of *pied-noir* dispossession, the motif readily articulates such sub-themes as that of the patriotic settlers' naïveté in dealing with duplicitous metropolitan administrations.

L'abandon was followed by *l'exode* [exodus], as the hasty 'repatriation' of the European population in the spring and summer of 1962 is invariably characterized[42]. Not surprisingly, this emergency transfer of the better part of a million *pieds-noirs* to a 'mother country' which the vast majority of them had never come from in the first place has its own mythology. This strand is most intriguingly represented by the work of Daniel Saint-Hamont, whose hilarious *Le Coup de Sirocco* [The Sirocco's Blast] (1978) is a fascinating blend of myth and demystification.[43] Take, for instance, his opening scene of *pied-noir* exile:

> Quand le bateau a démarré, beaucoup de gens sont restés à l'arrière. Ils écrasaient une larme en voyant disparaître la belle Algérie. Nous non, parce que ce jour-là, avec le brouillard on pouvait à peine voir à trois mètres: alors on a rien vu. Juste un peu sur le grand mur dans le port d'Oran les lettres: ICI LA FRANCE, et déjà tout était gris autour de nous. Ma mère pleurait. D'abord qu'elle était triste, et aussi qu'on avait perdu deux valises. C'était pas grave parce que dans ces deux valises, on avait que les choses qui servaient à décorer le salon: les bibelots, les chandeliers de mon père (il était le seul à croire que c'était de l'argent massif: on les soulevait, jusqu'au plafond ils envolaient . . .) et les peintures. C'est pas que je connais beaucoup en peinture, mais nos tableaux j'étais sûr que ceux qui les avaient faits n'étaient pas des génies inconnus, ou alors ils risquaient de le rester jusqu'à la mort. (7)

> When the ship cast off, many people stayed back in the stern. They wiped away a tear as they saw their beloved Algeria disappear. But not us, because it was so foggy that you could hardly see more than a few yards: so we didn't see anything. Just a brief glimpse of these letters written on the great wall in the port of Oran: THIS IS FRANCE, and then everything was grey all around us. My mother was crying. For a start, she was sad, but we had also lost two suitcases. It didn't really matter because all we had in the cases were things which used to decorate the living room: knick-knacks, my father's candlesticks (he was the only one who believed they were solid silver: if you picked them up, they would just about float up to the ceiling

[42] See e.g. Bacri, *Et alors? et oilà!*, 193–212.
[43] A successful film version of the book was produced by Alexandre Arcady in 1979.

by themselves . . .), and the paintings. Now I don't know much about painting, but I'm sure that our pictures were not painted by some undiscovered genius, or if they were he ran the risk of staying undiscovered until the day he died.

At first glance, the young narrator's disabused commentary on events would seem to provide a counter to more conventionally lachrymose versions of the settler diaspora. However, its bathetic approach to the community's suffering may, on closer inspection, be seen to utter a number of previously identified mythical themes. So, the clichés of European exile may be gently mocked—hence the tears as 'la belle Algérie' disappears forever over the stern rail—but the despair of this archetypal *mère de famille pied-noir* is clearly genuine. In short, the family are not the colonizers of history, but rather the hapless victims of *pied-noir* mythology. They are typical *petits blancs*, who have in no way profited from Algeria and the Algerians, as the references to their pathetically humble baggage make clear. Their naïveté may be comically evoked as regards the father's attachment to his worthless candlesticks, but it is revealed to have a serious edge when the official fiction of a 'French' Algeria is referred to: these people's only real sin is to have believed the declarations of generations of politicians, it would seem. With the introduction of the lost suitcases, meanwhile, we not only have an image of personal loss, but a stock symbol of the *pieds-noirs*' dilemma: exile or death, the suitcase or the coffin (*la valise ou le cercueil*).[44] Torn between the forces of French imperialism and Algerian nationalism, the settlers of *Le Coup de Sirocco* are sacrificed to history, their lives blown apart by the North African winds of change evoked by the novel's title.

As for the European terrorist organization which rendered inevitable this mass evacuation, the work of Henri Martinez is again an obvious reference. Himself a member of an OAS commando in Oran, Martinez predictably presents an extended apology for the organization and its often horrific acts of violence. His account derives the major part of its interest from the author's patent inability to pierce the attendant mythology of the OAS; and this, twenty years after the demise of *Algérie française*. So, for Martinez, the OAS was truly military in its structures and aims; it incarnated the spirit of the wartime French Resistance; its violence was a necessary response to that of the FLN; it was itself a nationalist

[44] This theme is best exemplified by A. Loesch, *La Valise ou le cercueil* (Plon, 1963).

movement, fighting for a *pied-noir* 'Israel'; it was the victim, not the aggressor, in its terminal conflict with the French military. When Henri Martinez's fictional *alter ego* joins the OAS, therefore, it is to defend his 'patrie algérienne' [Algerian homeland] (*Dernières nouvelles*: 16). For her part, Micheline Susini, wife of the infamous OAS leader Jean-Jacques Susini, explains her decision to fight in Mediterraneanist terms:

> Je me battrai pour mon soleil, pour la mer parce qu'ailleurs je ne pourrai pas vivre, même si j'ai envie d'aller en vacances dans un autre pays. Jamais je ne pourrai vivre en France, prendre le métro à Paris et porter un manteau dix mois de l'année. (13)

> I'll fight for my sun and for the sea, because I cannot live anywhere else, even if I do like to visit other countries when I am on holiday. I will never be able to live in France, take the underground in Paris, or wear an overcoat for ten months of the year.

When she does eventually, leave Algeria, it is, in the best traditions of Louis Bertrand, for Rome (259). Henri Martinez's anonymous protagonist, in contrast, decides at the end of the novel that he has made the wrong choice between *la valise* and *le cercueil*: so the OAS fighter buys another suitcase and returns with it, still empty, to a certain but happy—and thus appropriately Camusian—death in the newly independent Algeria (*Dernières nouvelles*: 268–76).[45]

Yet the most enduring of these tactical myths is, without doubt, that of the wasted opportunities for improving and thereby preserving French Algeria. A particularly frequent focus for thinking of this kind is the European-Muslim fraternization which occurred on the Algiers 'Forum' in the days which followed the settler agitation of 13 May 1958. The literary treatment accorded to this much-debated phenomenon turns on the old myth of the eternal Mediterranean: those who advocate a new and just version of *Algérie française* thus only succeed in revealing their enduring attachment to the ideology of the old one. A case in point is to be found in *De soleil et de larmes*, Micheline Susini's 1982 apology for the OAS:

> Dans toute l'Algérie, les Arabes et les Européens participent aux manifestations, unis dans le même désir. La paix se montre à l'horizon. Les musulmans aux côtés des pieds-noirs sont admirables. . . . Les paroles d'un

[45] Several of the younger generation of exiled *pieds-noirs* have written about their own, less permanent, returns to their native land, e.g. R. Bacri, *Le Beau Temps perdu*; D. Saint-Hamont, *La Valise à l'eau ou le voyage en Alger* (Fayard, 1981); Vircondelet, *Alger l'amour* (Presses de la Renaissance, 1982).

Agha, au Forum, me poursuivront longtemps: 'Vive la France, nous sommes tous Français!'. (60)

Throughout Algeria, Arabs and Europeans are taking part in demonstrations, united by a common desire. Peace has appeared on the horizon. The Muslims are magnificent by the side of the *pieds-noirs*. . . . The words of an Agha, on the Forum, stay with me for a long time: 'Long live France, we are all Frenchmen!'

The key notion of a colonial fraternity capable of transcending racial barriers will be considered in its own right in Chapter 7. For the time being, it is simply worth underlining the depoliticizing nature of any such inter-ethnic brotherhood: the Algerian revolution ceases at the point where Mediterraneanist *fraternisation* commences. As for the myth of missed opportunities, this was to prove so extraordinarily tenacious that such a clear-sighted critic of the *pieds-noirs* as Jules Roy would, even with the benefit of hindsight, continue to look on the conflictual relations between colonizer and colonized in terms of what he had called in *Autour du drame* [Concerning the Drama] (1961) 'une brouille amoureuse' [a lover's tiff] between France and Algeria.[46] So, in *Le Tonnerre et les anges* [The Thunder and the Angels] (1975), the final volume of his epic treatment of the French presence in Algeria, he will describe the work done for the Arabs by Dr Paris as the result of 'love' (6: 69), while the attitude adopted to Camus by the *pied-noir* critics of his planned civil truce is explained as the product of 'hatred' (6: 65). This emotional account of political developments extends to the FLN bomber who tries to murder the doctor. Passing himself off as just another patient, the young man will almost give his deadly game away:

Le docteur appliqua le stéthoscope sur ses épaules, écouta le murmure des bronches comme des vagues mourant sur la plage, puis un battement précipité du coeur qui l'étonna: un vrai tambour nègre . . . le rythme forcené, l'affolement du coeur après un effort violent ou le spasme amoureux. (6: 71)

The doctor put his stethoscope to the patient's shoulders and listened to the murmur of the bronchial tubes, like waves dying on a beach, and then was surprised by the rapid beating of the heart: a real jungle drum . . . the frenzied rhythm, the turmoil produced by the heart after a violent effort or a sexual climax.

So the emotional agitation of the Muslim terrorist may be likened

[46] p. 190.

to the consummation of a tragically perverted love affair. By the same sort of logic, a failed personal relationship may be taken to explain a female settler's lifelong antipathy towards the colonized (6: 65). Such images of inter-ethnic conflict are to be understood as part of Roy's all-embracing and parting vision of the colonial enterprise in Algeria as 'un mirage épique vers quoi des millions d'hommes et de femmes ont marché en portant les douleurs et les enchantements de l'amour' [an epic mirage towards which millions of men and women have stridden, bearing the suffering and the joy of love] (6: 429). This mystification of the Algerian war's historicity may have helped Roy and his fellow *pied-noir* liberals to rationalize the doubtless personally traumatic events which occurred in their native land, but it must also be seen to have detracted from Roy's own literary contribution to the debate surrounding those events. As we shall see in the following chapter, considerations of inter-racial sexuality are very much to the fore in the French fictional representation of the indigenous Algerians and their role in the 1954–1962 hostilities. Indeed, they will frequently provide the key to those few attempts which have been made by *pieds-noirs*, as well as by metropolitan French authors, to come to terms honestly with that new Algerian reality.

7
LE MÊME ET L'AUTRE: IMAGING THE ALGERIANS

The single most characteristic feature of *Algérie française* was its radical dualism. As John Talbott puts it:

> In colonial Algeria, linguistic, religious, and racial differences ran parallel along either side of one vast cultural fault, Algerians on one side, Europeans on the other. No institution served, at any point in the society, to join the two sides of the fault together . . .[1]

This fundamental dichotomy has its origins in the exploitative economy of the colonial relationship, which is itself both articulated through and, crucially, legitimized by an all-encompassing colonial discourse. Such sub-varieties of this discourse as the administrative, juridical, academic, and anthropological *paroles* were all drawn upon and added to by that of the prose fiction produced in an attempt to come to terms with militant Algerian nationalism's challenge to the existing social order. The primary thrust of this specifically literary contribution to the defence of the European ascendancy may be said to consist in the ideological manipulation of the linguistic/philosophical categories of the Self and the Other.[2]

As the object of the colonizer's discourse, rather than a partner in it, the colonized must inevitably be its victim. Indeed, this basic relationship is at the very heart of the colonial mode of speaking (about) the native, and reveals both its psychological motivation and its internal contradictions. Put simply, the colonizer is perma-

[1] *The War Without a Name: France in Algeria, 1954–1962* (London, Faber & Faber, 1981), 14.

[2] See H. Gourdon *et al.*, 'Roman colonial et idéologie coloniale en Algérie', *Revue algérienne des sciences juridiques, économiques et politiques*, 11/1 (March 1974), 100–14. For a useful survey of the major role played by this dialectic in postwar French philosophy, see V. Descombes, *Le Même et l'Autre* (Minuit, 1979).

nently tempted by the idea of physically exterminating the Other, whose mere existence is a reminder of the daily usurpation upon which colonial privilege is founded.[3] Yet to do so would clearly be to destroy the entire colonial edifice, and an alternative means of deflecting this permanent challenge to the settlers' communal self-image therefore has to be found. The most obvious method of endowing the colonial enterprise's objective usurpation with a mythical legitimacy is the dual one of insisting upon the merits of the colonizer and the demerits of the colonized. The literary elevation of the colonizer described in the previous chapter is thus properly understood as but one half of a single ideological strategy, with its negative pole—from the early days of the *Algérianistes* on—being the insistence upon the colonized's inferior alterity. In short, the *indolence* and *indigence* so easily connoted by the term *indigène* are the logical corollaries of the settler myths of pioneering creation and civilizing mission; they also serve to disqualify the original inhabitants of the colonized land. The category of the Other can thus be regarded as the mythical antithesis of that of the colonial Self: an essentially negative value, systematically contrasted with the positively evoked *pied-noir*. *L'Autre* may, in consequence, be alluded to in a variety of ways, but any such reference will always form part of a broader vindication of the French colonial enterprise.

Whether or not they were overtly likened to animals (*bicots*, *ratons*) or even to vegetable forms of life (*melons*, *troncs de figuiers*), the native Algerians were typically comprehended by the European settlers of the territory as an essentially passive and homogeneous mass: *ils*, *les Arabes*, *les bougnoules*. This reassuring colonial image was shattered by the nationalists' armed threat to the European ascendancy: as the initially isolated acts of terrorist violence spread and intensified, a new and specifically Algerian image of militant otherness would thus come to replace the common colonial emphasis on the laziness, dirtiness, dishonesty, and general incompetence of the colonized population. So the partisans of *Algérie française* might still insist upon the Algerians' disqualifying failure to cultivate the land[4], but they would also seek to make sense of their increas-

[3] The fact that the European settlers of North Africa did not, in fact, exterminate the territory's native inhabitants was regularly appealed to by politicians and writers after 1954, and particularly in response to American criticism of France in Algeria.

[4] See F. Châtelet, *Les Idéologies*, iii: *De Rousseau à Mao* (Verviers, Marabout, 1981), 223.

ingly frequent attacks on the property and persons of European farmers. It was the unmistakable signs of a hitherto unsuspected, or denied, Algerian dynamism, in other words, that the colony now sought to rationalize.

Perhaps the most typical literary response in the early years of the war was a scandalized reaffirmation of the French nation's civilizing mission as the blame for the burning, stabbing, shooting, and, above all, throat-cutting was placed not on the political development of the Other, but rather on his/her cultural retardation. The essential foundation of the settlers' faith in their own *mission civilisatrice*, this belief in Algerian backwardness could easily be combined with a favourable account of paternalistic colonial advance in order to explain away the nationalist revolt. As a senior army officer puts it in Cécil Saint-Laurent's *L'Algérie quand on y est* [Algeria, When We're Over There] (1958): 'La crise actuelle, je crois qu'elle tient à ce que nous avons porté des hommes comme Ferhat Abbas au même siècle que nous' [I believe that the present crisis stems from the fact that we have brought men like Ferhat Abbas into the same century as ourselves] (130).

Such thinking was by no means confined to the right wing of French politics, with liberals like Pierre-Henri Simon being just as willing to evoke 'l'état de mineurs . . . [d'une] race inégale en génie et en moyens' [the minor status of a race which has neither the genius nor the means of the French] (77). Typically, the leaders of the insurrection are depicted as *évolués* [developed], and as such the products of France's civilizing *œuvre* in Algeria: 'Français d'esprit et de langue . . . dans un combat contre la France' [French in spirit and French-speaking . . . and involved in a war against France] (75), as Simon puts it.[5] With this simple transformation of the militant colonized into a double of the colonial Self, the increasingly troublesome specificity of the Other is avoided, at least temporarily. Moreover, the literally unthinkable nationalist revolt is reduced to the status of a by-product of colonial assimilation: the educated colonized is only rebelling against France because the civilizing colonizer has made all such Algerians so 'French'. France has brought its colonial subjects this far, and, so the argument runs, only France can lead them properly into the future. As for the supposedly passive mass of the Algerian population, it is ultimately swayed only by force in the fictive universe of *Algérie française*:

[5] *Portrait d'un officier* (Seuil, 1958).

supersitious and fatalistic, the child-like natives all to easily fall victim to the coercion of what successive French administrations were to characterize as 'a handful of rebels'.

In retrospect, it would appear that it was the historical refusal of the European authorities to countenance even limited nationalist opposition to the colonial order that led directly to the outbreak of politically inspired violence in Algeria. It was thus the settlers' own cult of force, not that of the indigenous population, which rendered inevitable an insurrection in the colony. As for the precise nature of that insurrectionary violence, the guerrilla war waged by the FLN from 1954 to 1962 was all too often interpreted in the light of this presumed subordination of Algerian political consciousness to terrorism. For if the nationalists' acts of violence were so often horrific —as they undoubtedly were—it could only be because its leaders were seeking to coerce an otherwise uncommitted, if not actually unsympathetic, body of native opinion. Moreover, the murders (especially by throat-cutting), mutilations, arson attacks, and so forth were confidently interpreted as atavistic, a throwback to that pre-colonial barbarism which supposedly characterized the social organization of North Africa from the end of the Roman period to 1830.

If the results of the FLN's hit-and-run attacks were only too painfully apparent, then the perpetrators themselves remained frustratingly difficult to lay hands on. In contrast to its classically organized and clearly identifiable adversary, the rebel army was made up of small units scattered across the countryside, and was difficult to isolate from the indigenous Algerian community, which not only provided it with all of its recruits and the bulk of its intelligence, but also continued to feed it and frequently to house it. The French army's recourse to a 'dirty' war was inevitable in the face of the guerrilla campaign waged by an adversary which, in line with Mao's dictum, lived in the population 'like a fish in water'. It is this reality which French writers at the time and since have sought to communicate by referring to the FLN guerrillas as *invisibles* or, more accurately, *insaisissables* [elusive, imperceptible].

It is precisely the extreme difficulty involved in attempting to 'seize' the FLN guerrilla, both militarily and conceptually, that accounts for the paradoxical tendency of French writers of every stripe to depict the Other, *qua* combatant, as the double of the military Self. By depicting the FLN guerrilla as the worthy adversary of the French combatant—and often, with some historical justification, as a more or less nostalgic former member of the French army—the unknown, and perhaps even unknowable, reality of the nationalist *moudjahidin* is replaced by something which is reassuringly familiar: the enemy equal of the western military-romantic tradition.[6] This literary response is not difficult to understand in the context of the conflict itself, but its continued appeal in the years since the war points to a continuing need on the part of French writers and readers to render Algeria's unknown majority unthreateningly comprehensible to the European imagination. So, for instance, in Bernard Clavel's *Le Silence des armes* (1974), a reassuring inversion of the historical transformation of France's Algerian military servants into dangerous rebels is proposed. In this variation on the theme of the traumatized Algerian war veteran, a turning-point is reached with Jacques Fortier's refusal to return *là-bas*. The climactic armed confrontation with the military authorities which results from this decision permits the articulation of the conceit of the veteran's magical transformation into his erstwhile enemy: 'Il n'était plus un soldat français, mais un fellagha traqué par toute l'armée' [He was no longer a French soldier, but a fellagha hunted by the whole army] (174).

In this literary tribute to the 'tripwire veteran',[7] the metamorphosis of the military Self into the Other is directly prompted by the experience of what Clavel—following both Jean Guéhenno and Albert Camus—terms 'la mort des autres' [the death of others].[8] As the traumatized hero retreats increasingly from a society whose colonial war he is no longer prepared to wage, he moves ever deeper into a private universe inhabited by the dead of Algeria,

[6] It is a matter of record that many of the rebellion's key military figures had indeed served in the French army. Ahmed Ben Bella, the focus of the external FLN leadership and destined to be the first president of an independent Algeria, was only the most visible of the nationalists' *anciens combattants*. Personally decorated for valour by General de Gaulle, the future head of state had served with distinction in the armed forces of the very country whose rule in Algeria he now sought to overthrow, an experience common to many of the FLN's fighters and one which was found at all levels of the rebels' political hierarchy. Jean Lartéguy's guerrilla leader, Si Lahcen, is a typical figure in this respect: *Les Centurions* (Presses de la Cité, 1960), 341–74. This method of deflecting the rebellious colonized's challenge to the colonizer's ideological hegemony is taken to ridiculous lengths in Jean-Jacques Rochard's *Max Skoda* (L'Esprit Nouveau, 1965), in which the eponymous hero actually 'becomes' the Other by betraying his fellow Foreign Legionnaires and taking to the hills with the FLN.

[7] See L. Heinemann, '"Just Don't Fit": Stalking the elusive "tripwire" veteran', *Harper's*, Apr. 1985, 55–63.

[8] This theme is also the focus for a harrowing children's story: V. Buisson, *L'Algérie ou la mort des autres* (La Pensée Sauvage, 1978).

together with other symbolic victims of humankind's chronic inhumanity. The psychic trend is always downward, with the protagonist's suicidal last stand against the forces of order being depicted as a self-consciously Christian rite of expiation for the damage that he and his kind have done in Algeria.

The genuine power to defamiliarize of this variation on the 'death-of-others' theme derives from its linking, in a single troubled consciousness, of individual and collective culpability. In particular, the juxtaposition of childhood memories of pastoral creativity and the recent experience of military destruction, of an idyll which cannot be recaptured and a vision of horror which cannot be forgotten, serves to underline and intensify this fundamental linkage as the protagonist's mental condition deteriorates and gives way to a hallucinatory confusion (190–1). What is more, the suffering of the Algerian population is used by Clavel as the basis for something very like a heroic presentation of the FLN guerrilla. So the emphasis which the author places on the overwhelming numerical superiority of the rebel's military opponents is to be read as an indication of individual bravery—on the model, most obviously, of the *Résistance* (43–4 & 179–80)—rather than a confirmation of the official myth of the rebellion as merely the work of 'a handful of terrorists'.

In spite of its inability wholly to resist the temptation to portray the Algerian insurrection in terms borrowed from the French experience of Occupation and Resistance—a perspective which means that the Other, although depicted in a favourable light, can only ever be a pale reflection of the colonial Self—Clavel's novel must be reckoned a positive contribution to the French imaging of the Algerians. As such, it may fairly serve as an introduction to a number of notable fictional challenges to the long colonial denial of the colonized's identity. These narratives will, of necessity, be examined from a thematic rather than a chronological perspective: after all, the discursive victimization of the Algerian Other both predated the 1954–62 conflict and continued long after it, whilst its key rhetorical figures may still contribute to negative French perceptions of the Maghreb and Maghrebians.

If the French presence in Algeria was so readily comprehended in terms of the European *mission civilisatrice*, and the terrorism of the FLN perceived as just the latest manifestation of an age-old savagery, then much of the responsibility lies with the literary delineation of native barbarism. Indeed, the *barbare* is perhaps the most enduring image of the FLN combatant to have been presented both for domestic and international consumption. Clearly, the figure is a core element in the orientalist conception both of the Maghreb and the wider Arab world; the myth of *Barbarie*, complete with pirates and slave-traders, sultans and their harems, heathen religious beliefs and unspeakable sexual practices, and a variety of other, equally frightening and fascinating, exotica.[9] It is this European tradition of misrepresentation that is exposed to a sharply demystifying light in Claude Bonjean's remarkable novel, *Lucien chez les barbares* [Lucien in the Land of the Barbarians] (1977).

Bonjean's use of the barbarian theme is to be distinguished from the conventional one in two crucial respects: its insistence on the original, properly linguistic, sense of the word and its derivates; and its resistance to the familiar abusive connotations of the term as habitually applied to the Other. For Bonjean, in fact, *barbare* serves primarily as a synonym for 'Algerian': his novel never refers to the French colony, nor to the war there, by name; and the term is employed to make the reader aware that the action is, indeed, set in North Africa, the Barbary Coast of maritime history and lore.[10] With Algeria established as the geographical entity, *la Barbarie*, the adjective *barbare* may quite properly be applied to the inhabitants of the land and, above all, to their language. Bonjean, in fact, is one of the few French authors to have paid any real attention to what Memmi identifies as the 'linguistic drama' of colonialism[11], the clash of the colonizer's mother tongue with that of the Other, be it Arabic or Berber. So, for instance, his typically spare account of a revolt by native troops testifies to an unusual preoccupation with the role of linguistic conflict within the broader pattern of the Algerian war:

> Cette révolte couvait. Elle éclata en apostrophes barbares lorsque Terneuse pénétra sous les tentes avec l'intention d'en évacuer les occupants. Le son de la langue barbare évoque le fracas des lames entrechoquées. Le ferrailleur le plus bruyant portait un chiffon en huit sur la tête et une moustache

[9] Edward Said's seminal *Orientalism* (London, Routledge & Kegan Paul, 1978) is the obvious reference here. Also of interest is R. Kabbani, *Europe's Myths of Orient: Devise and Rule* (London, Macmillan, 1986). It must, of course, be acknowledged that the history of the French literary usage of the term 'barbare' is a peculiarly long and complex one. However, even the apparent enthusiasm for non-European cultures displayed by a writer like Leconte de Lisle in his *Poèmes barbares* (1862) relies for its effect upon a myth of oriental savagery and primitivism.

[10] Cf. the title chosen by Jules Roy for his fascinating (and best-selling) autobiography: *Mémoires barbares* (Albin Michel, 1989).

[11] See Ch. 4, n. 19.

noire. Le noir de sa moustache accentuait le gris mauvais du teint. Ce scélérat s'appelait Rohour, se prétendait le fils d'un chef de tribu, était fâché qu'on ne l'eût pas embarqué avec ses camarades, éparpillait furieusement de la pointe du pied le fumier qui servait de lit; en un mot, il en avait assez. (206–7)

This revolt had been brewing for some time. It burst out in barbaric shouting when Terneuse went into the tents intending to clear out the occupants. The sound of the barbarians' language conjures up the din of swords clashing together. The noisiest of these scrap merchants wore an old rag on his head, done up in a figure of eight, and had a black moustache. The blackness of his moustache emphasized the unhealthy grey colour of his skin. This rascal was called Rohour, and claimed to be the son of a tribal chief. He was angry that he had not been transported along with his friends, and was furiously kicking about the muck that he had to make do with as a bed; in a word, he had had enough.

This passage successfully draws attention to the linguistic predicaments both of the French soldier and the native auxiliary: the NCO's invasion of the auxiliaries' tents gives rise to an outburst, not in the language of the country whose cause they have been recruited to serve, but rather in that of their colonized homeland. The very sound of their speech, meanwhile, emphasizes its alien quality to French ears: an alterity that is the precise opposite of the orientalist comprehension of the Other. It also introduces what is Bonjean's central theme: the predicament of the *rallié* or *harki* [i.e. the Algerian recuited as an irregular by the French army], which we might describe as the untenable position of the Other when actually transformed into the French military Self.

Unlike the positively motivated *harkis* to be found in the work of colonial apologists, Bonjean's locally recruited auxiliaries join the French forces for that least romantic of reasons: harsh economic necessity. As for their likely fate, this is strongly hinted at in an earlier account of the murder of a native sentry by French troops. In the meantime, the recruits will be treated with contempt, brutality, and, above all, suspicion. Regarded as worthless from the outset, it is scarcely surprising that Bonjean's pitiful mercenaries should quickly discourage their instructors by their combined indiscipline and ineptitude. Two of their number never return from their first leave, while another deserts, killing a soldier and wounding two others in the process. The military's response to this not unexpected betrayal is predictably swift and merciless.

In a very significant development, the body of the dead deserter will be used by the army as a means to compromise (*mouiller*) the remaining recruits. Ordered to shoot the corpse, their terrified acquiescence will be interpreted, not as an indication of their good faith, but rather as a sign of their cowardice, and thus of their essential colonizability. There is no pretence at asserting the homogeneity of the French military's European and Algerian elements here, with the officer's description of the dead man as 'l'un des vôtres' [one of your lot] (129) being particularly eloquent. In fact, the *ralliés* are in a brutal dilemma: if they go along with the military's brutality, then they are cowards and doomed to servility; if they resist, then they are the objects of even more intense suspicion.

Yet in spite of the appalling treatment to which they are subjected by their French 'comrades', the natives continue to come forward in response to army appeals for recruits. Lucien therefore joins Terneuse, a driver, and a native interpreter in a mobile recruiting team. It is the native auxiliary who puts the recruiting team's message over, most effectively, to his fellow *indigènes*:

> Ils seront deux cents rameutés par porte-voix à accepter de rejoindre Tovar dans son chien et loup. Pourtant il ne leur promettait pas la lune, ni reconnaissance de la Patrie, ni évacuation en cas de désastre, mais, traduisant toujours Terneuse 'une bonne solde, du tabac, et la fraternité des combats'. (193)
>
> Two hundred of them were rounded up with a megaphone and persuaded to join Tovar in his twilight world. Yet he did not promise them the moon, nor that the Homeland would be grateful, nor that they would be evacuated in case of disaster, but rather, still translating Terneuse, 'a good wage, tobacco, and the brotherhood of arms'.

The predicament of the Other as *rallié* is here epitomized by the interpreter's own twilight existence: the characteristic and characterizing alienation of the native recruit, from both French 'friend' and Algerian 'foe', from military dog and FLN wolf. Similarly to the fore is the scandalous indifference of the French nation to the eventual fate of its Algerian defenders: the list of things not promised by Tovar is a sure indication that the French army's brotherhood of arms—like its obvious civilian counterpart, the much vaunted fraternization of *pieds-noirs* and Algerians in the wake of the 13 May 1958 events—is destined to end in the violent deaths of those natives unable to resist the temptations of the colonizer. Summarily dismissed as the end of the war approaches, the recruits will all be brutally murdered by their vengeful fellow countrymen.

As was so often the case in the history of French decolonization, it is the colonized who must pay the ultimate penalty for the delusions of the colonial power. Thanks to Bonjean's detailing of the Other's suffering at the hands of the French—including the torture and public execution of hostages taken at random in the wake of an FLN ambush on Lucien's regiment—a whole tradition of literary appeals to the myth of the *barbare* is terminally undermined. The reader of *Lucien chez les barbares* is thus presented with a demystified version of the barbarian theme which serves not to validate the gloss given to historical events by the mythology of *Algérie française*, but rather to draw critical attention to one of the key figures of its rhetoric. Moreover, in Bonjean's fictive Algeria, the nationalist challenge to the continued rule of the colonial power is to be found in everything and everyone. Consider the following exchange between Lucien and the mother of a dead comrade:

> 'Où est la guerre?' questionnait-elle.
>
> Il la conduisait alors au sommet de la colline et montrait les noires montagnes qui fortifiaient l'horizon.
>
> 'La guerre est là,' expliquait-il.
>
> Puis son doigt dessinait la plaine jaune et orange.
>
> 'Et là également.'
>
> Il désignait les enfants indigènes dégringolant la rue devant eux, sur des planches munies de roulettes.
>
> 'Là encore,' poursuivait-il.
>
> Et d'une pauvresse et d'un vieillard sur le trottoir:
>
> 'La guerre, aussi, c'est eux . . . Tous, ennemis.' (106)

> 'Where is the war?' she asked.
>
> So he took her to the top of the hill and showed her the black mountains which stood guarding the horizon.
>
> 'The war is there,' he explained.
>
> Then he pointed to the yellow and orange plain.
>
> 'And it is there too.'
>
> He pointed out the native children tearing down the street in front of them on home-made go-karts.
>
> 'There as well,' he went on.
>
> Seeing a poor woman and an old man on the pavement, he concluded:
>
> 'The war is them too . . . Every one of them is an enemy.'

Lucien's brutally lucid reply is, perhaps, the single most convincing literary evocation of the total nature of the Algerian conflict. In a revolutionary war, such as that fought by the FLN guerrillas against the French, only two positions are possible: *pro* and *contra*, with no intermediate stance being recognized either by the forces of colonial order or their insurrectionary challengers. There are thus only friends and foes in the Manichaean universe of this 'dirty' colonial war: who is not with us is, of necessity, against us, while no credence is given by either side to French liberal appeals to spare the innocents. Indeed, the doctrine of *guerre révolutionnaire*, whether as applied by the FLN or by its French military opponents, denies the very existence of innocence: the original sin of racial belonging, of European and Arabo-Berber ethnicity, determines each individual's role in the colonial drama, each individual's status as Self or Other, once and for all.

The ultimate fate of the French army's locally recruited *harkis* is still a painfully vexed question for commentators on the 1954–62 conflict. Whether left behind to face the wrath of the victorious FLN, or, in far fewer cases, 'repatriated' to a profoudly alien and generally hostile France, those tens of thousands of Algerians who had been persuaded or pressured to opt for the colonial cause were, and continue to be, very shabbily treated. This generally ignored subject was notably described in Saïd Ferdi's harrowing testament *Un enfant dans la guerre* [A Child in the War] (1981), whilst its long-term impact on subsequent generations has more recently been explored in *beur* [second-generation immigrant] novelist and film-maker Mehdi Charef's *Le Harki de Meriem* [Meriem's Harki] (1989). Perhaps most intriguingly, however, *le sort des harkis* is the principal theme of anti-gaullist right-winger Vladimir Volkoff's formally ambitious novel, *La Leçon d'anatomie* (1980).[12]

Set in the final, senselessly bloody days of the war, and dominated by one truly imposing fictional character, the narrative's sustained attack on French callousness and cynicism is a continuation of the critique of de Gaulle's Algerian policy to be found in the author's best-selling thriller in the Le Carré mode, *Le Retournement* [translated as *The Turn-Around*] (1979). The seigneurial protagonist of *La Leçon*

[12] For an overview of this subject see Stora, *La Gangrène et l'oubli: la mémoire de la guerre d'Algérie* (La Découverte, 1992), 200–2, 'Le Massacre des harkis', and 206–8, 'Les Harkis, des témoins gênants'. See also B. Moinet, *Ahmed? Connais pas . . .* (Lettres du Monde, 1980). The 1991 demonstrations by alienated 'fils de harkis' in the Narbonne region briefly succeeded in raising the profile of this generally forgotten group.

d'anatomie, Colonel François Beaujeux, is a regular officer of extensive experience who, at the height of an impressive career, is offered the singularly unglamorous mission of guarding an oil pipeline and its associated port facility in the period leading up to Algerian independence. The colonel's posting *là-bas* is not designed to combat the FLN, but rather to keep the violent outbursts of the various factions still involved in the conflict within acceptable limits, in order that the imminent transfer of sovereignty should be achieved as smoothly as possible.

If Beaujeux is prepared to accept this posting, it is only in order that he should be able to organize a secret operation, code-named *Riwbeodeam* or 'Expiation' in his private code. Designed to go some way towards repaying what he regards as France's debt of honour towards its Algerian defenders, the operation involves the illegal transfer across the Mediterranean of just a few hundred of the most seriously implicated members of his locally recruited troops, together with their wives and families. The colonel explains his thinking on the subject to a junior officer, who will consequently join him in the enterprise and thus in the sacrifice of both military career and personal liberty. For both men, it is necessary to do something to protect at least some of those Algerians who, having been obliged to bear arms in the French colonial cause, are now being left to face the terrible consequences. As Beaujeux makes plain, the French abandonment of these locally recruited troops to the victorious FLN is the final act in a long colonial assault on the Other's identity:

> . . . voilà des gens à qui on avait dit qu'ils étaient Français eux-mêmes, et à qui, maintenant, on arrachait cette qualité, et on s'attendait à les voir résignés, d'abord à devenir Français malgré eux, puis étrangers de force, et ils y mettaient un tact et une bonne volonté sans limite, se traitant successivement d'indigènes, de F.S.N.A., de musulmans, de Français-musulmans, de Français, et maintenant ils ne savaient plus de quoi . . . (202)

> . . . here were people who had been told by us that they themselves were French, and yet whom we were now stripping of that Frenchness. We expected to see them resign themselves to becoming French in spite of their own opposition, and then to being obliged to become foreigners once again. And they did just that, showing a limitless capacity for tact and goodwill, calling themselves in turn 'natives', 'Frenchmen of North African stock', 'Muslim Frenchmen', 'Frenchmen', and now they no longer knew what . . .

This passage is remarkable for its profound insight into the plight of the Algerian colonized in the face of the French colonizer's constant and seemingly whimsical revision of the political status of the indigenous population: it is as moving as it is demystifying. Indeed, the author's insistence on the variety of euphemisms applied to the Algerians can only serve to underline the fact that, whether Arabs or Kabyles, *harkis* or civilians, they were never French, and, moreover, could never hope to become French. The futility of all such colonialist dreams of assimilation is further evidenced by Beaujeux's account of the nature of the welcome which awaits those few Algerian troops lucky enough to be 'repatriated'. Their otherness becomes ever more apparent as Beaujeux stresses the alien nature of the land for which they are bound and the profound and abiding hostility of its inhabitants:

> . . . nous les déracinerons, nous les arracherons à leur petit village, à leur petite mosquée, nous les jetterons dans un pays qui n'est pas de leur foi, qui est à peine de leur langue, où ils ne connaîtront personne . . .
>
> Nous tenterons de leur faire passer la mer et puis nous en ferons des égoutiers, des balayeurs de métro, des valets de ferme, et nous les paierons le moins que nous pourrons, et nous les exploiterons le plus que nous pourrons, et quand nous les croiserons dans la rue, nous marmonnerons 'Sales Nord-Afs! Tous les mêmes.' (385–6)

> . . . we shall uproot them, tear them away from their little village and their little mosque, and then we'll throw them into a country which does not share their faith, which barely speaks their language, and where they don't know anyone . . .
>
> We'll try to get them over the sea and then we'll turn them into sewer workers, platform sweepers on the underground, or farm labourers, and we'll pay them as little as we can, and we'll exploit them as much as we can, and when we pass them in the street we'll mutter: 'Dirty North Africans! They're all the same.'

An overtly nostalgic chronicler of the last days of French imperial power, Vladimir Volkoff plainly has few illusions as regards the lot of the Algerian immigrant in French society. This is a subject to which we shall return a little later in the discussion.

Whether exiled in France or back home in Algeria, the Other is liable to regular literary mystification of his/her sexuality. Indeed, sexual relations between Europeans and Algerians are regularly portrayed in terms which favour the colonizer to the detriment of the colonized, in spite of the historical absence of such inter-racial liaisons.[13] However, the Other has also been depicted as a lover to more constructive effect. Indeed, I shall argue that it is this theme which has provided the focus for some of the most artistically satisfying and durably relevant fiction of the Algerian war.

The myth of an all-consuming Arab sexuality may usefully be understood as a French North African equivalent of the 'black peril' so feared by European wives and daughters in colonies further to the south. In both cases, a preoccupation with the sexual life of the Other tells us far more about the colonizer than it ever does about the colonized. In particular, the image of the Algerian male as a violent sexual predator has its psychological roots in the post-1945 boom in the indigenous birthrate, which far outstripped that of the European population and thus constituted a very real basis for the settlers' fear of demographic swamping. This French obsession with the Other's sexual behaviour was predictably fuelled by the FLN's systematic recourse to rape and genital mutilation as instruments of terror.

As previously described, the very special case of the *fellaghas*' rape of captured French soldiers is presented as the cause of the most profound and abiding personal trauma, although there is no suggestion that it was suffered by the writers themselves, in the work of such veterans of the war as Daniel Zimmermann and Gilles Perrault.[14] Ex-conscript Claude Bonjean, for his part, provocatively combines the standard themes of Muslim power-worship and all-consuming Arab sexuality to produce a knowing antidote to a whole tradition of sexually oriented literary obfuscation. The crucial passage occurs towards the end of Bonjean's 1977 novel, as the French hold over the local population is increasingly challenged by the nationalist rebels:

Les autorités furent bientôt submergées par les révoltes qui éclataient en

[13] Talbott, *The War Without a Name*, 14: 'This lack of social contact [between Europeans and Muslims in Algeria] manifested itself in countless ways. One of the most telling was the absence of intermarriage between Europeans and Algerians. Such liaisons took place at the rate of fewer than 100 per year. If marriages were rare, illicit relationships were unheard of. Half-castes were remarkably scarce. Sexual encounters between Europeans and Algerians were limited to the furtive meetings of homosexuals and the commercial transactions of prostitutes.' The remarkable absence of miscegenation in 'French' Algeria may be attributed, at least in part, to the resilience of pre-colonial structures and values among its indigenous population, including particularly those relating to the traditional role of women in Islamic societies. The near-total lack of inter-racial sexual relations in the territory may thus be understood as the most fundamental expression of two mutually hostile—and yet, in this strictly limited regard, paradoxically complementary—mind-sets: European colonialism's radical denial of the colonized Other; and proto-nationalism's quasi-visceral rejection of the colonial 'foreign body'.

[14] See Ch. 5.

chaîne à travers le pays. Les populations versatiles se donnaient à d'autres maîtres.

Sur les murs des casernes, on placarda des affiches aux couleurs ennemies. Et les militaires étaient hués; lorsqu'ils défilaient, s'efforçant à un maintien martial, on les accablait de gestes ridiculisant leur virilité. Des bandits descendirent même de la montagne pour sodomiser une patrouille de chasseurs alpins sur la place publique afin que chacun sût de quel côté était la force mâle.

Alors, la grande ville s'offrit, femelle, aux rebelles. (229–30)

The authorities were soon overwhelmed by the succession of revolts which broke out right across the country. The fickle populations were devoting themselves to new masters.

The walls of army barracks were covered with posters in the enemy's colours. And the soldiers themselves were booed; when they paraded, doing their best to maintain a military bearing, they were showered with abusive gestures deriding their virility. A group of bandits went so far as to come down from the hills to sodomize a patrol of *chasseurs alpins* in the town square so that everyone might see who had masculine vigour on their side.

So the great town offered itself, like a female, to the rebels.

This exaggerated image of the Other's sexuality as conceived by the military and colonial Self is significantly complemented by the narrative's grisly accounts of homosexual relations between French soldiers and Algerian youths, and of the military's rape of native women (177–85; 163–4). Indeed, rape and homosexuality are, together with the much-evoked use of Arab prostitutes, literary themes which, whether or not they are used self-consciously, as here, serve to draw the attention of the critical reader to the fundamentally unsatisfactory nature of sexual relations between the races in colonial Algeria. Given this general background, what are we to make of the *ménage à trois* which is the dominant theme of Jean-Pierre Millecam's novel, *Sous dix couches de ténèbres* [Beneath Ten Layers of Shadow] (1968)?

Millecam's contribution to the French literature of the Algerian war would be worthy of particular note were it only for his quite exceptional first-hand experience of the conflict: left for dead in 1956 following a murderous attack prompted by his anti-colonialist views, the young colonial schoolmaster was to make a miraculous recovery. In *Sous dix couches de ténèbres*, this incident is mentioned only in passing, and does not occupy the central ground that it would later do in Millecam's *Une Légion d'anges* [A Legion of

Angels] (1980).[15] Instead, it is the troubled relationship between a Frenchwoman and her two suitors, one a *pied-noir*, the other an Arab, which is to the fore. The treatment accorded to this peculiarly Algerian variation on the theme of the eternal triangle is an intriguing one, not least because of the relatively inaccessible nature of the narrative.

The difficulty of Millecam's writing can be explained in terms both of form and content. On the one hand, the narration is characterized by that self-conscious disruption of formal conventions so typical of literary modernism; whilst on the other, the bare bones of the plot give little indication of the thematic richness of the story told. So while *Sous dix couches de ténèbres* may conveniently be summarized as the tale of the terminal collapse of Laurent's and Rachid's childhood friendship under the combined pressures of their shared passion for Isabelle and the onset of the Algerian war, such a synopsis gives no real indication either of the novel's narrative complexity, or of its psychological depth; nor, in truth, does the fact that the two young men take opposite sides in the conflict, Rachid as an FLN militant, Laurent as a policeman. It is in the latter capacity that the young *pied-noir* will come into direct and violent conflict with his boyhood friend, now Isabelle's lover. Although brutally tortured by the doubly spurned Laurent, Rachid does not crack, and is eventually released from police custody in a predictably pitiful condition. He is taken off to the mountains to recuperate, whilst Isabelle, obsessed with the suffering inflicted on her beloved, invites Laurent to her home and kills him.

Yet, fascinating as this very unusual perspective on historical events undoubtedly is, the real interest of Millecam's tragic tale lies elsewhere, at the level of form. For the story of this peculiarly Algerian *ménage à trois* is not related in classic realist fashion, and lacks such features of conventional literary texts as an obvious hierarchy of discourses and a straightforwardly linear chronology. So the novel may open with Isabelle's final preparations for Laurent's murder and follow her through the day to its bloody conclusion, but everything else is recounted in a series of highly cinematic flashbacks, much as in a *nouveau roman*, with the constituent elements of the three young people's lives together being juxtaposed and intertwined in what is, superficially at least, a most

[15] J.-P. Millecam, *Sous dix couches de ténèbres* (Denoël, 1968). The latter work is part of what we might regard as Millecam's mature Algerian tetralogy—*Et je vis un cheval pâle* (Gallimard/NRF, 1978), *Un vol de chimères* (ibid. 1979), *Une légion d'anges* (ibid. 1980) and *Choral* (ibid. 1982).

bewildering fashion. Like the work of Butor, and, even more obviously, that of Robbe-Grillet, the text is obsessional in character, and as such does not behave in a fashion which makes either for easy reading or straightforward criticism. Events are typically presented out of sequence, with no situating context, and from multiple perspectives; physical details are dwelt on with just as much insistence as mental states; questions are put by characters who are not always clearly identified, and frequently remain unanswered. However, the result of this very demanding mode of narration is a properly Racinian psychological intensity, which may also be explained in terms both of the classical density of the *topos* and the bold concentration of the action into a single, climactic day.

It is not altogether surprising that it should be the contribution made by Millecam's fiction to the furtherance of the myth of colonial fratricide which critics have hitherto tended to single out for praise. I should wish, however, to draw attention to an altogether more perceptive aspect of Millecam's Algerian *œuvre*, namely the literary exploration of the psychological fantasy world of colonial Algeria, in which every relationship was a combination of attraction and repulsion, underpinned, more often than not, by an ambiguous sexuality. By choosing to focus on what is a historically unrepresentative image of French Algeria—that of an inter-racial *ménage à trois*—Millecam has, paradoxically, brought into the light a number of key elements of the colonial psyche which were previously 'under ten layers of shadow'. Improbable individuals and situations assume a new and demystifying significance when considered not as history, but rather as symbol: the binary opposition of attraction and repulsion is thus revealed to be of fundamental importance in the colonial context, with sexuality—in spite of, or perhaps precisely because of the general historical absence of inter-racial sexual relations—appearing as a privileged area of study for anyone seeking to understand what Memmi has identified as 'the contradictory complementarity' of the colonizer and the colonized.[16]

Millecam's grasp of these psychological truths is overtly manifested in such character-mediated observations as the following, in which Rachid challenges Isabelle's understanding of their relationship:

[16] A. Memmi, 'Une littérature de la séparation', in *Anthologie des écrivains français du Maghreb* (Présence Africaine, 1969), 14. See also G. Tillion, *Les Ennemis complémentaires* (Minuit, 1960).

Nous sommes ennemis, c'est pour ça que nous nous aimons, l'Algérie indépendante en réalité ça te fait horreur, ça te raye d'un coup, toi, ta mère, tes chiennes, vos propriétés, ne me dis pas le contraire ... Note bien que je ne te fais pas de reproche, j'aime que tu sois comme ça, fidèle à toi, mon ennemie, ma meilleure ennemie, la seule sur qui je puisse compter ... (22)

We're enemies, that's why we love each other; in truth an independent Algeria terrifies you, it gets rid of you at a stroke, you, your mother, your dogs, your houses; don't tell me different, don't tell me otherwise ... Don't think that I'm criticizing you, I'm glad that you're like that, true to yourself, my enemy, my best enemy, the only one I can rely upon ...

Similarly, Lancelot—the two young men's former teacher and mentor, and the transparent incarnation of the author himself—reveals Millecam's understanding of the profound ambiguity of personal relations in the colonial context when he addresses Isabelle:

En vérité, ils [Rachid et Laurent] se mouvaient l'un et l'autre sous le ciel de la fascination: dès la prime enfance ils étaient fascinés l'un par l'autre ... Mais la fascination peut déboucher sur l'impossible et la violence ... Lorsque l'écart qui sépare les [individus] devient celui qui sépare les races, les choses deviennent mille fois plus violentes, la fascination mille fois plus grande. Vous aimez Rachid: cet amour aurait pu tout aussi bien être de la haine, car l'amour et la haine sont le recto et le verso de la même fascination. L'amitié de Laurent a laissé la place à une haine qui s'est étendue aussitôt à l'ensemble d'une race: cette haine n'est qu'un amour inverse. Bref, si vous aimez Rachid, Isabelle, c'est par racisme ... (226–7)

Truth to tell, they [Rachid and Laurent] were both moving under the heavens of fascination: from a very early age they were fascinated by one another ... But fascination can result in the impossible and in violence ... When the gap between [individuals] becomes the one between races, things become a thousand times more violent, and the fascination a thousand times greater. You love Rachid: that love could just as well have been hatred, for love and hate are the two sides of the same fascination. Laurent's friendship has given way to a hatred which immediately extended to a whole race: his hatred is only a love which has been reversed. In short, if you love Rachid, Isabelle, it is out of racism ...

While we might wish to dispute the notion that the permanent enmity of colonizer and colonized in Algeria gave rise to a love of some strange kind, there can be little disputing the justice of

Millecam's emphasis on race in the colonial context, together with the economic, political, and social advantages, and disadvantages, which it brings. Indeed, the narrative's exploration of the protagonists' web of psychic confusions and contradictions serves to reveal the fault-lines of *Algérie française*, a society in which, in spite of its rhetoric, ethnicity was all.

In fact, what we are presented with in Millecam's symbolic fiction is a psychoanalytical critique of the colonial situation, in which, as Albert Memmi has argued, both losers and winners were isolated and alienated: the former by their defeats, the latter by their victories.[17] This demystifying project extends to the ethnocentric world-view upon which the colonial edifice is constructed, and thus, in a rare and fascinating departure, to the form of the literary text itself. For it is in its refusal to accede to the demands for transparency and stability of a readership brought up in the tradition of colonial realism that *Sous dix couches de ténèbres* most subtly calls into question habitual procedures of representation, together with the meanings which they generate.

By retaining a large measure of incompleteness—a significant element of *scriptibilité* or 'writerliness', in Roland Barthes's terms—Millecam's narrative serves to draw attention to the linguistic and psychological conditions of its own production. More specifically, in Russian Formalist terms, the text systematically foregrounds its *syuzhet* (discourse) at the expense of its *fabula* (story) by leaving what are very obvious 'holes' in its narrative fabric. This organizational propensity bears a significant resemblance to the successful literary practice of the most celebrated French theorist of artistic commitment, Jean-Paul Sartre. As described by Rhiannon Goldthorpe, Sartre's fictions rely for their defamiliarizing effect upon 'those silent gaps between the lines . . . those suspensions of the act of writing which contest its power as transcription, expression or convention . . . and frustrate the reader's readiness to settle for an accessible and superficial meaning'.[18]

It is precisely in its determined disruption of the comforting verisimilitude of the apparently seamless narrative that Jean-Pierre Millecam's novel displays its radical formal dynamism: it obliges its readership to find a substitute for representational stability, together with the apparent ideological coherence which conventional

[17] 'Une littérature de la séparation', 20.

[18] *Sarte: Literature and Theory* (Cambridge, Cambridge Univ. Press, 1984), 60; see also 128–33.

methods tend both to reflect and to reinforce. The text's shattered image of *Algérie française* thus challenges the reader to produce new meanings on the basis of the narrative fragments provided: a formal defiance of convention which encourages a broader reassessment of accepted colonial wisdom. No less than Kateb Yacine's masterly *Nedjma* (1956), properly regarded as the most remarkable Algerian novel of French expression of the war years, *Sous dix couches de ténèbres* explodes narrative form to political ends. In Goldthorpe's terms, once again, the novel is one in which 'the disjunction rather than the convergence of action, history, meaning and representation is dramatised in order to undermine the stabilising functions of representation, definition, stereotype or interpretation'.[19] Pandering neither to those who harbour nostalgia for the colonies, nor to those who yearn for the lost certitudes of classic realist fiction, Millecam's narrative is, perhaps, the nearest thing to a proof of what Barthes claims to be the necessary connection between radical formal innovation and ideological defamiliarization.

In truth, Jean-Pierre Millecam's writing transcends the specific conflictual situation in which it is rooted, just as surely as does that of, for instance, André Malraux in *La Condition humaine* [published as *Man's Estate*] or T. E. Lawrence in *Seven Pillars of Wisdom*.[20] Nevertheless, as the one novel which best encapsulates Millecam's treatment of the Algerian war, *Sous dix couches de ténèbres* usefully draws attention to those aspects of his work which illuminate the inextricably linked predicaments of colonizer and colonized.

The observation that the literary treatment of inter-racial sexuality may act as a touchstone for judging attitudes to the colonial relationship as a whole underlines the importance of a number of alternative approaches to the imaging of the Other as lover. The most remarkable of these is Xavier Grall's *Africa Blues* (1962),[21] a novel by a liberal Catholic member of the *contingent* which displays an impressive artistic maturity, coupled with a developed insight into both the psychology and the politics of colonial Algeria. Though produced while the war was still in progress, the novel is

[19] Ibid. 132–3

[20] Pierre Enckell makes this point particularly strongly, maintaining that it would be quite improper to categorize Millecam's work as part of the 'French literature of North Africa': 'L'œuvre de Jean-Pierre Millecam', in J.-R. Henry *et al.*, *Le Maghreb dans l'imaginaire français* (Aix-en-Provence, Edisud, 1985), 191–4,

[21] (Calmann-Lévy, 1962; Quimper, Calligrammes, 1984); refs. are to the latter edn.

thus more akin to the major post-1962 treatments of the theme of sexuality.

Grall's narrative possesses not only an impressive formal symmetry, but also a genuine thematic density, with its concentration on the devastating impact on the very strong central figure of the conflictual relations between colonizer and colonized being as original as it is intense. From its powerful opening scene, which describes the *pied-noir* protagonist's hanging of a would-be Algerian arsonist, to its close, with his own death on the same tree, *Africa Blues* sharply focuses the reader's mind on the contradictions of the colonizer's rhetoric. These are personified by the diehard settler, José Montfort, who is revealed to be the offspring of a scandalous union between his now-dead mother and one of the many *indigènes* employed on the family farm. Introduced as the proud upholder of the colonial tradition, 'le dernier des Montfort' [the last of the Montfort family] (10) will thus be transformed into the ultimate colonial aberration, a half-caste, condemned to pay for the sins of the colonial fathers, or rather mothers. As his own unfaithful wife will put it in her diary: '"José Montfort, fils de Driss", me disais-je, prenant soudain conscience de sa tare originelle, de ce qu'il avait de monstrueux, dans le sang, la chair et l'âme' ['José Montfort, the son of Driss', I said to myself, suddenly becoming aware of his original flaw, of what was monstrous in his blood, his flesh, and his soul] (160). The Self will become the Other, and *vice versa*, as the details of José's original sin are revealed.

Throughout his novel, Grall displays the ability to imagine the world of the Other in an unusually challenging fashion. In particular, he is one of the very few French writers to appreciate the 'redemptive' and genuinely revolutionary character of nationalist violence, including especially rebel atrocities (19–20). He also provides a number of refreshing counter-images of *Algérie française*, including notably a powerfully sensual adversary vision of the growth of nationalism in the Mitidja, the jewel in the crown of French colonial creation: 'la luxuriante, la verte, la plate, la riche Mitidja, la Mitidja impure, celle qui avait le plus forniqué avec les Français, celle qui sentait le plus fortement la prostitution, le luxe, la graisse de lard, celle qui sentait le vin et l'alcool . . .' [the luxuriant, green, flat, rich Mitidja, the impure Mitidja which had fornicated the most with the French, which stank most of prostitution, luxury, pork fat, wine, and spirits . . .] (21).

This harshly physical personification of the Mitidja, generally seen as the greatest triumph of settler creation *ex nihilo*, serves not only to draw attention to the ethnocentricity of all such conventional views of the colonial *mise en valeur*, but also to emphasize both the breadth and the depth of the Algerian insurrection. Indeed, for the author of *Africa Blues*, the nationalists' revolt against the established order is as total as its success is inevitable. Yet it is in his depiction of the colonizer's attitude to the colonized that Grall displays his real originality. Specifically, the ex-*appelé* recognizes that his fellow troops, caught up in a war for which they have never been prepared (78–9), can only respond to the Other in a way which bears a striking similarity to that of the *pieds-noirs*. For both the soldier and the settler, in fact, fears and resentments readily manifest themselves in a fierce loathing of the colonized: 'Leur drame n'avait qu'un seul nom: le raton, le fel, le bounioul, et c'était un nom qu'ils ne supportaient pas, le poivre dans leur sang, le sel dans l'iris, le poison au ventre' [Their drama had only one name: 'little [Arab] rat', 'fel[lagha]', 'wog'; and that was a name that they could not bear, the pepper in their blood, the salt in their eyes, the poison in their bellies] (82).

In colonial Algeria, Grall makes plain, the single really important distinction is that between the colonizer and the colonized, the privileged Self and the impoverished Other. For the military representatives of the *Français de France*, just as for the *Français d'Algérie*, in fact, the Algerian is, and must always be, perceived as a permanent affront to the Self's individual and communal identity:

> Ce chancre, cette crasse, cette saleté, l'Arabe! Cette obsession légendaire, transmise de père en fils! Avec, pour toile de fond, cette crainte latente de leur ressembler, à eux, ces bouniouls. Tout doux, tout bons, quand ils ne bougent pas et qu'ils baissent la tête. Insupportables, littéralement insupportables comme une vermine, dès qu'ils se mettent à remuer, à montrer qu'ils existent. (137)
>
> That canker, that scum, that filth: the Arab! That legendary obsession, passed on from father to son! With, as its backdrop, that latent fear of being like them, those wogs. They are no trouble at all when they keep quiet and show some respect. But they are intolerable, literally intolerable like vermin, as soon as they make a move, as soon as they show that they exist.

Grall's insistence on the neurotic character of this primary colonial relationship bears out that of Jean-Pierre Millecam, while his suggestion that the *pieds-noirs* are unconsciously afraid of resembling the indigenous inhabitants of Algeria is to be regarded as a demystifying inversion of the supposed Mediterranean fraternity so loudly trumpeted by the literary defenders of *Algérie française*. Not surprisingly, this novel variation on the theme of the settler's fear of the Other comes across most powerfully, and most ironically, in the person of José Montfort. Consider the character's account of his adolescent attempt to deny the truth of his mixed race:

> Je me regardais tous les jours dans la glace. Je craignais que mon visage ait ce teint olivâtre des bâtards arabes, et qu'il trahisse mon horrible secret. . . . J'étais obsédé. 'T'es le fils d'un raton, t'es le fils d'un raton.' Dès mes vingt ans, je fréquentais les bouzbirs et là je choisissais la putain la plus typiquement arabe et me vengeais sur elle. Le complexe du colonisé quoi! . . . Mon corps lui-même haïssait l'Arabe. Il le sentait. Il le flairait. Il en avait des répulsions. (114–5)

> I looked at myself every day in the mirror. I was afraid that my face had that olive tone that Arab half-castes have, and that it would give away my terrible secret. . . . I was obsessed. 'You're the son of a wog, you're the son of a wog.' When I was twenty, I started going to brothels and I would choose the most typically Arab-looking whore and get my own back on her. The good old colonial complex! . . . My very body hated the Arabs. It could feel them. It could smell them. It felt complete revulsion for them.

In this colonial inversion of the Lacanian 'mirror-phase', the young colonizer's position of identification with a unitary Self gives way to a demented awareness of the essential dualism of his own existence, and by extension that of the colonial situation itself. For the mature José, the revelation of the scandalous circumstances of his conception will mark the onset of a terminal decline. When the narrative opens, the protagonist is only too ready to kill the Other in order to preserve his property and privilege; when it closes, he has come to terms with the contradictions of his life as a 'European' and is only too ready to die.

The end will finally come for José as he sits drinking one night on his veranda. Shot in the leg by an unseen assailant, he does not cry out for help, attempting instead to staunch the flow of blood by applying more and more earth to the wound. The resulting mess functions as a grotesque symbol of the settler community's attachment to its adopted land, and also serves to explain the character's terminal delirium. Though convincingly jumbled, these last fevered thoughts contain flashes of intense clarity, the most significant of which is the central figure's recognition that his mother's unthinkable adultery has not only ruined his own life, but has also undermined colonialism's entire symbolic order:

> Le sirocco ne faiblissait pas. Face à José, près de l'agonie maintenant, il s'engouffrait dans la vieille, la vénérable, l'austère, l'intrépide maison coloniale dressée sur le haut plateau comme une maison forte, quelque donjon arc-bouté contre la fatalité du ciel, maison d'un siècle où tant de joies humaines, où tant de bonheurs ruraux, prodigieusement simples et bons, avaient régné, sous les murs crépis au blanc, cerclés par la bague lumineuse de la véranda, bercés par l'immémoriale chanson des récoltes de septembre quand l'Algérie livrait dans la paix faillible mais si désirable de l'automne, les ouvriers à leur travail sous l'œil noir des Montfort, tout allant pour le mieux jusqu'à ce que cette femme, Eve infidèle et pantelante, eût fait signe au vieux Driss dont le membre impatient dans la culotte de coutil attendait ce jour pour bousculer l'ordre établi et heureux, pour rompre irrémédiablement le bail et la féodalité. (196–7)

> The sirocco was still blowing just as strongly. Opposite José, who was now nearing death, it swept into the ancient, austere, and intrepid colonial dwelling, which stood on the high plains like a fortress, as if it were some castle bracing itself against fate and the heavens; a house which had stood there for a century, and in which so much human joy, so much wonderfully simple and decent country happiness, had reigned. Within these whitewashed walls, surrounded by the bright ring of the veranda, and rocked by the immemorial lullaby of the September harvests, Algeria gave way to the fragile but so wonderful peace of autumn; while the workers laboured under the dark gaze of the Montfort family, everything had been for the best, until that woman, that unfaithful and panting Eve, had given the nod to old Driss, whose eager member had long awaited this opportunity to burst out of his coarse trousers and overturn the happy established order, thus making a break forever with tutelage and feudalism.

This climactic passage exposes to view the underlying fallacy of that myth of Franco-Algerian *métissage* [interbreeding] once uttered by Gabriel Audisio and other *pied-noir* liberals: such a blending of the races failed to occur in *Algérie française* precisely because it would have brought to an end the radical dualism upon which the economy of colonial exploitation relied. No North African equivalent of the formalized 'separateness' of the Cape Dutch was needed to protect French interests against the subversive potential of their own sexuality; the *pieds-noirs*' own sense of racial 'apartness' provided adequate insurance against such a revolution from within.

Xavier Grall's literary treatment of the Other includes a typically incisive depiction of the condition of the Algerian worker in France itself, with the FLN guerrilla responsible for José Montfort's death reflecting bitterly upon his experiences on the Citroën assembly line in Paris. Here it was that he first learnt that 'la misère d'un manœuvre nor'af n'a pas la même valeur que la misère d'un manœuvre français . . . que la fraternité ouvrière était un leurre et que la haine des classes n'était qu'une galéjade comparée à la lutte des races . . .' ['the woes of a North African labourer do not count for as much as those of a French labourer . . . that workers' unity was an illusion, and that class hatred was just a tall story compared with racial conflict'] (29–30).

This passage introduces what we may conveniently term the theme of the Other in our midst or *parmi nous*.[22] Grall was not the first French writer to portray this durably relevant aspect of Algerian suffering, however, with a particularly important contribution to the immigration debate having been made as early as 1958 by Jacques Lanzmann, a long-standing leftist opponent of the war in North Africa. In *Les Passagers du Sidi-Brahim* (1958), this political campaigner became a literary pioneer, using fiction to draw attention to the plight of the eponymous exiles, who have been obliged to quit their homeland in order to avoid an even greater suffering there. Their segregated voyage—with the French travellers in the ship's cabins and the Algerians in the hold (89)—is an accurate foretaste of the systematic dicrimination that awaits them on the other side of the Mediterranean.

Lanzmann's depiction of the harsh world of the Other is convincingly hard-edged: if an immigrant quarter in his Marseilles is 'just like home', then it is only because it is over-populated, squalid, and cruel (105).[23] Moreover, his narrative serves to underline the fundamental difference in kind between the suffering of the proletariat and that of the colonized peoples. It is leftist mystification of this underlying relationship that Claire Etcherelli looks to expose, together with all such convenient distortions of the complex reality of the Algerian immigrant, in what is perhaps the best known novel devoted to the idea of the Other as lover, her *Élise ou la vraie vie* [Élise or Real Life] (1967).

Produced just five years after the Algerian conflict ended, *Élise* remains as pertinent to the France of the 1990s as it was to that of

[22] This term is suggested by J. Leriche, *Les Algériens parmi nous* (Éditions Sociales, 1959).

[23] In contrast, that of André Stil, the principal literary apologist for the PCF in this period, is characterized by the very brand of 'proletarian' mystification against which Grall takes such a determined stand. See especially *Le Dernier quart d'heure* (Éditeurs Français Réunis, 1962; Grasset, 1978).

the 1960s. The foundation of this abiding relevance is to be found in the novel's thematic orientation, with the narrative addressing itself less to the 1954–62 conflict as such, and more to the enduring tensions and contradictions of the Franco-Algerian relationship. Though a readily accessible narrative, *Élise* possesses a genuinely classical concentration of emotional effect. This quality may be attributed, much as in Millecam's novel, to the fact that the novel's action is recounted in flashback over a single night, as the central figure spends her final hours in Paris. Moreover, the text regularly manages to defamiliarize, and thereby to demystify, metropolitan French perceptions of the Other.

A tale of unremitting depression, *Élise* is a love story stripped bare of romantic frills, with the traditional happy ending being ruled out from its desperate opening sentence: 'Surtout ne pas penser' [Above all, don't think] (11). In stark prose, the text details the oppression of the weak by the strong, and that of those even weaker in turn, and is at least as inclined to explode the myth of proletarian solidarity as it is that of Arab sexuality. By concentrating its resources on a very restricted segment of French society, it manages to tell us infinitely more about metropolitan attitudes as a whole than most of the wider-ranging novels generated by the Algerian conflict. By the same token, Élise, the first-person narrator, is the text's exclusive point of focus: the Algerian war, like everything else, is only real for the reader to the extent that it is lived and recounted by the protagonist. Though seemingly limiting, this mediation is, in fact, extremely productive. For as she leaves behind her psychologically debilitating provincial upbringing, in quest of the 'real life' sought by Rimbaud and other doomed poets, this simple soul will, indeed, achieve enlightenment, albeit fleetingly and very traumatically: an emotional awakening will thus bring her to a new, but by no means comfortable, political awareness.

The Parisian heart of *Élise* is the car plant where the eponymous heroine goes to work on the production line, the very appropriately named 'chaîne' (100); with extensive use made of immigrant labour, race inevitably dominates relations at all levels. Into this bleak vision of an industrialized humankind comes Élise, timid, well-intentioned, and caring. In spite of 'friendly' warnings from both her employers and her fellow employees, Élise will become involved not only with the union, but also, and more importantly, with the immigrants who work alongside her. Ignoring the self-serving counsel of her 'superiors', she will refuse to ignore the Algerians and their problems: she will argue, will politicize, and will not spare the sacred cows of the Left any more than she will those of the Right. Her naïveté is precisely what underpins her *provocation*, and, as such, is the principal cause of her alienation from her French co-workers and managers.

Like its central figure, Etcherelli's narrative is determined to be political: its abiding interest resides in the fact that it insists on discussion, rather than settling for the reassuring statement of myth. Moreover, *Élise*, following its protagonist, may wear its political heart on its sleeve, but it does so in a way which constantly challenges the reader and is thus rarely comfortable. Typically, when Élise becomes involved in the metropolitan anti-colonialist and anti-war movement, it is not this overtly political side of a general awakening that will take her—and us—nearer to an understanding of the whole Franco-Algerian relationship, but rather its emotional aspect. Élise's love for an immigrant fellow car-worker, Arezki, brings her both to the fringes of involvement with the FLN and to a radically new understanding of Self. In addition, it offers the reader of the tale a demystified and demystifying insight into the Algerian war. That it is able to do so is a function of the narrative density gained by eschewing an illusory comprehensiveness: for what *Élise* lacks in coverage as a result of its exclusive concentration on a single character's limited experience is more than made up for in communicative intensity.

The principal demystifying strategy which may be identified in Etcherelli's novel is the regular constrasting of the confident generalities of both Right and Left with the modest details of the protagonist's halting love affair. The specious certainties of the two apparent adversaries thus give way to a necessarily messy world—both emotionally and politically—of personal tensions, complexities, and contradictions: *la vraie vie* as lived rather than dreamed. There is absolutely no place for illusion in *Élise*'s scheme of things: what little progress the largely unhappy couple do make is consistently undermined by events, and is ultimately demolished by them. All that the central figure is able to cling to is hope, though of a wholly disabused kind. In a demystifying inversion of the Pandora or Eve figure—woman perceived as the origin of mankind's ills—this particular female is revealed to be the helpless victim of a wider social malaise.

The key to an appreciation of the novel's force is to be found in an awareness of its central figure's severely restricted psychological capabilities: the last thing that her emotionally deprived home life has prepared her for is the transgression of one of metropolitan French society's most rigorously observed taboos. The depiction of her relationship with Arezki through her own, desperately honest, eyes immediately puts the text, and the reader, at a distance from the vast majority of male-written and male-centred French treatments of the Algerian war. With *Élise*, we cut through the multiple layers of sexually-focused military romanticism which mediate so much discussion of the conflict. Here, we are in the rarely considered world of metropolitan women, a world which, *via* Élise's love for Arezki, impinges on an even less frequently visited domain: the universe of the Other. Uniquely regarded as the loved one, the Algerian is inescapably present in Etherelli's *métropole*, as is the war itself.

The protagonist's love for an Algerian worker—a literally unspeakable crime for so many of her contemporaries, writers included—permits the articulation and simultaneous exposure of a variety of immigrant-related myths. Central among these is the durable myth of all-consuming Arab sexuality. This theme is voiced and demystified in a variety of ways, of which the most overt centres on the French women who work alongside Élise, and whose cloakroom conversations evoke the prevailing atmosphere in all its banal hostility. Crucially, Etcherelli does not shy away from the limited sociological insights contained in the women's crude observations regarding 'les Arabes': on the contrary, the wolf-whistles, cat-calls, and similar manifestations of shop-floor sexual harassment are dutifully recorded. However, these overt expressions of Algerian male sexuality are placed in the social and cultural context necessary for a demystified understanding of them.

In the process, Arezki's gentle mocking of Élise's emotional limitations takes the argument a crucial stage further; for his playfully expressed, but perfectly legitimate, awareness of her underdevelopment (185–6) undermines the central colonial thesis of the chronic backwardness of the Other. This inversion of the standard European perspective is thus potentially subversive, in that it should lead the reasonably aware reader to question the state of his or her own emotional and political development. Of prime importance in this regard is Élise's own ambivalence as a consumer of myth. Although it would be all too easy for her heroine to appear blameless in the midst of institutionalized French racism, Etcherelli's fictive reality is persuasively complex, and Élise is as prone to suspect Arezki's intentions as anyone. Real demystification thus comes not so much from attacks on obvious targets—ignorant workmates, loud-mouthed drinkers, the police, *Monsieur et Madame tout un chacun* [Mr and Mrs Average]—as from the systematic undermining of the central figure's own well-intentioned and avowedly anti-racist attitudes. So, for instance, the common-sense notion of Arab sexuality is, in the following extract, exploded all the more effectively for Elise's unattractive susceptibility to it; she learns from experience, and the reader learns with her:

> Imprégnée d'idées reçues, j'avais pensé, le soir où nous nous promenions dans les jardins du Trocadéro et où, choisissant un trou d'ombre, Arezki m'avait violemment embrassée: ça y est, maintenant, il va m'emmener dans sa chambre. Mais rien ne s'était produit. (184)
>
> My head was full of other people's prejudices. One evening, as we were walking in the Trocadéro gardens, Arezki, choosing a dark spot, had kissed me violently. I thought: here we go, he's going to get me into bed now. But nothing happened.

Similarly, whilst the reader might wish Etcherelli's heroine to be stronger and admit openly to her relationship with Arezki, Élise's own attitude is both more convincing and more constructive. Thus, Arezki's accusation that Élise is embarrassed to be seen in public with him might be denied by her, in all good faith and to his apparent satisfaction, but a serious doubt remains. Indeed, the protagonist's own inability to fool herself for long soon reveals a harsher truth:

> Chaque fois que nous nous séparions, Arezki me recommandait le secret, et cela m'agaçait un peu. A la vérité, cela me convenait tout à fait. (184)
>
> Each time that we parted, Arezki would remind me to keep quiet about us, which annoyed me slightly. To tell the truth, it suited me perfectly.

What is more, even a distinctly Barthesian or Memmian capacity for understanding the mechanics of colonial mystification does not guarantee the protagonist immunity from its pernicious influence:

> Irène sortit. Il y eut des murmures dans le groupe des femmes. Je saisis cette phrase:
>
> '. . . elle marche avec les Algériens.'
>
> C'était l'expression d'usage: marcher avec, toujours suivi du pluriel. Et c'était l'injure suprême: marcher avec les Algériens, marcher avec les Nègres . . .
>
> Demain, elles diraient de moi 'elle marche avec les Algériens'. Ces mots évoquaient des bouges tristes où la même femme passe successivement dans les bras de beaucoup d'hommes. (175)

Irène went out. There was some muttering amongst the group of women. I caught the sentence:

'. . . she goes with the Algerians.'

That was the expression which everybody used: 'go with,' always followed by the plural. It was the supreme insult: go with the Algerians, go with the niggers . . .

Tomorrow they will say about me 'she goes with the Algerians'. The words conjured up miserable hovels where the same woman was passed around between a lot of different men.

For all her demystifying insight into the linguistic workings of her colleagues' prejudices, Élise cannot wholly resist them. In the same breath, she wishes she could confide in these women, could share their secrets along with their bench: fearing their condemnation, she longs to be one of them, with predictably self-destructive consequences (175). This flawed awareness of myth's power is deeply persuasive. The same approach is used, with considerable success, to expose a complex of immigrant-centred myths. One by one, the notions of Arab inhumanity, homogeneity, touchiness, and unfitness for serious work are held up for critical appraisal; and not by a self-assured individual, confident in the rightness of her words and deeds, but by Élise. Her hesitant insights into the mystification of the Franco-Algerian relationship leave no comfortable position intact for the reader, and this is the real basis of its abiding importance and appeal: the text demands that the issues presented be considered anew by each reader, on something very like their own, historically specific, terms.

The inability of Élise wholly to break free of her condition and conditioning is symbolized most forcefully, perhaps, by her persistent unwillingness to write to her grandmother informing her about Arezki. This has its mythological counterpoint in the Algerian militant's patent lack of revolutionary *grandeur*. He is not the glamorous figure dreamed of by the French Left, any more than he is the bogeyman of the Right. All that remains when the layers of metropolitan mystification have been stripped away is that most demanding of rhetorical figures, that ultimately unassimilable but irresistibly challenging construct: a fellow human being, with the full quota of frailties and contradictions. Depicted as such, Arezki is a determinedly anti-romantic figure, and is thus genuinely representative of the Algerian revolution as a whole:

Je suis comme les autres. Moi aussi, j'ai envie de casser la figure à quelques types, moi aussi j'ai envie de me saouler quand j'ai le cafard ou pour oublier, moi aussi j'ai bu en cachette. J'ai eu aussi envie de tricher avec le trésorier, et je ne vais pas aux réunions sans peur. Je voudrais passer mon dimanche au lit et non pas me lever à six heures pour courir le quartier, ne plus rendre des comptes, ne plus être commandé; et il y a des frères que je ne peux pas souffrir. . . . Il y a des gais, des vaniteux, des sournois, des naïfs, des durs, des salauds, des timides. Des hommes. Et le miracle, c'est qu'on ait réussi à empêcher l'explosion de cent ou de mille caractères condamnés à se supporter, à se brimer. (211–12)

I'm like all the others. I too feel like punching a few faces in, and I too feel like getting drunk when I'm fed up or when I want to forget, and I too have had a drink on the quiet. I too have been tempted to cheat on the fund-collectors, and I can't go to meetings without feeling scared. I would like to spend my Sundays in bed and not have to get up at six o'clock to run around the neighbourhood; I would like not to have to give any answers any more, and not to be ordered around; and there are some 'brothers' that I cannot stand. . . . Some of them are happy, some of them are conceited, some of them are deceitful, some of them are gullible, some of them are hard cases, some of them are bastards, some of them are scared. Men. And the miraculous thing about it is that we have managed to prevent the explosion of a hundred or a thousand characters who are obliged to put up with one another, in spite of the aggravations.

Interestingly, Arezki's most disturbing shortcoming concerns not his revolutionary will but rather his love for Élise. In particular, his apparently pointless cruelty towards her on occasion—for instance, when she wishes to visit her brother in hospital (256)—means that an element of enigma remains disturbingly present in the character: the reader, like Élise, never knows precisely why Arezki acts as he does; just as the Algerian's disappearance at the end of the narrative can never be satisfactorily explained either by Élise or by us. The text's movement towards closure—the classically satisfying dissipation of the mystery which it has itself created—is, in consequence, neither as consistent nor as final as that exhibited by the bulk of Algerian war fiction. In his terminal absence, just as in his transient presence, Arezki retains an important measure of unseizability, of openness. Moreover, the metropolitan France in which he lives, and perhaps dies, and the Algerian revolution which he modestly furthers are likewise possessed of this ideologically challenging brand of diegetic openness. We, the readers, are patently not provided with all the facts about the Algerians' clandestine struggle, no more than we are able to see clearly into the state's overt and covert responses: how could we be? Rather, history is played out in the shadows of metropolitan France by aesthetically unsatisfactory figures, and we only hear the echoes of their bitter clash: 'les murmures de la guerre', as Roger Ikor put it.

Fought by essentially messy characters, the Algerian conflict of *Élise* is very much the 'dirty' war of historical record. Just as she foregrounds Arezki's contradictions, so Etcherelli faces up to the less palatable aspects of the nationalist revolt, not shying away, in particular, from the FLN's use of coercion as often as conversion among its own people. In the fictive universe of *Élise*, the Algerian struggle for national liberation is the antithesis of romance. As Arezki sums it up for his old alcoholic uncle: 'La révolution . . . est un bulldozer' (205).

At the heart of the metropolitan leftists' misreading of the Algerian war is their own myth of working-class solidarity. This notion is regularly undermined, and thus gives way to a less attractive but considerably more constructive vision of chronic economism aggravated by a particularly acute form of racist nationalism. Élise sees through the French Left's institutionalized appeals to the nobler sentiments of the proletariat very early on, and it is but a short step for her from this discovery to a *tiers-mondiste* critique of the totality of colonialist power-structures, including the oppression of colonized workers by their supposed counterparts in the mother country. Informed by Arezki about the harsh realities of his childhood and adolescence in colonial Algeria, she will thus come to realize that the suffering of the colonized South is different in kind from that of the colonizing North (197).

The logical corollary of this inherent tension in the Franco-Algerian relationship as lived at the industrial workplace is that participation in the French Left's anti-war agitation, however well-intentioned, can only ever be a negation of the very solidarity that it is designed to incarnate. This paradox is most clearly illustrated by Élise's unwished but definitive estrangement from Arezki as a result of her idealistic enthusiasm, in the wake of the events of 13 May 1958, for a leftist march against the Algiers' insurrection and in support of the Fourth Republic. It is the Algerian militant's hard-headed recognition that the demonstration will serve no useful purpose that is borne out by subsequent historical developments. Misled by her emotional reaction to political events, Élise neglects Arezki, and is very shortly to lose him forever. Sacked from the plant following an altercation with a foreman, Arezki is deprived of the all-important proof of employment, and is consequently in grave danger of arrest and detention, or worse. Élise turns down his offer to meet her in order to attend the demonstration, and never sees him again: she subsequently discovers that Arezki was arrested after his final telephone call to her, on the eve of the futile demonstration.

The radical inability of metropolitan observers to come to a full awareness of the condition of the Other is thus seen to extend even to Élise: her objectively privileged position may allow her to sympathize with the lot of the inhabitants of the Nanterre shanty town (*bidonville*), but not to live it. Crucially, this deep inability to empathize is not merely noted by the text, but rather integrated into its narrative structure. So in the following extract, the limits of the narrator and of the narration are admitted in a self-conscious rejection of earlier literary and journalistic treatments of the *bidonville* theme. The result is precisely the defamiliarization lacking in those earlier accounts:

> Tant de journaux, de témoins, de récits ont décrit, depuis, ces lieux où, parqués, agglutinés, survivaient des centaines d'êtres; le faire, ce serait dire et répéter les mêmes mots, accumuler les mêmes adjectifs, tourner en rond autour des mêmes verbes: entassement misérable, souffrance physique, maladie, pauvreté, froid, pluie, vent qui secoue les planches, flaques qui se coulent sous la porte, peur de la police, obscurité, parcage inhumain, douleur, douleur partout. (209–10)

> So many newspapers, eye-witnesses, accounts have since described these places where hundreds of human beings were packed in and stuck together, and yet survived; to do it here would be to say and repeat the same words, to pile up the same adjectives, to go round in circles with the same verbs: wretched overcrowding, physical pain, illness, poverty, cold, rain, winds which rattle the boards, puddles which come in under the doors, fear of the police, darkness, inhuman dumping, suffering, suffering everywhere.

This self-conscious admission of the narrative's limitations is of considerable strategic significance: the text does not merely recount Élise's failed attempt, as protagonist-narrator, to turn Life into Literature, it makes that failure a principle of its narration. The process of aesthetic estrangement thus encouraged by *Élise* is part of the relentless concentration on the prosaic that constitutes the narrative's abiding strength. Etcherelli's portrayal of the humdrum horror of metropolitan France draws on both the naturalism of Zola and the monstrous logic of Kafka, for hers is a fictive universe in which abnormality is the norm—at least as far as Algerians are concerned: 'La disparition d'Arezki était naturelle, elle s'inscrivait dans une fatale logique dont j'étais la seule à m'émouvoir' [The disappearance of Arezki was natural, it conformed to a fatal logic which I alone found distressing] (274).

The concluding section of the narrative, in which Élise is driven home by a friend, is a climactic indictment of metropolitan French indifference to Algerian suffering. Shocked into mute receptivity, the protagonist penetrates the ugly truths behind the superficial calm of the passing Paris streets. Above all, she realizes that her efforts to discover the whereabouts of Arezki are doomed to failure:

> . . . la vie d'un Arabe est de quel prix ici? Le goût de l'ordre sue de ces maisons. On l'a refoulé, renvoyé là-bas, dans la guerre. Je pourrai bien crier, qui m'écoutera? S'il vit, où est-il? S'il est mort, où est son corps? Qui me le dira? Vous avez pris sa vie oui, mais son corps qu'en avez-vous fait? . . . Qui se souciera d'Arezki? . . . Je pressens que je ne verrai plus jamais Arezki. (271–2)

> What is the life of an Arab worth here? These houses ooze a love of order. He has been turned away, sent back over there, back to the war. I could shout out, but who would hear me? If he's alive, then where is he? If he's dead, then where's his body? Who will tell me? Alright, you have taken his life, but what have you done with his body? . . . Who will spare a thought for Arezki? . . . I have a premonition that I shall never see Arezki again.

An immense success, both as a novel and in Michel Drach's Cannes-premièred film version, Claire Etcherelli's *Élise ou la vraie vie* was awarded the 1967 Prix Fémina. It is to be hoped that this distinction will not result in the mythical recuperation, as Great Literature, of what is a profoundly disturbing text. Indeed, the work's firmly established position in the new literary canon should not be allowed to blind us to its durable power to subvert.

Arezki's mysterious disappearance/death at the hands of the most shadowy forces of the Gaullist state serves to combine the major themes of *l'autre parmi nous* and *la mort des autres*; and, moreover, to situate them both within the central problematic of the Algerian war, namely, the failures of individual and collective memory. The same could be said, *a fortiori*, of the historical disappearance/deaths of hundreds of the fictional character's real-life counterparts on 17 October 1961.[24] On that rainy night, Algerians assembled in large

[24] The bloody repression perpetrated in Paris on 17 October 1961 is painstakingly and harrowingly reconstructed by Jean-Luc Einaudi in *La Bataille de Paris* (Seuil, 1991).

numbers to protest against the curfew recently introduced to curb the FLN's activities in the city. The unarmed and largely silent mass of men, women, and children met an unprecedented show of force orchestrated by police chief Maurice Papon, previously a key figure in Vichy's deportation of French Jews. With the *Palais des Sports* replacing the *Vel' d'Hiv'*, the Algerians were rounded up, beaten, imprisoned, and, in an estimated 200 cases, brutally murdered.

The subject of a predictably intense, but surprisingly successful government cover-up, this violence was effectively replaced in the collective memory by the deaths of 9 anti-OAS demonstrators in the Charonne 'massacre' of 8 February 1962: while their funerals drew an incredible half a million mourners, the events of 17 October were forgotten. It was in a noble effort to penetrate this wall of silence that Didier Daeninckx produced *Meurtres pour mémoire* [Murders for the Record] in 1984.[25] A further example of the *polar* which exploits the medium of detective fiction to analyse the official and mediatic occultation of the memory of the Algerian war, Daeninckx's novel also functions as an indictment of those responsible for this atrocity: most obviously the Paris police and the de Gaulle government, but ultimately a whole society which has been all too wilfully forgetful about its actions on both sides of the Mediterranean in the period 1954–62:

> Au petit matin il ne restait plus sur les boulevards que des milliers de chaussures, d'objets, de débris divers qui témoignaient de la violence des affrontements. Le silence s'était établi, enfin. (37)

> In the early morning, all that was left on the boulevards were thousands of shoes and other objects, a range of debris which bore witness to the violence of the clashes. Silence reigned, at last.

As we shall see in the next chapter, this durable 'silence' was to preoccupy a number of French film-makers, just as it had literary commentators on the war.

[25] This work was to win both the Prix Vaillant-Couturier and the Grand Prix de la Littérature Policière in 1984.

Part 3

Filming the War Without a Name, 1954–1992

8

CINEMA IMAGES OF THE ALGERIAN CONFLICT, 1954–1992

It has long been a critical commonplace to bemoan the lack of a French cinema of the Algerian war.[1] More recently, however, the publication of substantial critical inventories of this supposedly non-existent corpus has forced a reappraisal of the cinematic representation of the 1954–62 conflict.[2] It is as part of this reassessment that Benjamin Stora, the leading historian of the French collective memory of the war, has sought to analyse not an objective absence, but rather a perceived one. Stora looks to the doubly partial—both fragmentary and partisan—character of the approximately fifty feature films which have so far dealt, directly or indirectly, with the Algerian conflict, in an attempt to account for this abiding impression of a cinematic absence.[3] In what follows, I shall propose both a chronology and a typology of the corpus which draws on this and other contributions to the recent debate. However, as I turn in this final chapter to the processes of mediation performed by cinematic 'texts', it is the pivotal relationship between the ideological stances and the narrative strategies of the films in question that will constitute the primary object of my analysis.

[1] See e.g. J.-P. Jeancolas, 'Le Cinéma des guerres coloniales', in the same author's *Le Cinéma des Français: la Ve République (1958–1978)* (Stock, 1979), 156–62. Jeancolas talks of 'the strange silence of the French cinema regarding decolonization', 156. Cf. J. Daniel, *Guerre et cinéma* (Cahiers de la Fondation Nationale des Sciences Politiques/Armand Colin, 1972), 335–55.

[2] See esp. A. Garel, 'Le Cinéma français et la guerre d'Algérie', *Grand Maghreb*, 57 (19 Apr. 1989), 18–25; P. Ory, 'L'Algérie fait écran', in Rioux, *La Guerre d'Algérie et les Français* (Fayard, 1990), 572–81; P. Guibbert, 'La guerre d'Algérie sur les écrans français', in L. Gervereau, J.-P. Rioux, and B. Stora (eds.), *La France en guerre d'Algérie* (MHC-BDIC, 1992), 247–55. A major festival of films about the war, 'France-Algérie: images d'une guerre', was held at the Institut du Monde Arabe in Paris, 1–29 Mar. 1992.

[3] B. Stora, *La Gangrène et l'oubli: la mémoire de la guerre d'Algérie* (La Découverte, 1992), 248–55, 'Images: cette sensation d'absence'.

A second, and no less frequently voiced, criticism of the French cinema of the Algerian war is that it compares badly with the American films inspired by the second Vietnam conflict.[4] What is certain is that there is nothing to compare with the huge success at the box-office or worldwide critical acclaim enjoyed by films such as *The Deerhunter*, *Full Metal Jacket*, *Hamburger Hill*, and *Platoon*. Still less is there anything which might reasonably be likened to the grandiose self-indulgence of *Apocalypse Now*. But then nor is there any obvious equivalent of Hollywood's exploitation of star vehicles from *The Green Berets* to *Rambo* to effect a cinematic rehabilitation of military and political failures in South-East Asia.[5] It is thus no coincidence that the only conventionally heroic 'war film' inspired by the Algerian conflict should be *Lost Command* (1966), the American Mark Robson's screen adaptation of Jean Lartéguy's *Les Centurions*, featuring Anthony Quinn as Raspéguy and Alain Delon as Esclavier. Indeed, on closer inspection, this unfavourable comparison may be seen to involve not only a somewhat uncritical acceptance of the merits of the American cinema's representation of the country's South-East Asian war, but also a tendency to underestimate the value of the very varied French production on Algeria.

It is important to recognize that the French cinema of the Algerian war was born of a combination of crises; for to the major geopolitical and institutional challenges presented by decolonization, and the social and economic revolutions of *les trente glorieuses*, must be added the French film industry's own process of mutation. It is this background of conflict, structural change, and symbolic reassessment which must be borne in mind if we are to be in a position to appreciate the cultural specificity of this aspect of the imaging of the Franco-Algerian conflict. This is particularly true of what is, in contrast to the necessarily private production and consumption of the war's literature, a quintessentially social medium of artistic expression and political commentary. Indeed, it is scarcely an

[4] Ibid. 255. Jeancolas, meanwhile, suggests that the French film industry might have used the nation's recent experience of defeat in Indo-China as an 'alibi' for commenting on Algeria, much as American directors had used the 1943–5 war with Japan as a means of denouncing American involvement in Korea, 1950–3, *Le Cinéma des Français*, 156. Guibbert, 'La Guerre d'Algérie', 248–50 is notably critical of all such 'simplistic' US–French comparisons.

[5] For a useful intro. to this subject, see P. Melling, 'The Vietnamese in a fatal light', in P. Melling and J. Roper, *America, France and Vietnam: Cultural History and Ideas of Conflict* (Aldershot, Avebury, 1991), 129–51.

exaggeration to say that an ideologically informed reading of the cinematic corpus—regarded as 'shown texts' or 'performative narratives'[6]—will tell us almost as much about three decades of rapid social evolution as it will about the history of French perceptions of the Algerian war. For it is necessary, as Pierre Guibbert reminds us, to appreciate these films for what they are: cultural products, which it would be particularly ridiculous to compare mechanically with the 'realities' of the conflict in order to appreciate their 'fidelity' to the events portrayed.[7]

It was in the late 1950s and early 1960s that the technical, aesthetic, and thematic assumptions of the officially encouraged Tradition of Quality were first challenged by the New Wave of previously unknown and consciously authorial film directors. Having grown accustomed to stability in the postwar period, thanks to the system of financial support instituted by the laws of 1948 and 1953, and administered by the state-run Centre national de la cinématographie (CNC), the mainstream French film industry now found itself threatened on three fronts; for not only was it confronted, as were other European film industries, by falling audiences and the rise of television, but it also had to deal with the emergence in the 1958–62 period of a rash of young, talented, and determinedly disrespectful new directors. Whether coming to feature films from a background in documentaries, as did Alain Resnais, or moving directly into cinematic production with little or no practical experience, like Jean-Luc Godard, the very different members of this 'nouvelle vague' would, in many cases, have their word on the Algerian question.[8]

Yet to say this is not to suggest that the relevant productions appeared either early or easily in the history of the French remembrance of the Algerian conflict. Indeed, if there is a genuine cinematic 'absence' to be accounted for, then it is in the period 1954–7: three years which saw no reflection in cinematic productions of the moral and political issues raised by Algeria. However,

[6] These terms are suggested by Seymour Chatman, in his *Coming to Terms: The Rhetoric of Narrative in Fiction and Film* (Ithaca, Cornell Univ. Press, 1990), 3–4.

[7] 'La Guerre d'Algérie', 247. Cf. Jeancolas on film's ambiguous relationship with history, *Le Cinéma des Français*, 8–10.

[8] Jeancolas provides a list of 97 film-makers whose first commercial films came out between 1958 and 1962 and thus might legitimately be considered part of this broadly-defined 'New Wave'. In addition to Resnais and Godard, the list includes such directors as Alain Cavalier, Jacques Demy, Michel Drach, Robert Enrico, Chris Marker, and Pierre Schoendoerffer. *Le Cinéma des Français*, 114, n. 3.

there is a straightforward historical explanation for this apparent failure of the film industy to take account of the war. Quite simply, the French people as a whole remained largely ignorant in this period of the scale and intensity of the Algerian insurrection. The *Toussaint* rising itself had gone generally unreported or unappreciated, and it was only with the gradual spread of violence from the mountains of the Algerian hinterland and into the European cities of the littoral in 1955 and 1956 that the war would begin to make itself felt in metropolitan France. This awareness would initially be based on the heavily censored reporting of the official news media, and only much later, if at all, on the first-hand evidence of returning conscripts. The inevitable time-lag was such that the first important examples of this adversary *témoignage* only appeared in 1957,[9] and it is hardly surprising that their cinematic equivalents—with their more complex and time-consuming processes of production and distribution—should not have appeared before 1958. Nor, given the French record on censorship as regards colonial issues, is it surprising that mainstream commercial studios should have continued to avoid the subject even when it became clear that things were going badly wrong on both sides of the Mediterranean. With the return to power of de Gaulle in June 1958, established producers and directors were generally ready to leave the field clear for the hero of a wartime Resistance which their state-sponsored industry had sought to celebrate since 1944. In this, no doubt, they revealed both their political pragmatism and their commercial acumen, for there can be few doubts that the bulk of the French population had little appetite for breaking this soothing cinematic consensus for the sake of Algeria: with the providential leader once again in charge, they were only too happy to turn their attention to the economic and social challenges posed by the construction of a modern, technologically adventurous, and consciously 'hexagonal' France.

It was therefore left to other voices to break the film establishment's largely self-imposed silence on the final demise of *la plus grande France*. First to make itself heard was the so-called 'parallel' cinema which developed precisely in order to make and show its own films about Algeria. Taking advantage of the same advances in film technology that would enable the New Wave to emerge and to develop its characteristically raw style,[10] such consciously opposi-

[9] See Ch. 5, n. 2.

[10] Examples of these technological advances include lightweight, easily portable

tional directors as Pierre Clément and René Vautier produced a series of documentary shorts which, in their case, did indeed result in direct state intervention. The secret projection of banned films like Clément's *Sakiet Sidi Youssef* and *Réfugiés algériens*, and Vautier's *Algérie en flammes* (all 1958) thus became a regular act of defiance for anti-war militants, with the premises of trades unions and leftist *ciné-clubs* typically being used for the often unannounced, and not infrequently raided, screenings.

The pioneering work of Clément and Vautier was significantly added to by that of returning *appelés* with experience of the film industry, such as Guy Chalon's *58 2/B* (a reference to the conscript's *classe*, or year of mobilization) and Philippe Durand's *Secteur postal 89 098* (both 1959), while the parallel cinema movement as a whole may be said to have culminated in the projection and seizure of the Vérité-Liberté collective's *Octobre à Paris* (1962), which sought to publicize the appalling repression of the peaceful Algerian demonstration which occurred in the French capital on 17 October 1961.[11] Yet, as Jean-Pierre Jeancolas has argued, the really important thing about these militant screenings was not what was actually shown at them, but the fact that they took place at all. For this anti-colonialist attack on the post-1944 cinematic consensus marked a turning point in the French public's relationship with the medium itself: the unitary cinema which had existed to serve—or, perhaps more accurately, to produce—a homogeneous audience under the Fourth Republic was permanently shattered and replaced by a variety of cinemas playing to discrete sets of ideologically affiliated spectators. This is a pattern which, at least as far as the cinema of the Algerian war is concerned, has been maintained into the 1990s.[12]

The first move from a complete absence to an illicit marginality was to be followed by a second, and much more celebrated, challenge to the political, commercial, and technical constraints of mainstream cinema: that of the New Wave itself. As Jill Forbes has observed, the early iconoclasm of this movement itself gave way to a new orthodoxy, which later directors would feel themselves obliged to respect or to reject: 'in France *nouvelle vague* signifies a specific kind of film practice, a complex of aesthetic, technical,

16mm cameras, and synchronous sound-recording equipment. See A. Williams, *Republic of Images: A History of French Filmmaking* (Cambridge, Mass., Harvard Univ. Press, 1992), 364.

[11] See Jeancolas, *Le Cinéma des Français*, 158–61, and cf. Guibbert, 'La Guerre d'Algérie', 248.

[12] Jeancolas, *Le Cinéma des Français*, 158. See also Stora, *La Gangrène et l'oubli*, 254.

political and social positions . . . [in relation to which] we can perceive a constant necessity for the film maker to position himself —or more rarely herself—positively or negatively'.[13] Central to this cinematic legacy is the shift in both the content and style of French films which occurred as the industry's own financial troubles combined with the profound social restructuring of the period to allow new opportunities for artistic self-expression and political commentary.[14] These opportunities were grasped most dramatically by Jean-Luc Godard, whose epoch-making *À bout de souffle* [released as *Breathless*] (1960) has been hailed as the most startling of the New Wave films, on account both of its technical innovation and its accurate dramatization of the frustrations, hostility, and sense of foreboding of the French youth of the day.[15] Indeed, for Benjamin Stora, the film is a mirror-image of the collapse of the established social order in the late 1950s, with Jean-Paul Belmondo's doomed anti-hero perceived as the screen representative of that young generation of Frenchmen condemned to serve, suffer, and even die in Algeria.[16]

If Belmondo's rebellious, chain-smoking, Bogart-inflected criminal was intended to portray the alienation of the *génération algérienne*, Bruno Forrestier, the bafflingly contradictory protagonist of Godard's second major film, *Le Petit Soldat* [The Little Soldier] (1960), epitomizes its political and emotional confusions in the face of the radical choices posed by the Algerian conflict.[17] A far more conventionally linear narrative than *À bout de souffle*—the film lacks, in particular, the celebrated and disconcerting 'jump cuts' of the earlier work—*Le Petit Soldat* was shot on location in Switzerland in 1959. The action centres on the highly implausible adventures of a deserter and self-declared *emmerdeur* [trouble-maker], who becomes caught up in the secret terrorist war being fought out in Geneva by the FLN and the forerunners of the OAS. Having been obliged to assassinate an FLN sympathizer, Bruno is himself captured and tortured by the Algerian nationalists, before escaping and only then converting to their cause. His lover, Véronica, will herself be murdered by right-wing terrorists for her pro-FLN

[13] *The Cinema in France: After the New Wave* (Macmillan/British Film Institute, 1992), 3.

[14] See Williams, *Republic of Images*, 327–53.

[15] See W. Wolf, *Landmark Films: The Cinema and Our Century* (New York, Paddington Press, 1979), 248–57.

[16] Stora, *La Gangrène et l'oubli*, 40.

[17] Michel Marie draws attention to the protagonist's expressed wish, which he shares with other Godard characters, to 'hide his soul': '"It really makes you sick!": Jean-Luc Godard's *À bout de souffle* (1959)', in S. Hayward and G. Vincendeau (eds.), *French Film: Texts and Contexts* (Routledge, 1990), 208.

sympathies, leaving the protagonist existentially alone as the film closes. Though far from favourable to the FLN in its detailed depiction of the nationalists' use of torture, the film said enough about the French role in the Algerian conflict to be banned until 1963;[18] an outcome which was not only to reinforce mainstream film producers in their determination to avoid provoking the new Gaullist state, but also to postpone the Algerian activity of even the New Wave directors. Meanwhile, the fact that the film's brand of amoral political activism should have been violently denounced by the Left when it did finally appear on French screens is indicative of precisely that ideological fragmentation of cinema audiences identified by Jeancolas.

It is Bruno, the confused deserter, who claims that 'le cinéma, c'est vingt-quatre fois la vérité par seconde' [cinema is the truth, twenty-four times a second]. In *Le Petit Soldat*, as Stora has pointed out, that 'truth' is subjective and contradictory, the emphatically first-person account of a confused individual's incoherent attempt to make sense of the historical absurdity in which he finds himself.[19] Homodiegetic (first-person) narration of this kind is particularly well suited to the evocation of memory, the single most important problematic for both literary and cinematic commentators on the Algerian war, in that the formal imposition of a manifestly limited perspective may be used to hint at the gaps in both individual and collective recollections of historical events.[20] Indeed, it was through the variously subtle mediation of one or more character-narrators, and more specifically as imperfectly repressed memories of trauma, that the Franco-Algerian conflict would shortly and most effectively be represented by the directors of the New Wave.

As with much of the French fiction of the Algerian war, it is the painful reinsertion of the traumatized members of the *contingent* into a rapidly modernizing society which provides the focus for the majority of war-inspired films released in the period immediately following the cessation of hostilities.[21] So, for instance, such works

[18] Véronica's statement that the Algerians have an ideal to fight for, just as the French did during the Resistance to the German Occupation, and that they will win as a result, is the most obvious example of the film's oppositional politics. See Stora, *La Gangrène et l'oubli*, 38–42, on 'Le Cinéma sous la censure'.

[19] *La Gangrène et l'oubli*, 249. The highly personal nature of this properly existential quest is emphasized by the regular use of Bruno's voice-over narration.

[20] See Chatman, *Coming to Terms*, 144–5.

[21] Obvious exceptions are the adaptation of Jean Pélégri's *Les Oliviers de la justice* directed by the American James Blue (1962), and Alain Cavalier's *Le Combat dans l'île*

as *Adieu Philippine* (Jaques Rozier, 1963) and *La Belle Vie* [The Good Life] (Robert Enrico, 1963) are set in metropolitan France and evoke the war at a distance—typically, through reference to it in radio broadcasts and newspaper headlines—whilst the protagonists themselves remain stubbornly silent about what they have seen and done in Algeria. If the war itself is condemned by Rozier and Enrico, then it is, as Guibbert has noted, on the basis of very pragmatic and very personal brands of pacifism, rather than in the name of great humanitarian or political principles.[22] Echoes of these troubling memories are also to be found in films not directly inspired by events in Algeria, and most notably in Agnès Varda's celebrated exercice in the use of 'real time', *Cléo de cinq à sept* [Cléo from Five to Seven] (1962). As the eponymous heroine wanders through Paris for the two hours which must pass before she receives the results of a test for cancer, she meets and chats pleasantly with a young soldier, who has been widely interpreted as a symbol of the Algerian war's 'gangrenous' contagion of French society.[23] Even a big-budget commercial production like the technically innovative musical *Les Parapluies de Cherbourg* [released as *The Umbrellas of Cherbourg*] (1964), by Varda's husband, Jacques Demy, refers obliquely to the drama of separation prompted by compulsory military service in Algeria. However, it was Alain Resnais, the New Wave's most celebrated student of the mechanics of individual and collective memory, who was to deal with this aspect of the Algerian experience most convincingly.

Having previously fallen foul of government censorship with *Les Statues meurent aussi* [Statues Die Too] (1953), an anti-colonialist documentary about African art which he had produced in collaboration with Chris Marker, Resnais was to tread somewhat more warily when he came to deal with the Algerian question. A signatory, like François Truffaut and Marguerite Duras, of the famous 'Manifeste des 121', the intellectuals' September 1961 proclamation of the right of French youth to refuse military service in

and *L'Insoumis* (1962; 1964). Cavalier's work is more akin to that of Godard and Kané in its emphasis on the secret war being fought out in France itself by the supporters and opponents of an increasingly discredited *Algérie française*.

[22] See 'La Guerre d'Algérie', 248. Cf. Stora, *La Gangrène et l'oubli*, 41.

[23] See Jeancolas, *Le Cinéma des Français*, 137, and Ory, 'L'Algérie fait écran', 575. Attention has previously been drawn to both Gilbert Cesbron's use of the cancer image for the Algerian war (Ch. 3) and the commonplace 'gangrene' metaphor (Ch. 6). Stora's own study obviously draws attention to this latter theme in its title.

Algeria (*le droit à l'insoumission*), the director himself has suggested that his celebrated documentary treatment of the Holocaust, *Nuit et Brouillard* [released as *Night and Fog*] (1955) is to be read on one level as an allegory of the French army's activities in North Africa.[24] More obviously, *Muriel* (1963) is one of the most technically innovative and thematically ingenious films to have been inspired by the Algerian war.[25] As Alan Williams points out: 'Many critics consider *Muriel* to be Resnais's greatest film, though audiences often find it hard to follow because of its jagged, Eisensteinian editing and highly elliptical screenplay'.[26] The reasons both for the film's deliberately unpolished style and its indirect approach to its subject may be better appreciated if we now consider *Muriel*'s historical importance as the first work to lift the cinematic taboo on the French military's use of torture in Algeria.

Like French films before and since, *Muriel* undoubtedly conforms to the general pattern of metropolitan preoccupation with the troubled memory of the traumatized conscript survivors of the Algerian war. Indeed, the film epitomizes this tradition, which is as least as much literary as cinematic, and represents its most sophisticated fictional expression. To this extent, the Algerian writer Rachid Boudjedra is quite justified in describing the film as one which has nothing to do with Algeria as such, and everything to do with the French perception of Algeria as an imperfectly repressed memory.[27] The point, however, is that the film should not be dismissed in consequence, for it casts a particularly revealing light on the radical incommunicability of the 'Algerian experience', as previously noted by directors like Rozier and Enrico, and even earlier by writers like Vladimir Pozner. That it should have done so in 1963 and should continue to do so today is a result of its exceptionally productive juxtaposition of the individual and collective will to forgetfulness

[24] Williams, *Republic of Images*, 369: 'When, almost three decades after its release, Charles Krantz asked Resnais about the film's political intent, the director replied, "The whole point was Algeria" . . . '. If this was, indeed, the case, then Resnais's opposition to the Algerian conflict began remarkably early on.

[25] Resnais's alternative title for the film—*le temps d'un retour*—is peculiarly difficult to render in a single phrase, suggesting, as it does, both the duration of the return and the (appropriate? inappropriate?) moment at which it occurs, together with the idea of an about-turn or (physical? mental?) turn-around.

[26] Williams, *Republic of Images*, 372. Jill Forbes has quite rightly pointed out that Resnais's oblique and elliptical approach to the Algerian war was a response to the still oppressive censorship in operation at this time: *The Cinema in France*, 14.

[27] *Naissance du cinéma algérien* (Maspero, 1971), 27. Cited by Stora, *La Gangrène et l'oubli*, 41.

as regards events in Algeria, with its characters' and the French nation's obsessive remembering of the Second World War: by hinting at convenient omissions in the memory of that earlier devastation, it serves to emphasize, if not quite to define, the officially encouraged silence surrounding recent events on the other side of the Mediterranean.

With a screenplay by Jean Cayrol, a writer essentially preoccupied by the memory of the Second World War,[28] *Muriel* is set in Boulogne, and combines the tale of a wartime lover's return with that of an *appelé* just back from Algeria: an approach which serves to illuminate both of these historical traumas. Early on, the film presents a series of rapidly juxtaposed images of the Channel port to evoke both its suffering between 1940 and 1944, and its post-war reconstruction: stark high-rise buildings and modern shops thus alternate with shots of street signs commemorating the Occupation and especially the local Resistance to it. There are regular references to the cold, the rain, and the sea, and a general impression is created of being, as one character puts it, 'au bout du monde' [at the end of the world]. For we are at the northern extremity of the French empire—almost in sight of the boreal pole of the colonial Dunkirk-Tamanrasset axis[29]—and if there are no equivalent public memorials to the Algerian war to be found here, ample evidence will at least be provided of its durable grip on individual imaginations.

From the outset, the New Wave's characteristic 'fascination with the details and small rituals of everyday life: lighting cigarettes, shopping, conversing in cafés, walking in the street' is given a narrative significance—and, ultimately, a political one—by the intrusive use of suspenseful, and even intimidating, music.[30] This impression of hidden meanings is intensified both technically, through the use of discontinuous cuts and disconcerting compressions of time, and thematically. The awkward silences of Bernard, the returned conscript, are just the most obvious indication of a world where little is as it first seems: Bernard is not Hélène's real son; Alphonse (her wartime lover) is not, as he claims to be, the uncle of Françoise, the young actress whom he has brought with

[28] See e.g. *Je vivrai l'amour des autres* (Seuil, 1947).

[29] This dimension of the setting has been remarked upon by Ory, 'L'Algérie fait écran', 575. A similar use of Brittany has been noted in the conscript literature of the Algerian war (see Ch. 5, n. 24), and is also a feature of Pierre Schoendoerffer's film *Le Crabe-Tambour* (1977).

[30] Williams, *Republic of Images*, 338. See Forbes, *The Cinema in France*, 97, on Resnais's use of music as both a structuring and narrative element in his work.

him; Hélène is a secret gambler; and above all, there is the mystery of 'Muriel', the conscript protagonist's 'fiancée', who is often referred to, but never seen. By the same token, Bernard refers to his Algerian experiences with considerable reticence, and only when directly questioned, as here by Françoise:

FRANÇOISE. Vous n'avez pas l'air de beaucoup vous amuser. Qu'est-ce que vous faites?
BERNARD. Je vous l'ai déjà dit. Je reviens d'Algérie.
FRANÇOISE. Qu'est-ce que vous avez fait là-bas?
BERNARD. Comme tout le monde.
FRANÇOISE. C'est tout? Et maintenant?
BERNARD. Je rentre.

FRANÇOISE. You don't seem to have much fun. What do you do?
BERNARD. I've already told you. I've just come back from Algeria.
FRANÇOISE. What did you do over there?
BERNARD. The same as everyone else.
FRANÇOISE. Is that all? What about now?
BERNARD. I'm back.

In fact, the verb *rentrer* is ambiguous, and can be understood not only intransitively, in the obvious senses of returning and picking up the normal routine, but also transitively, to suggest the interiorization of the conscript's painful recent experiences. The specific Algerian memories which he vainly seeks to repress are those of the torture and murder of a woman in Algeria: the mysterious 'Muriel', which we learn is not her real name, and which seems to refer more to the whole episode than to its victim. Significantly, the narrative will make the self-conscious reference to the actual process of narration a feature of its construction of this historically specific meaning, with Bernard's own efforts as a film-maker performing the same kind of self-referential function that photography—and Bruno's celebrated comment on cinematic 'truth'—had done in *Le Petit Soldat*. The revelation of the nature of Bernard's Algerian crimes—which he committed, to pick up his own expression, 'comme tout le monde'—will thus be inextricably bound up with a characteristically modernist reflection on the generation of fictional meaning itself. Moreover, the narrative will ultimately resort to an ingenious combination of properly literary and documentary strategies to convey its vision of the Algerian conflict.

In fact, it is in two particularly dense narrative sequences that the true story of Muriel unfolds. In the first of these, Alphonse, rudely searching through his host's apartment in her absence, discovers an old exercise book concealed in Bernard's room. This symbol of childhood is revealed, much as in Vladimir Pozner's short story 'Les Étangs de Fontargente', to be the traumatized conscript's attempt to write his way out of his Algerian predicament. The viewer of the film is encouraged to participate in this intrusion on private grief, sharing the perspective of the uninvited reader, as Alphonse flicks nonchalantly through Bernard's searing memories. We are thus offered tantalizing fragments from the Muriel episode—references are made to a ditch, a tarpaulin, Muriel's closed eyes, Bernard's wish to be dead (a theme reinforced by an old holiday photograph of the young man, in which his face has been completely blacked out)—and are invited to construct a coherent explanation for these inadequate snapshots of France's latest, and officially denied, war.

This 'literary' sequence is part of a knowing exploitation of the cinematic medium's unique richness of signification. So, having established Bernard as a secret and shameful writer, the narration points to its own lack of innocence by depicting him in turn as a consumer and a producer of film. In the second of the two crucial sequences, film's two-track capacity[31] is skilfully exploited to combine apparently disparate images and auditory elements into an interpretative whole which is only gradually revealed. With a home movie of military service in Algeria completely filling the narrative's visual space, Bernard's confession of his role in the torture and murder of Muriel is made in a monotonous and apparently preoccupied voice-over. As the camera pulls back from the screen, we realize that Bernard too is concentrating on the flickering images. Subsequent scenes will concentrate on the fracturing of the protagonist's personality and on the inadequacies of the cinematic representation of history; we see him, for instance, in close-up through a kaleidoscope, whilst a freeze-frame of Algerian women melts into non-existence as Hélène, another trespasser on Bernard's memories, turns on the lamp of his projector without running the film.[32]

As for the documentary which he himself is seen working on, this is revealed to be an accumulation of evidence against Robert, a fellow veteran who is, moreover, also implicated in the suffering and death of 'Muriel'. Although Bernard will eventually kill Robert, it is the latter's statement of his belief in his impunity

[31] See Chatman, *Coming to Terms*, 135–6.

[32] On this aspect of the film, see esp. C. Britton, 'Broken Images in Resnais's *Muriel*', *French Cultural Studies*, 1/1, 1 (Feb. 1990), 37–46.

which is worthy of particular note. Having confronted Bernard about his filming, he explains his reasoning against the backdrop of a busy street-scene:

> Tu veux raconter Muriel. Mais Muriel ne se raconte pas. . . . Chaque Français se sent seul. Il crève de peur. Il mettra lui-même des barbelés autour de sa petite personne. Il n'aime pas les histoires.

> You want to talk about Muriel. But Muriel's story can't be told. . . . Every Frenchman feels alone. He's frightened to death. He'll put the barbed wire up around his little world all by himself. He doesn't like trouble.

It is not so much *les histoires* that the frenetically modernizing France of *Muriel* is afraid of, as *l'histoire*, *tout court*, be it the history of the Algerian conflict or that of the Occupation. As we shall see, Bernard's attempt to capture the essence of a profoundly foreign experience through a resolutely domestic documentary points the way forward to the ultimate cinematic breaking of the taboos on these very different French experiences of war.

Alain Resnais's sophisticated use of the quasi-obligatory reference to the Second World War may usefully be contrasted with the mechanical and reductive variations on this theme to be found in those leftist treatments of the Algerian conflict which were produced in the early 1970s. For the intervening period, 1964–70, is remarkable primarily for the impact of foreign films about the Algerian war, such as Robson's *Lost Command* (1966) and, above all, the Italian Gillo Pontecorvo's *La Bataille d'Alger* [released as *The Battle of Algiers* and *La Battaglia di Algeri*, 1965]. For the first time, the war in Algeria became the subject proper of major features, and whilst Robson's exercise in Hollywoodian heroics was not perceived as a threat to the French national memory and was consequently widely distributed, Pontecorvo's masterful handling of the paratroopers' 1957 campaign against the FLN's Algiers bomb networks was not granted certification until 1970. Awarded the prestigious 'Golden Lion' at the 1966 Venice film festival—which the French delegation walked out of in protest—the film met with considerable hostility from groups of *anciens combattants* and repatriated *pieds-noirs* when it did eventually reach a few French screens, with a number of violent incidents being recorded. A scrupulously researched film, made on location in Algiers with the approval of the newly independent state and the participation of a number of high-ranking veterans of the liberation struggle, *La Bataille d'Alger* is characterized by a quasi-documentary style which makes extensive use of voice-overs of official communiqués from both sides in the conflict. The remarkable political balance of this intense celebration of cinematic realism is such that the *para* colonel Matthieu is sympathetically depicted as a rational military technician rather than a demonic sadist, while the film presents not only a series of shocking images of torture, but also close-ups of carefree youngsters and a child eating ice-cream as the FLN's bombers, the undoubted heroes of the film, place their bombs in the 'Milk Bar' and the 'Ottomatic'. Yet this startling representation of *la sale guerre* would not be seen in France until the end of the decade, and by then new and more urgent conflicts would preoccupy French film-makers.

It is no doubt symptomatic of the considerable time-lag afflicting the French collective memory of its wars of decolonization that one of the few domestic references to the Algerian war to have been made in this period should have occurred at the close of Pierre Schoendoerffer's *La 317^e^ Section* [The 317th Platoon] (1965), a film which deals in a remarkably convincing fashion with the French defeat at Dien Bien Phu in 1954.[33] That relative rarity of the period, an avowedly right-wing French director, Schoendoerffer would take up the cudgels for the professional soldier, as confirmed leftists like René Vautier and militant ex-conscripts like Yves Boisset returned to the Algerian war of the *contingent* in the wake of 1968, and its radical questioning of French society's values and structures.

What Vautier's *Avoir vingt ans dans les Aurès* [To Be Twenty Years Old in the Aurès] (1972) shares with Boisset's *RAS* [*rien à signaler*, or 'nothing to report', in contemporary military jargon] (1973) is third-person narration, an authentic North African location, and a desire, in response to the prodding of Pontecorvo and even Robson, to show for the first time the 'dirty' war fought by French conscripts in Algeria. What the two films also share, however, is an all-too-obvious desire to make up for lost time, which is reflected in a bludgeoning emphasis on the horrors of the war and the impossibility of avoiding contamination once exposed to its brutal and brutalizing logic: we thus see a succession of images of torture, rape, murder, and the destruction of Algerian villages; all of which is aurally reinforced in Vautier's film with a string of anti-war dirges.

[33] Filmed in Laos, very near the actual site of the battle, where Schoendoerffer, a former army cameraman, had himself been taken prisoner, this film has claims to be ranked with the best American cinema of the Vietnam war, and is certainly far superior to *Dien Bien Phu* (1992), the director's own big-budget return to the theme.

As Jean-Pierre Jeancolas has shrewdly observed, it is at least as much the presence of these images in the cultural landscape of 1972–73 as their absence in 1956 and 1962 which is historically significant.[34] For the early 1970s saw the release, in turn, of Michel Drach's Cannes-premièred film version of Claire Etcherelli's successful *Élise ou la vraie vie* [Élise or Real Life] (1970), Marcel Ophuls's epoch-making reassessment of the Occupation period, *Le Chagrin et la Pitié* [released as *The Sorrow and the Pity*] (1971), and *Français, si vous saviez* [Frenchmen, if (only) you knew] (1972), a 'new documentary' by André Harris and Alain de Sédouy which sought, above all, to explode the myth of de Gaulle, including his role in the Algerian war.[35] Against this backdrop, which includes the new interest in political thrillers in the wake of the enormous success of Costa-Gavras's *Z* (1969), both Vautier's and Boisset's militantly left-wing films are seen to be part of a much deeper re-evaluation of French society: a process of questioning, indeed, which went far beyond their outmoded political certainties. In particular, the two films' heavy-handed equation of the behaviour of the French forces in Algeria with the actions of the Nazis during the Occupation is in complete contrast to the genuine attempts made, in their different ways, by Drach, Ophuls, and Harris and Sédouy, to understand the nature of past sins and abiding guilts. For, whether they desert with their prisoners, as in Vautier's work,[36] or kill their superiors and then commit suicide as in Boisset's film, the congenitally anti-militaristic French youths who are tricked or coerced into fighting for the colonial cause by their uniformly brutal and fascistic superiors, are, in fact, the ideological mirror-images of the noble defenders of *Algérie française* to be found in such right-wing ripostes as René Gainville's *Le Complot* [The Plot] (1973) and Pierre Schoendoerffer's *Le Crabe-Tambour* [The Drum-Crab] (1977).

Whereas Gainville's apology for the OAS may be straightforwardly situated within the conflictual problematic of the early 1970s, the altogether more self-assured reaffirmation of activist

[34] *Le Cinéma des Français*, 200–1.

[35] See Forbes, *The Cinema in France*, 33–8 on the phenomenon of the 'new documentary', and compare Wolf, *Landmark Films*, 338–49. Also worthy of note is Chris Marker's *Le Joli Mai* (1963), an exercise in *cinéma-vérité* which includes the Algerian war amongst the multitude of questions raised with Parisian passers-by in May 1962.

[36] It is not the least of the ironies of the French cinema of the Algerian war that the part of 'Nono', transparently based on Noël Favrelière's *Le Désert à l'aube* (Minuit, 1960), should have been played by Alexandre Arcady, who as a director was to go on to produce a string of films devoted to *pied-noir* nostalgia.

military values in Schoendoerffer's film may be understood as the first stage in a cinematic dedramatization of the Algerian conflict.[37] In this film, and in those less consciously oppositional films which followed it, the war becomes a setting, rather than a subject: an ideologically charged backdrop to the exploration of more universal themes, or a modern metaphor for tragic destiny, as Pascal Ory puts it.[38] More specifically, the preoccupation with the young individual in search of an identity—a theme which had previously become something of a cliché with the New Wave—made its Algerian reappearance. This figure is as much to the fore, for instance, in Alexandre Arcady's version of Daniel Saint-Hamont's *Le Coup de sirocco* [The Sirocco's Blast] (1978), as it is in Jacques Davila's *Certaines Nouvelles* [Certain News] (1979), and Pascal Kané's *Liberty Belle* (1983). Whether it be Arcady's amused adolescent's view of the *pied-noir* 'exodus', Davila's juxtaposition of beach parties and OAS bombs, or Kané's reworking of the figure of the secret war, fought out this time by students and teachers on the Parisian 'home front', the pattern is the same: Algeria serves as a decor for the exploration of broader, and less obviously historical, themes.

Against this background, Gérard Mordillat's *Cher Frangin* [Dear Brother] (1989) is revealed to be something of a throwback to the discredited Manichaeanism of Vautier and Boisset in its tale of the familiar anti-war radical's opposition to the war, disciplinary incorporation into a combat unit, experience of *la sale guerre*, desertion, and aid to the FLN in Tunisia.[39] In complete contrast, *La Guerre sans nom* [The War Without a Name] (1992), a documentary filmed by Bertrand Tavernier on the basis of interviews conducted by Patrick Rotman, makes what is probably the definitive cinematic statement of the conscript's experience of the Algerian war.[40] Although this film has been widely compared with *Le Chagrin et la*

[37] Schoendoerffer's 1982 courtroom drama on the French military's use of torture in Algeria, *L'Honneur d'un capitaine*, is in a similar ideological mould.

[38] 'L'Algérie fait écran', 579.

[39] The film's juxtaposition of official media images of the war and accounts taken from the conscripts' contemporaneous correspondence does, however, resemble that used to good effect in recent television documentaries such as *Lettres d'Algérie*. This programme in the 'Envoyé spécial' series formed the basis for Martine Lemalet's *Lettres d'Algérie, 1954–1962: la guerre des appelés, la mémoire d'une génération* (Jean-Claude Lattès, 1992).

[40] The film is 'completed' by an accompanying book: P. Rotman and B. Tavernier, *La Guerre sans nom: les appelés d'Algérie, 1954–1962* (Seuil, 1992). Tavernier was also involved in the production of Laurent Heynemann's 1976 screen version of Henri Alleg's *La Question*.

Pitié, with the focus on the Grenoble region providing the same kind of locational unity that Clermont-Ferrand does in Marcel Ophuls's celebrated study, Tavernier himself has, quite rightly, been at pains to emphasize the differences between the two films, and particularly the relative simplicity of his own work.[41] For not only did Ophuls free French documentary from the traditional format of an authoritative voice-over interpretation of coherently presented, and essentially illustrative, archive footage, replacing it with a complex interview-based juxtaposition of frequently contradictory information and opinions, but he thereby 'restored the image to a position of supremacy'.[42] This cannot, in truth, be said of Tavernier's work, which, although both fascinating and moving in its resolute determination to let a cross-section of *appelés* speak for themselves, is, with some important exceptions, dominated by the auditory channel.

Nevertheless, it is important to recognize the real efforts which Rotman and Tavernier make to let their conscript witnesses share in the discourse of the film. Tavernier himself explains in an introductory voice-over that a conscious decision was made not to include archive material in the documentary, and the accompanying images are thus restricted to shots of the speakers themselves, stills of their private photographs and sketches, and the occasional image of a wintry Isère and a pointedly similar Djurdjura. Speaking, in many cases, for the first time about their Algerian war(s), the thirty veterans are drawn from all walks of life and are of all political persuasions. Their experiences of the Algerian war take in the whole period 1954–62; they cover the European cities and the Algerian hinterland, its mountains, plains, and electrified frontiers; they range from conscientious objection to combat with the *paras*, taking in 'pacification' with the SAS, 'self-defence' with the *harkis*, and the provision of specialized medical care; they describe their diverse experiences of fear, boredom, brutality, and death; they record their suffering, their sense of loss, and their shame, together with their amusements, their friendships, and even their adventures.

The generally sympathetic close-ups of the veterans' talking heads undoubtedly develop a genuine communicative intensity on those not infrequent occasions when their answers to Rotman's

[41] See e.g. the interview with Michel Pascal and Alain-Gérard Slama, '"Ils y ont laissé une part de leur jeunesse"', *Le Point*, 22 Feb. 1992, 58–9.

[42] Forbes, *The Cinema in France*, 36.

probing questions dry up. The resulting silences, head-shaking, tears, requested and actual cuts serve to underline the intensity of the lived experience and its psychological after-effects in a fashion which does, indeed, invite comparison with the work of Marcel Ophuls. Whether prompted by the failure to take a stand against the war, the recollection of torture, the proximity of death, the loss of a limb, or impotent outrage at the fate of the *pieds-noirs* or the *harkis*, it is this—literally spectacular—release of long-denied emotions by solid, and even superficially stolid, pillars of French society which is the key to the exceptional dramatic intensity of Tavernier's film.

By allowing the gradual and cumulative expression of the sheer variety of the veterans' disparate experiences, the film undoubtedly reveals a war which, in its mundaneness just as in its extreme situations, was clearly every bit as 'real' as those commemorated by so many earlier French films. That it is able to do so—and in this it does bear an uncanny resemblance to *Le Chagrin et la Pitié*—only after an interval of three decades is as much an indication of the failure of cinematic fictions as it is of loudly proclaimed ideological convictions. It only remains to be hoped that in an age dominated by an all-consuming television, this insightful production will not itself be recuperated as just one more edition of 'Le Débat de l'Écran'.[43]

[43] For Guibbert, 'La Guerre d'Algérie', 250–1, it is precisely the notion that a 'good' film about the Algerian war should be able to serve as the pretext for a television debate that accounts for what he sees as a paralyzing cinematic cult of realism. Cf. Stora, *La Gangrène et l'oubli*, 248, 255, on the absence of televison images of the conflict in the 1970s and 1980s. Stora himself has attempted to fill this cultural gap as one of the co-producers of the first French television history of the Algerian war, A2's four-part series *Les Années algériennes* (1992).

CONCLUSION

The foregoing discussion will, I hope, have given some indication of the historical importance and the critical interest of the Algerian theme—or, more accurately, the Algerian thematic—in contemporary French fiction and film. By way of a conclusion, I should, perhaps, make it plain that my own attempt partially to remedy the chronic neglect of this extensive corpus of literary texts and feature films may itself reflect, and even encourage, a perceptual imbalance. Let me therefore stress my consciousness of the need not to overestimate the cultural significance of this body of narratives; for I should certainly not wish to claim that the Algerian war has at any stage come close to dominating French writing and cinema, despite the mass of material which most definitely exists, and which the present book has sought to introduce to a wider audience.

For there is really nothing in the French artistic experience that could be said to equal the virtually total preoccupation with the 1954–62 conflict on the part of Algerian producers of fiction and film, whether of Arabic, Berber, or French expression. As Christiane Achour has recently pointed out, the grip exerted by the 'Revolution' on the Algerian artistic imagination has been such that the war of national liberation is present, either as the principal theme or as the backdrop, in virtually every work produced since 1954.[1] This state-encouraged, and even state-sponsored, collective obsession may have resulted, in many cases, in a brand of socialist realism *à l'algérienne*, but has also given rise to the remarkable literary and linguistic innovation of at least two generations of Algerian artists as they atempt to construct an authentically national identity and

[1] 'La Guerre de libération nationale dans les fictions algériennes', in the collective *Trente ans après: nouvelles de la guerre d'Algérie* (Le Monde-Éditions/Nouvelles-Nouvelles, 1992), 145: 'La guerre de libération nationale est au cœur de la littérature nationale, comme thématique dominante, comme toile de fond ou comme réminiscence: présence à la mesure de l'événement lui-même. La prendre en charge dans toutes les œuvres où elle apparaît serait prendre en compte la quasi-totalité de la littérature depuis 1954.'

history. The now classic works of Kateb Yacine, Mohammed Dib, and Assia Djebar have thus been followed by the writings of such talented representatives of a younger literary generation as Rabah Belamri, Rachid Boudjedra, and Yamina Mechakra. (Perhaps inevitably, given the Algerian state's tight control of cinematic output, the successors to such celebrated directors as Tewfik Farès and Mohamed Lakhdar Hamina remain to be discovered). It is hardly a coincidence that the work of these, the most artistically challenging of literary producers, should also have been the most politically adventurous, questioning the FLN both in its self-appointed role of guardian of the national memory, and in its management of the independent Algeria for which so many fought and died.[2] The fact that this artistic struggle for nationhood should have been conducted in and through, as well as against, the language of the former colonial power, and, moreover, with the often crucial support of French publishing houses, is one of the abiding ironies of the Franco-Algerian relationship.

In contrast, the French literature and cinema of the Algerian war are primarily remarkable for their frequently alleged non-existence. Yet the reality of this body of discursive and performative narratives may not reasonably be denied, a fact which reflects the intensity of the private French determination to bear witness to historical events in the face of both official denials and public apathy. While the academic and journalistic commemoration, in 1992, of the thirtieth anniversary of the ending of the Algerian war undoubtedly marked the conflict's entry into the mainstream of French historiography, its definitive assimilation into the broader national consciousness is far from obvious. If the passage of time has finally allowed a collective French reassessment of a conflict which caused so much blood and so much ink to be spilled,[3] then the need for a literary and/or a cinematic replacement for the physically absent *lieux de mémoire* [places of remembrance] may eventually disappear. For the time being, however, the flow of novels and films inspired by the dark days of 1954–62 shows no sign of abating. From this point of view, *Le Monde*'s self-consciously 'balanced'—and even more self-

[2] Ibid. 149: 'Les œuvres les plus incisives . . . mettent en scène la guerre pour éclairer ou condamner l'Algérie au présent. La lutte n'a pas tenu ses promesses: elle reste un espace de réflexion et de possibles encore ouverts, si l'on veut bien prendre la peine de le réveiller.'

[3] Benjamin Stora has described this development as the granting of a national 'permission to return' to the subject of the colonies and decolonization: 'Indochine, Algérie, autorisations de retour', *Libération*, 1 May 1992, 5.

consciously 'literary'—celebration of the Évian peace agreements, 'thirty years on', is very likely to be of less significance than the apparently undiminished desire of various interested parties to have their far-from-impartial say on the Algerian question, some forty years after the *Toussaint* rising.[4]

One of the best-crafted contributions to this latest wave of French attempts to capture the Algerian 'experience' in fiction is undoubtedly Phillipe Doumenc's *Les Comptoirs du Sud* [The Southern Trading Posts], an ambitious and genuinely original work which was awarded the 1989 Prix Renaudot. Set in the highly mysterious North African trading post of 'Chella', the action of the novel is brought to a close with an intriguing image of yet one more conscript's difficult reinsertion into French society:

> Tout disparut. Dans le taxi qui roulait vers Paris, je retrouvai les lèvres tendres et soumises de Catherine. En même temps que je l'embrassai, je me disais qu'il me faudrait bien, un jour ou l'autre, tenter d'élucider ce qui, dans mon histoire, était vrai ou n'était pas vrai. Cette pensée m'occupait sans plaisir, comme celle d'une corvée inutile et au fond dangereuse dont j'espérais remettre l'exécution au plus tard possible. (408–9)

> Everything disappeared. As the taxi headed for Paris, I rediscovered Catherine's soft and willing lips. While I was kissing her, I thought to myself that I really must, sooner or later, try to find out which parts of my story were true and which were not. This thought did not fill me with any great pleasure, seeming rather like a futile and even dangerous chore that I hoped to put off doing for as long as I possibly could.

The outrageously stereotypical image of submissive femininity communicated by this variation on the theme of *le repos du guerrier* [the warrior's rest and/or homecoming] should alert us to the ironically manipulative games being played in Doumenc's investigation both of the remembrance and the forgetting of Algerian things past. For the reader has previously been made aware that the Catherine who so lovingly greets the returning protagonist-narrator has, in fact, long since deserted him. Indeed, the narrative periodically hints that her erstwhile partner may even have been killed in an accidental explosion during his military training, i.e. *before* his

[4] Among the more noteworthy of the recently published novels are the following: G. Caban, *Retour à Alger* (Denoël, 1988); M. Sportès, *Outremer* (Grasset, 1989); and O. Todd, *La Négociation* (Grasset, 1989). By far the most interesting recent film is Brigitte Rouan's *Outremer* (1990), an incisive feminist critique of both colonialism and patriarchy which focuses on the decline and fall of *Algérie française* from World War II to Algerian independence. (It should be noted that this film is quite unrelated to Morgan Sportès's novel of the same title.)

posting to Algeria. With this ingenious variation on the very familiar theme of the traumatized *appelé*, Doumenc undermines the central figure's testimony in its entirety, and thus manages to focus attention on what is arguably the key to the French failure of collective memory as regards the Algerian conflict.

For it is precisely the reluctance to engage with a turbulent colonial past which has, until very recently, and with one or two honourable exceptions, typified the response of official and academic historians to the Algerian 'experience'. In the absence of a properly consensual history, the collective memory of a war which for long did not dare to speak its name has been preserved by all those with a case to plead or an axe to grind. It is these partisan commentators, above all, who have looked to fictional narratives as a privileged means of fixing and communicating their personal or communal recollections of a peculiarly traumatic complex of events. A failure of French historiography, then, lies behind the telling of so many conflicting tales about what went on in Algeria. Hence the blurring of generic distinctions—between fiction and documentary, polemic and autobiography—as politically motivated writers and film-makers search for a generally elusive 'authenticity'.

Indeed, 'faction' is a doubly apt description for many of the literary and cinematic narratives produced in response to the Algerian war: stridently 'real' accounts of the war as it is, or was, and yet which may readily be revealed, on closer inspection, to be little more than varieties of an immutably conflictual rhetoric. Thus we see the balancing myths of the angelic and demonic paratrooper, the decadent Parisian intellectual and the liberal soul-searcher, the courageous pioneer and the greedy exploiter of the natives, the treacherous *fellagha* and the valiant *moudjahidin*. The fictive space of the Algerian war is, in very many cases, a narrow and frozen one, in which stereotypes, clichés, and euphemisms predominate: a world of prejudices where ingenious narrative strategies serve all too often to confirm the reader in his or her partisan certainties. Algeria, thus regarded, is above all a screen against which essentially domestic conflicts are endlessly replayed.

Considered in this light, the corpus is eminently to be recommended to anyone with a personal or professional interest in scratching the sore spots of our nearest neighbour. Indeed, it is very much against the background of conflicting and conflictual interpretations of the Algerian war that I have sought throughout to situate the present study. Taking as my point of departure the foreign observer's astonishment at the continued French preoccupation with a period of history which may be seen—admittedly, with the benefit both of hindsight and cultural distance—to be just one episode among many in the global process of decolonization, I have looked to the prose fiction and feature films produced in response to the 1954–62 conflict in an attempt to understand and explain the remarkable intensity of the Algerian 'experience'.

An approach of this kind necessarily implies a focus on the sociological and political aspects of texts, and a systematic selection of materials which are primarily, and sometimes exclusively, of interest from this point of view. The resulting extra-literary and extra-cinematic method of reading has been characterized as ideological, with my principal criterion of textual worth being each work's contribution to the mystification or demystification of the Algerian war. I have consequently considered a range of texts produced by French soldiers, settlers, and metropolitan commentators, concentrating throughout on the affective images which these works communicate of the writers' own interest-groups, and of the other parties to the conflict. This approach has revealed the existence of a body of discursively communicated ideological myths, an informed reading of which may, I believe, help to explain the singularity of the French experience of decolonization.

All of which may be useful from a sociological point of view, but does it amount to an experience of art? The literature and cinema of a historical failure, does the corpus itself point to a failure of these media? Almost in spite of the fact that it became the last great battle waged by the committed French artist, the Algerian war did generate a number of literary and cinematic texts which may outlast their still-immediate social relevance. I hope to have shown why I believe the 'Algerian' output of such different cultural producers as Jean-Pierre Millecam, Claire Etcherelli, Alain Resnais, and Bertrand Tavernier to be of lasting worth. However, it must be recognized that the end of empire coincided to a large extent with the decline of both literature and cinema in the face of the rise of a mass televisual culture, with the dramatic relaxation of official censorship since the Algerian war accurately reflecting the eclipse of the established media. Whether this new communicative regime will seek to address the officially defunct symbolic order of French colonialism, and if so, to what ideological ends, remains to be seen.

Bibliography

PRIMARY SOURCES

(The place of publication of all books is Paris unless otherwise stated.)

ALLEG, HENRI, *La Question* (Minuit, 1958).
——*Prisonniers de guerre* (Minuit, 1962).
ALQUIER, JEAN-YVES, *Nous avons pacifié Tazalt* (Robert Laffont, 1957).
BACRI, ROLAND, *Et alors? et oilà!* (Balland, 1971).
——*Le Beau Temps perdu: Bab-el-Oued retrouvé* (Lanzmann & Seghers, 1978).
BARDERY, JEAN-PIERRE, *La Longue Mémoire* (La Table Ronde, 1984).
BENSOUSSAN, ALBERT, *La Bréhaigne* (Denoël, 1973).
BOIS, PIERRE, *La Friche* (Denoël, 1963).
BOISSEL, PIERRE, *Les Hussards perdus* (Éditions Saint-Just, 1966).
BONHEUR, GASTON, *La Croix de ma mère* (Julliard, 1976).
BONJEAN, CLAUDE, *Lucien chez les barbares* (Calmann-Lévy, 1977).
BOURGEADE, PIERRE, *Les Serpents* (Gallimard, 1983).
BRUNE, JEAN, *Cette haine qui ressemble à l'amour* (La Table Ronde, 1961).
——*Journal d'exil, suivi d'une lettre à un maudit* (La Table Ronde, 1963).
——*La Révolte* (Robert Laffont, 1965).
——*Interdit aux chiens et aux Français* (La Table Ronde, 1967).
BUIS, GEORGES, *La Grotte* (Julliard, 1961; Seuil, 'Points', 1988).
BUISSON, VIRGINIE, *L'Algérie ou la mort des autres* (La Pensée Sauvage, 'Folio Junior', 1978).
CABAN, GÉVA, *Retour à Alger* (Denoël, 1988).
CAMUS, ALBERT, *Théâtre, récits, nouvelles* (Gallimard/NRF, 'Pléiade', 1962).
——*Essais* (Gallimard/Calmann-Lévy, 'Pléiade', 1965).
CARDINAL, MARIE, *Écoutez la mer* (Julliard, 1962).
——*Les Mots pour le dire* (Julliard, 1975).
——*Au pays de mes racines* (Grasset, 1980).
CASTANO, JOSÉ, *Les Larmes de la passion* (Robert Laffont, 1982).
CASTELBAJAC, BERTRAND DE, *La Gloire est leur métier* (Éditions Françaises et Internationales, 1958).
——*L'Officier perdu* (La Table Ronde, 1963).

CESBRON, GILBERT, *Entre chiens et loups* (Robert Laffont, 1962).
CHAREF, MEHDI, *Le Harki de Meriem* (Mercure de France, 1989).
CLAVEL, BERNARD, *Le Silence des armes* (Robert Laffont, 'J'ai Lu', 1974).
—— *Lettre à un képi blanc* (Robert Laffont, 'J'ai Lu', 1975).
CONESA, GABRIEL, *Bab-El-Oued: notre paradis perdu* (Robert Laffont, 1970).
CROUSSY, GUY, *Ceux du djebel* (Seuil, 1967).
—— *Ne pleure pas, la guerre est bonne* (Julliard, 1975).
CURUTCHET, JEAN-MARIE, *Je veux la tourmente* (Robert Laffont, 1973).
DAENINCKX, DIDIER, *Meurtres pour mémoire* (Gallimard, 'Série Noire' & 'Folio', 1984).
DELTEIL, GÉRARD, *N'oubliez pas l'artiste!* (Fleuve Noir, 1985).
DESSAIGNE, FRANCINE, *Journal d'une mère de famille pied-noir* (L'Esprit Nouveau, 1962).
DOUMENC, PHILIPPE, *Les Comptoirs du Sud* (Seuil, 'Points', 1989)
DUBOS, ALAIN, *L'Embuscade* (Presses de la Cité, 1983).
ETCHERELLI, CLAIRE, *Élise ou la vraie vie* (Denoël, 1967).
FAVRELIÈRE, NOËL, *Le Désert à l'aube* (Minuit, 1960).
—— *Le Déserteur* (Jean-Claude Lattès, 1973).
FERDI, SAÏD, *Un enfant dans la guerre* (Seuil, 1981).
FERRY, ALAIN, *El-Kous* (Seuil, 1978).
FLAMENT, MARC, *Les Hommes peints* (La Pensée Moderne, 1962).
FRANCO, GUY, *Le Jardin de Juan* (Fayard, 1976).
GENET, JEAN, *Les Paravents* (Marc Barbezat, 1961; L'Arbalète, 1976).
GRALL, XAVIER, *Africa Blues* (Calmann-Lévy, 1962; Quimper, Calligrammes, 1984).
GUEDJ, MAX, *Le 'Bar à Campora'* (Albin Michel, 1969).
GUYOTAT, PIERRE, *Tombeau pour cinq cent mille soldats* (Gallimard, 1967).
IKOR, ROGER, *Les Murmures de la guerre* (Albin Michel, 1961).
JOLY, FRANÇOIS, *L'Homme au mégot* (Gallimard, 'Série Noire', 1990).
KLOTZ, CLAUDE, *Les Appelés* (Jean-Claude Lattès, 1982).
LABRO, PHILIPPE, *Des feux mal éteints* (Gallimard, 1967).
LAGORCE, GUY, *Le Train du soir* (Grasset, 1983).
LANZMANN, JACQUES, *Les Passagers du Sidi-Brahim* (Julliard, 1958).
LARTÉGUY, JEAN, *Les Centurions* (Presses de la Cité, 'Presses Pocket', 1960).
—— *Les Prétoriens* (Presses de la Cité, 'Presses Pocket', 1961).
LE CARVENNEC, ALAIN, *La Mémoire chacale* (Hachette, 1983).
LEULLIETTE, PIERRE, *Saint Michel et le dragon: souvenirs d'un parachutiste* (Minuit, 1961).
LISCIA, RICHARD, *Le Conscrit et le Général* (La Table Ronde, 1980).
LOESCH, ANNE, *La Valise ou le cercueil* (Plon, 1963).
MARTINEZ, HENRI, *Et qu'ils m'accueillent avec des cris de haine* (Robert Laffont, 1982).
—— *Dernières nouvelles de l'enfer* (Robert Laffont, 1984).
MATTÉI, GEORGES, 'Jours kabyles', *Les Temps modernes*, July 1957.
—— *Disponibles* (Maspero, 1960).

MATTÉI, GEORGES, *La Guerre des gusses* (Balland, 1982).
'MAURIENNE' (JEAN-LOUIS HURST), *Le Déserteur* (Minuit, 1960; Manya, 1991).
MILLECAM, JEAN-PIERRE, *Sous dix couches de ténèbres* (Denoël, 1968).
—— *Et je vis un cheval pâle* (Gallimard/NRF, 1978).
—— *Un vol de chimères* (Gallimard/NRF, 1979).
—— *Une légion d'anges* (Gallimard/NRF, 1980).
—— *Choral* (Gallimard/NRF, 1982).
MOINET, BERNARD, *Ahmed? Connais pas . . .* (Lettres du Monde, 1980).
MONTAGNON, PIERRE, *Pas même un caillou* (St-Just, 1965; Pygmalion/Gérard Watelet, 1990).
MONTHERLANT, HENRY DE, *Romans et œuvres de fiction non-théâtrales* (Gallimard, 'Pléiade', 1982).
MONTUPET, JEANNE, *La Traversée de Fiora Valencourt* (Robert Laffont, 1961).
MOUSSY, MARCEL, *Arcole ou la terre promise* (La Table Ronde, 1953).
ORTUÑO, JOSÉ VICENTE, *Mort pour une chose morte* (Julliard, 'Presses Pocket', 1971).
PÉLÉGRI, JEAN, *Les Oliviers de la justice* (Gallimard, 1959).
—— *Le Maboul* (Gallimard, 1963).
PÉPIN, ROBERT, *Pavillon 114* (Flammarion, 1981).
PEREC, GEORGES, *Les Choses: une histoire des années soixante* (Julliard, 'J'ai Lu', 1965).
—— *Quel petit vélo à guidon chromé au fond de la cour?* (Denoël, 'Folio', 1966).
PERRAULT, GILLES, *Le Dossier 51* (Fayard/Delattre, 1969).
PONS, MAURICE, *Le Passager de la nuit* (Julliard, 1960).
POZNER, VLADIMIR, *Le Lieu du supplice* (Julliard, 1959).
REY, BENOIST, *Les Égorgeurs* (Minuit, 1961).
ROBLÈS, EMMANUEL, *Les Hauteurs de la ville* (Seuil, 1948; 1960).
—— *Saison violente* (Seuil, 1974).
ROCHARD, JEAN-JACQUES, *Max Skoda* (L'Esprit Nouveau, 1965).
ROSEAU, JACQUES, and FAUQUE, JEAN, *Le 13ᵉ convoi: chronique romanesque (1848–1871)* and *Le 113ᵉ été: chronique romanesque (1903–1962)* (Robert Laffont, 1987; 1991).
ROY, JULES, *La Guerre d'Algérie* (Julliard, 1960).
—— *Autour du drame* (Julliard, 1961).
—— *La Bataille de Dien Bien Phu* (Julliard, 1963).
—— *Les Chevaux du soleil* (Grasset, 1967).
—— *Une femme au nom d'étoile* (Grasset, 1968).
—— *Les Cerises d'Icherridène* (Grasset, 1969).
—— *Les Maîtres de la Mitidja* (Grasset, 1970).
—— *Les Âmes interdites* (Grasset, 1972).
—— *Le Tonnerre et les anges* (Grasset, 1975).
—— *Mémoires barbares* (Albin Michel, 1989).

SAINT-HAMONT, DANIEL, *Le Bourricot* (Fayard, 1974; 1982).
——*Le Coup de sirocco* (Fayard, 1978).
——*La Valise à l'eau ou le voyage en Alger* (Fayard, 1981).
SAINT-LAURENT, CÉCIL, *L'Algérie quand on y est* (Le Livre Contemporain, 1958).
——*Les Passagers pour Alger, i: Les Bons Motifs; ii: Le Moment venu* (Presses de la Cité, 'Presses Pocket', 1960).
——*Les Agités d'Alger, i: 'Quand pars-tu?'; ii: Promesses perdues* (Presses de la Cité, 'Presses Pocket', 1961).
SARTRE, JEAN-PAUL, *Les Séquestrés d'Altona* (Gallimard, 1960).
SCHOENDOERFFER, PIERRE, *La 317e section* (La Table Ronde, 'Folio', 1963; 1973).
——(1976) *Le Crabe-Tambour* (Grasset, 1976).
SERVAN-SCHREIBER, JEAN-JACQUES, *Lieutenant en Algérie* (Julliard, 1957).
SIMON, PIERRE-HENRI, *Portrait d'un officier* (Seuil, 1958).
SPORTÈS, MORGAN, *Outremer* (Grasset, 1989).
STIL, ANDRÉ, *Trois pas dans une guerre* (Grasset, 1978).
SUSINI, MICHELINE, *De soleil et de larmes* (Robert Laffont, 1982).
SUTRA, JOSETTE, *Algérie mon amour: L'histoire d'une institutrice pied-noir* (*Constantine 1920–1962*) (Atlanthrope, 1979).
SYREIGEOL, JACQUES, *Une mort dans le djebel* (Gallimard, 'Série Noire', 1990).
TODD, OLIVIER, *La Négociation* (Grasset, 1989).
[collective] *Trente ans après: nouvelles de la guerre d'Algérie* (Le Monde Éditions/Nouvelles-Nouvelles, 1992).
VALMAIN, FRÉDÉRIC, *Les Chacals* (Fayard, 1960).
VENAILLE, FRANCK, *La Guerre d'Algérie* (Minuit, 1978).
VIDAL, GUY, and BIGNON, ALAIN, *Une éducation algérienne* (Dargaud, 1982).
VIRCONDELET, ALAIN, *Maman la Blanche* (Albin Michel, 1981).
——*Alger l'amour* (Presses de la Renaissance, 1982).
VOLKOFF, VLADIMIR, *Le Retournement* (Julliard/L'Âge d'Homme, 1979).
——*La Leçon d'anatomie* (Julliard/L'Âge d'Homme, 1980).
YVANE, JEAN, *L'Arme au bleu* (Grasset, 1978).
ZIMMERMANN, DANIEL, *80 exercices en zone interdite* (Robert Morel, 1961).
——*Nouvelles de la zone interdite* (L'Instant, 1988; Manya, 1992).

SECONDARY SOURCES

(The place of publication of all books is Paris unless otherwise stated. PUF = Presses Universitaires Françaises. The Conseil National de la Recherche Scientifique is referred to throughout as CNRS; the *Nouvelle Revue Française* is similarly abbreviated to NRF.)

ACHOUR, CHRISTIANE, *Dictionnaire des œuvres algériennes en langue française* (L'Harmattan, 1991).

——'La Guerre de libération nationale dans les fictions algériennes', in the collective *Trente ans après* (see above), 145–68.

Adereth, Maxwell, *Commitment in Modern French Literature* (London, Gollancz, 1967).

Ageron, Charles-Robert, *Histoire de l'Algérie contemporaine, 1830–1970* (PUF, 1964; 6th edn. 1977).

——*L'Anticolonialisme en France de 1871 à 1914* (PUF, 1973).

——'L'Opinion française devant la guerre d'Algérie', *Revue de la France d'Outre-Mer*, Apr.–June 1974, 259–85.

——*France coloniale ou parti colonial?* (PUF, 1978).

——*Histoire de l'Algérie contemporaine, ii: De l'insurrection de 1871 au déclenchement de la guerre de libération (1954)* (PUF, 1979).

——'L'Exposition coloniale de 1931: mythe républicain ou mythe impérial?', in Nora, *Les Lieux de mémoire*, 561–91.

——(ed.) *Les Chemins de la décolonisation de l'empire colonial français (1936–1956)* (CNRS, 1986).

——*La Décolonisation française* (Armand Colin, 1991).

Albouy, Pierre, *Mythes et mythologies dans la littérature française* (Armand Colin, 1969).

——'Quelques gloses sur la notion de mythe littéraire', *Revue d'histoire littéraire de la France*, 5–6 (Sept.–Dec. 1970), 1059–63.

Alleg, Henri (ed.), *La Guerre d'Algérie* (3 vols., Temps Actuels, 1981).

Alliot, Bernard, 'Avoir vingt ans dans les djebels', *Le Monde*, 4 June 1982, 19.

Althusser, Louis, 'Idéologie et appareils idéologiques d'État', *La Pensée*, 151 (May–June 1970).

Ambler, John, *The French Army in Politics, 1945–1962* (Columbus, Ohio State University Press, 1965).

——*Soldiers against the State* (New York, Anchor, 1968).

Andrews, William G., *French Politics and Algeria: The Process of Policy Formation, 1954–1962* (New York, Meredith, 1962).

Armanet, François, and Armanet, Max, 'La Guerre d'Algérie: 30 ans après', *Le Nouvel Observateur* (Collection Dossiers, 9, 1992).

Aron, Robert, *Les Origines de la guerre d'Algérie* (Fayard, 1962).

Astier-Loutfi, Martine, *Littérature et colonialisme: l'expansion coloniale vue dans la littérature romanesque française, 1871–1914* (Mouton, 1971).

Audisio, Gabriel, *Jeunesse de la Méditerranée* (Gallimard, 1935).

——*Le Sel de la mer* (Gallimard, 1936).

——*Feux vivants* (Limoges, Rougerie, 1957).

——*L'Opéra fabuleux* (Julliard, 1970).

——[*ed.*]*Cagayous de Musette* (Balland, 1972).

August, Thomas G., *The Selling of the Empire: British and French Imperialist Propaganda, 1890–1940* (Westport, Conn., Greenwood Press, 1985).

Auvray, Michel, *Objecteurs, insoumis, déserteurs: une histoire des réfractaires en France* (Stock, 1983).

AYOUN, MONIQUE, and STORA, JEAN-PIERRE, *Mon Algérie: 62 personnalités témoignent* (Acropole, 1989).

AZOULAY, PAUL, *La Nostalgérie française* (Baschet, 1980).

BACRI, ROLAND, 'Le Pataouète', in Elia, 89–96.

—— *Trésors des racines pataouètes* (Belin, 1983).

BARKER, FRANCIS *et al.*, *Europe and its Others* (2 vols.) (Colchester, University of Essex, 1985).

BARTHES, ROLAND, *Le Degré zéro de la littérature* (Seuil, 1953).

—— *Mythologies* (Seuil, 1957).

—— *S/Z* (Seuil, 1970).

BATTY, PETER, *La Guerre d'Algérie* (Barrault, 1989).

BEAUVOIR, SIMONE DE, *La Force des choses* (Gallimard, 1963).

BÉDARIDA, FRANÇOIS, and FOUILLOUX, ÉTIENNE (eds.), *La Guerre d'Algérie et les chrétiens* (*Les Cahiers de l'Institut d'Histoire du Temps Présent*, 9, Oct. 1988).

BELAMRI, RABAH, *L'Œuvre de Louis Bertrand: miroir de l'idéologie colonialiste* (Algiers, Office des Publications Universitaires, 1980).

BELHADJ, A. *et al.*, *La Gangrène* (Minuit, 1969).

BELSEY, CATHERINE, *Critical Practice* (London, Methuen, 1980).

BERGOT, ERWAN, *Les Paras* (Balland, 1971).

—— *La Guerre des appelés en Algérie, 1956–1962* (Presses de la Cité, 1980).

BERQUE, JACQUES, *Le Maghreb entre deux guerres* (Seuil, 1962).

BERTRAND, LOUIS, *Le Sang des races* (Paris, Ollendorf, 1899).

BETTS, RAYMOND, *Assimilation and Association in French Colonial Theory, 1890–1914* (New York, Columbia University Press, 1961).

—— 'The Sources of French Imperialist Ideology Before World War I', *Proceedings of the Fourth Meeting of the French Colonial Historical Society* (Washington, DC, University Press of America, 1978), 165–73.

—— *France and Decolonisation, 1900–1960* (London, Macmillan, 1985).

BIDDISS, MICHAEL D., *Father of Racist Ideology: The Social and Political Thought of Count Gobineau* (London, Weidenfeld & Nicolson, 1970).

BIRCHALL, IAN H., 'Imperialism and Class: The French War in Algeria', in Barker *et al.*, ii. 162–74.

BOISDEFFRE, PIERRE DE, 'Le Phénomène Volkoff', *La Nouvelle Revue des deux mondes*, 7 (July 1980), 162–71.

BOLLARDIÈRE, JACQUES PARIS DE, *Bataille d'Alger, bataille de l'homme* (Desclée de Brouwer, 1972).

BOSQUET, ALAIN, 'Jules Roy, de Bugeaud à Bigeard', *La Nouvelle Revue Française*, 271 (July 1975), 93–5.

BOUDJEDRA, RACHID, *Naissance du cinéma algérien* (Maspero, 1971).

BOURDIEU, PIERRE, *Sociologie de l'Algérie* (PUF, 1958; 7th edn. 1985).

—— 'Guerre et mutation sociale en Algérie', *Études méditerranéennes*, 7 (Spring 1960), 25–37.

BOUSQUET, FRANÇOIS, *Camus le méditerranéen; Camus l'ancien* (Sherbrooke, Quebec, Naaman, 1977).

BRETON, MICHEL, and GÉRARD, JEAN-LOUIS, 'La Guerre d'Algérie au miroir de la fiction française', in the collective, *Trente ans après: nouvelles de la guerre d'Algérie* (Le Monde Éditions/Nouvelles-Nouvelles, 1992), 169–89.

BRITTON, CELIA, 'Broken images in Resnais's *Muriel*', *French Cultural Studies*, 1/1, 1 (Feb. 1990), 37–46.

BROSMAN, CATHERINE S., 'Sartre, the Algerian War, and *Les Séquestrés d'Altona*', *Papers in Romance*, 3/2 (Spring 1981), 81–9.

—— 'Les frères ennemis: Jules Roy et l'Algérie', *French Review*, 56/3–6 (1982–3), 579–87.

BRUA, EDMOND, *La Parodie du Cid* (Algiers, Heintz, 1941).

BRUCKNER, PASCAL, *Le Sanglot de l'homme blanc: tiers monde, culpabilité, haine de soi* (Seuil, 1983).

BRULLER, JACQUELINE, *Vladimir Volkoff: 'L'exil est ma patrie'* (Le Centurion, 1982).

BRUNSCHWIG, HENRI, *Mythes et réalités de l'impérialisme colonial français, 1871–1914* (Armand Colin, 1960).

—— *Noirs et blancs dans l'Afrique noire française, ou comment le colonisé devient colonisateur, 1870–1914* (Flammarion, 1983).

BUTLER, CHRISTOPHER, *Interpretation, Deconstruction, and Ideology* (Oxford, Clarendon Press, 1984).

CABRIDENS, VALÉRIE, '"Algérie perdue": Analyse de titres—Écrits de Français sur l'Algérie publiés après 1962', in Henry *et al.*, 175–89.

CALMES, ALAIN, *Le Roman colonial en Algérie avant 1914* (L'Harmattan, 1984).

CAMUS, ALBERT, *Actuelles* iii: *chroniques algériennes* (Gallimard, 1958).

CARROLL, DAVID, 'Representation or the End(s) of History: Dialectics and Fiction', *Yale French Studies*, 59 (1980), 201–29.

CAYROL, JEAN, *Je vivrai l'amour des autres* (Seuil, 1947).

CHALIAND, GÉRARD, *Mythes révolutionnaires du tiers monde* (Seuil, 1976).

CHÂTELET, FRANÇOIS, *Les Idéologies*, iii: *De Rousseau à Mao* (Verviers, Belgium, Marabout, 1981).

CHATMAN, SEYMOUR, *Story and Discourse: Narrative Structure in Fiction and Film* (Ithaca, Cornell University Press, 1978).

—— *Coming to Terms: The Rhetoric of Narrative in Fiction and Film* (Ithaca, Cornell University Press, 1978).

CHENNELLS, ANTHONY JOHN, 'Settler Myths and the Southern Rhodesian Novel', unpubl. D. Phil. thesis (University of Zimbabwe, 1982).

COATES, PAUL, *The Double and the Other: Identity as Ideology in Post-Romantic Fiction* (London, Macmillan, 1988).

COHEN, W.B., *The French Encounter with Africans: White Response to Blacks, 1530–1880* (Bloomington, Indiana University Press, 1980).

COHEN-SOLAL, ANNIE, *Sartre* (Gallimard, 1985).

—— 'Camus, Sartre et la guerre d'Algérie', in Guérin, 177–84.

Collective, *Ceux d'Algérie: lettres de rappelés* (Plon, 1957).

COLLINGWOOD-WHITTICK, S., 'The Colonial Situation in Algeria and its Literary Reflection', unpubl. Ph.D. thesis (University of London, Birkbeck College, 1980).

'Comité de Résistance Spirituelle', *Des rappelés témoignent* (Minuit, 1957).

COPFERMANN, ÉMILE, *La Génération des blousons noirs: problèmes de la jeunesse française* (Maspero, 1962).

CORNEVIN, ROBERT, 'Colonialisme littéraire et colonialisme politique', *Vie et langage*, 207 (June 1969), 309–11.

COURRIÈRE, YVES, *La Guerre d'Algérie* (4 vols., Fayard, 1968–1971).

CROCHET, MONIQUE, *Les Mythes dans l'œuvre de Camus* (Éditions Universitaires, 1973).

CROUZET, MICHEL, 'La Bataille des intellectuels français', *La Nef*, 12–13 (Oct. 1962–Jan. 1963), 47–65.

CRYLE, PETER, 'Bodily Positions and Moral Attitudes in *L'Exil et le royaume*', in Rizzuto, 35–41.

DALLOZ, JACQUES, *La Guerre d'Indochine, 1945–54* (Seuil, 1987).

—— *Textes sur la décolonisation* (PUF, 1989).

—— *Dien Bien Phu* (La Documentation Française, 1991).

DANIEL, JEAN, *De Gaulle et l'Algérie: la tragédie, le héros et le témoin* (Seuil, 1986).

DANIEL, JOSEPH, *Guerre et cinéma* (Cahiers de la Fondation Nationale des Sciences Politiques/Armand Colin, 1972), 335–55.

DAUDET, ALPHONSE, *Tartarin de Tarascon* (1st edn. 1872; Gallimard, 'Folio Junior', 1977).

DÉJEUX, JEAN, 'Essai de bibliographie algérienne, 1er janvier 1954–30 juin 1962: lectures d'une guerre', *Cahiers nord-africains*, 92 (Oct.–Nov. 1962).

—— 'Bibliographie algérienne des essais, récits et témoignages, 1945–1967', *Revue algérienne des sciences juridiques, politiques et économiques*, 5/1 (1968), 171–86.

—— *La Littérature algérienne contemporaine* (PUF, 1975).

—— 'De l'éternel méditerranéen à l'éternel Jugurtha', *Revue algérienne des sciences juridiques, économiques et politiques*, 14/4 (Dec. 1977), 658–728.

—— *Bibliographie de la littérature 'algérienne' des Français* (CNRS, 1978).

—— 'Romans algériens et guerre de libération', *L'Esprit créateur*, 26/1 (Spring 1986), 70–85.

DELAIN, MICHEL, 'Cinéma: trop tôt trop tard', *L'Express*, 1477 (3 Nov. 1979), 90–1.

DÉON, MICHEL, *L'Armée d'Algérie et la pacification* (Plon, 1959).

DESCHAMPS, HUBERT, *Les Méthodes et les doctrines coloniales de la France du XVIe siècle à nos jours* (Armand Colin, 1953).

—— *La Fin des empires coloniaux* (PUF, 1969).

DESCOMBES, VINCENT, *Le Même et l'Autre* (Minuit, 1979).

DESSAIGNE, FRANCINE, *Jean Brune: Français d'Algérie* (Albatros, 1983).

DOMENACH, JEAN-MARIE, *La Propagande politique* (PUF, 1956; 8th edn. 1979).

DROZ, BERNARD, 'Le Cas très singulier de la guerre d'Algérie', *Vingtième siècle*, 5 (special number on 'Les Guerres franco-françaises', Jan.–Mar. 1985), 81–90.

—— and LEVER, EVELYNE, *Histoire de la guerre d'Algérie, 1954–1962* (Seuil, 1982).

DUCHET, CLAUDE, 'The Object-Event of the Ram's Charge: An Ideological Reading of an Image', *Yale French Studies*, 59 (1980), 155–74.

DUPUY, AIMÉ, *L'Algérie dans les lettres françaises* (Éditions Universitaires, 1956).

DUQUESNE, JACQUES, *L'Algérie ou la guerre des mythes* (Desclée de Brouwer, 1958).

EINAUDI, JEAN-LUC, *La Ferme Ameziane: enquête sur un centre de torture pendant la guerre d'Algérie* (L'Harmattan, 1991).

—— *La Bataille de Paris* (Seuil, 1991).

ELIA, LUCIEN, and MYRIAM (eds.), *Les Pieds-Noirs* (Philippe Lebaud, 1982).

ELLUL, JACQUES, *Propagandes* (Armand Colin, 1962).

—— *Histoire de la propagande* (PUF, 1967).

ENCKELL, PIERRE, 'L'œuvre de Jean-Pierre Millecam', in Henry *et al.*, 191–4.

ERICKSON, JOHN, 'Abert Camus and North Africa: A Discourse of Exteriority', in Knapp, 73–88.

ÉTIENNE, BRUNO, *Les Européens d'Algérie et l'indépendance algérienne* (CNRS, 1968).

—— *Algérie, cultures et révolutions* (Seuil, 1977).

EVANS, MARTIN, 'A Story of Censorship and Forgetting: French Cinema and the Algerian War', *Modern and Contemporary France*, 39 (Oct. 1989), 46–9.

—— 'French Resistance and the Algerian War', *History Today*, 41 (July 1991), 43–9.

ÉVÉNO, PATRICK and PLANCHAIS, JEAN (eds.), *La Guerre d'Algérie: dossier et témoignages* (La Découverte/Le Monde, 1989).

FALL, BERNARD B., *Hell in a Very Small Place: The Siege of Dien Bien Phu* (New York, Lippincott, 1966).

FANON, FRANTZ, *L'An V de la révolution algérienne: sociologie d'une révolution* (Maspero, 1959).

—— *Les Damnés de la terre* (Maspero, 1961; La Découverte, 1984).

—— *Pour la révolution africaine* (Maspero, 1969).

FARÈS, A., *La Cruelle Vérité: de l'Algérie de 1945 à l'indépendance* (Plon, 1982).

FERRO, MARC (ed.), *Le 13 mai 1958* (La Documentation Française, 1985).

FLAUBERT, GUSTAVE, *Salammbô* (Garnier-Flammarion, 1964).

FORBES, JILL, *The Cinema in France: After the New Wave* (Macmillan/British Film Institute, 1992).

FORTIER, PAUL A., 'Le Décor symbolique de 'l'Hôte' d'Albert Camus', *French Review*, 46/3 (Feb. 1973), 535–42.

FOULETIER-SMITH, NICOLE, 'Les Nord-Africains en France: réalités et représentations littéraires', *French Review*, 51/5 (Apr. 1978), 683–91.

FOULKES, A. P., *Literature and Propaganda* (London, Methuen, 1983).

FOURASTIÉ, JEAN, *Les Trente glorieuses* (Fayard, 1979).

FRÉMONT, ARMAND, *Algérie-El Djazaïr* (Maspero, 1982).

GAREL, ALAIN, 'Le Cinéma français et la guerre d'Algérie', *Grand Maghreb*, 57 (19 Apr. 1989), 18–25.

GAUCHON, PASCAL, and BUISSON, PATRICK, *OAS: histoire de la résistance française en Algérie* (Éditions Jeune Pied-Noir, 1984).

GAULLE, CHARLES DE, *Mémoires d'espoir*, i: *le Renouveau, 1958–1962* (Plon, 1970).

—— *Discours et messages: avec le renouveau, 1958–1962* (Plon, 1970).

GENETTE, GÉRARD, *Figures, iii* (Seuil, 1972).

GERVEREAU, LAURENT, RIOUX, JEAN-PIERRE, and STORA, BENJAMIN (eds.), *La France en guerre d'Algérie* (MHC-BDIC, 1992).

GIRARDET, RAOUL, *La Crise militaire française, 1954–1962: aspects sociologiques et idéologiques* (Armand Colin, 1964).

—— *L'Idée coloniale en France de 1871 à 1964* (La Table Ronde, 1972).

—— *Mythes et mythologies politiques* (Seuil, 1986).

GOLDTHORPE, RHIANNON, *Sartre: Literature and Theory* (Cambridge, Cambridge University Press, 1984).

GORCE, PAUL-MARIE DE LA, *La République et son armée* (Fayard, 1963).

—— *Apogée et mort de la Quatrième République* (Grasset, 1979).

—— *L'Empire écartelé (1936–1946)* (Paris, Denoël, 1990).

GORDON, DAVID C., *The Passing of French Algeria* (Oxford, Oxford University Press, 1966).

GOURDON, HUBERT *et al.*, 'Roman colonial et idéologie coloniale en Algérie', *Revue algérienne des sciences juridiques, économiques et politiques*, 11/1 (special number on this theme, Mar. 1974).

GRALL, XAVIER, *La Génération du djebel* (Desclée de Brouwer, 1962).

GRASSIN, JEAN-MARIE *et al.*, *Mythes, images, représentations* (Didier Érudition, 1981).

GREENLEE, JAMES W., 'Camus' "Guest": the inadmissible complicity', *Studies in Twentieth Century Literature*, 2/1 (Spring 1978), 127–39.

GRILLO, RALPH D., *Ideologies and Institutions in Urban France: The Representation of Immigrants* (Cambridge, Cambridge University Press, 1985).

GRIMAL, HENRI, *La Décolonisation* (Armand Colin, 1965).

GROSSER, ALFRED, *La Quatrième République et sa politique extérieure* (Armand Colin, 1961).

GUÉRIN, JEAN-YVES, *Camus et la politique* (L'Harmattan, 1986).

GUERS-VILLATE, YVONNE, 'Rieux and Daru or the deliberate refusal to influence others', in Suther, 143–51.

GUIBBERT, PIERRE, 'La guerre d'Algérie sur les écrans français', in GERVEREAU, L. *et al.*, 247–55.

GUICHARD, JEAN-PIERRE, *De Gaulle et les mass-media: l'image du général* (Éditions France-Empire, 1985).

GUIRAL, PIERRE, and TÉMIME, ÉMILE (eds.), *L'Idée de race dans la pensée politique française contemporaine* (CNRS, 1977).

HABART, MICHEL, *Histoire d'un parjure* (Minuit, 1960).

HADDOUR, AZZEDINE, 'Algeria and its History: Colonial Myths and the Forging and Deconstructing of Identity in *Pied-Noir* Literature', in HARGREAVES and HEFFERNAN, 77–94.

HAMON, HERVÉ, and ROTMAN, PATRICK, *Les Porteurs de valises: la résistance française à la guerre d'Algérie* (Albin Michel, 1979).

HARBI, MOHAMMED (ed.), *Le FLN, mirage et réalité: des origines à la prise du pouvoir (1945–1962)* (Jeune Afrique, 1980).

—— *Les Archives de la révolution algérienne* (Jeune Afrique, 1981).

—— *1954: La Guerre commence en Algérie* (Brussels, Complexe, 1989).

HARGREAVES, ALEC G., *The Colonial Experience in French Fiction: A Study of Pierre Loti, Ernest Psichari and Pierre Mille* (London, Macmillan, 1981).

—— 'Personnes grammaticales et relations affectives chez Camus', *Revue Celfan/Celfan Review*, 4/3 (1985), 10–17.

—— 'Caught in the Middle: The Liberal Dilemma in the Algerian War', *Nottingham French Studies*, 25/2 (Oct. 1986), 73–82.

—— 'Camus and the Colonial Question in Algeria', *The Muslim World*, 77 (1987), 164–74.

—— and HEFFERNAN, MICHAEL J. (eds.), *French and Algerian Identities from Colonial Times to the Present: A Century of Interaction* (Lampeter, Edwin Mellen, 1993).

HARRISON, ALEXANDER, *Challenging de Gaulle: The OAS and the Counter-revolution in Algeria, 1954–1962* (New York, Praeger, 1989).

HARRISON, CHRISTOPHER, 'French Attitudes to Empire and the Algerian War', *African Affairs*, January 1983, 75–95.

HAYWARD, SUSAN, and VINCENDEAU, GINETTE (eds.), *French Film: Texts and Contexts* (London, Routledge, 1990).

HÉDUY, PHILIPPE, *Algérie française, 1942–1962* (Société de Production Littéraire, 1980).

HEGGOY, ALF ANDREW, *Insurgency and Counterinsurgency in Algeria* (Bloomington, University of Indiana Press, 1972).

—— (ed.), *Through Foreign Eyes: Western Attitudes Toward North Africa* (Washington, DC, University Press of America, 1982).

HEINEMANN, LARRY, '"Just Don't Fit": Stalking the elusive "trip-wire" veteran', *Harper's* (Apr. 1985), 55–63.

HENISSART, PAUL, *Wolves in the City: The Death of French Algeria* (St. Albans, Paladin, 1973).

HENRY, JEAN-ROBERT *et al.*, *Le Maghreb dans l'imaginaire français* (Aix-en-Provence, Edisud, 1985).

Historia, 'La Guerre d'Algérie' (special series, 1971–1974).

HOGUE, JANINE DE LA, 'Les Livres comme patrie', in Elia, 112–13.

HORNE, ALISTAIR, *A Savage War of Peace: Algeria, 1954–1962* (London, Macmillan, 1977).

—— *The French Army and Politics, 1870–1970* (London, Macmillan, 1984).

HUREAU, JOËLLE, *La Mémoire des pieds-noirs de 1830 à nos jours* (Olivier Orban, 1987).

ISER, WOLFGANG, *The Act of Reading* (London, Routledge and Kegan Paul, 1978).

ISNARD, HILDEBERT, *La Vigne en Algérie* (2 vols., Gap, Éditions Ophrys and CNRS, 1954).

JAMESON, FREDERIC, *The Political Unconscious: Narrative as a Socially Symbolic Act* (London, Methuen, 1981).

JAUFFRET, JEAN-CHARLES *et al.*, *La Guerre d'Algérie par les documents*, i: *'L'Avertissement, 1943–1946'* (Service Historique de l'Armée de Terre, 1990).

JEANCOLAS, JEAN-PIERRE, *Le Cinéma des Français: la Ve République (1958–1978)* (Stock, 1979).

JEANSON, COLETTE and FRANCIS, *L'Algérie hors la loi* (Seuil, 1955).

JEANSON, FRANCIS, *Notre guerre* (Minuit, 1960).

—— *Algéries: de retour en retour* (Seuil, 1991).

JEFFERSON, ANN, and ROBEY, DAVID (eds.), *Modern Literary Theory: A Comparative Introduction* (London, B. T. Batsford, 1982; 1986 edn.).

JOLY, DANIÈLE, *The French Communist Party and the Algerian War* (London, Macmillan, 1991).

JONES, ROSEMARY, 'Locations and Identity: Reflections in Three *Pied-Noir* Novels, 1949–1959', in HARGREAVES and HEFFERNAN, 95–108.

JOWETT, GARTH S., and O'DONNELL, VICTORIA, *Propaganda and Persuasion* (New York, Sage, 1992).

JULIEN, CHARLES-ANDRÉ, *L'Afrique du nord en marche: nationalismes musulmans et souveraineté française* (Julliard, 1952; 3rd edn. 1972).

—— *Histoire de l'Algérie contemporaine*, i: *La conquête et les débuts de la colonisation, 1827–1871* (PUF, 1964; 2nd edn. 1979).

KABBANI, RANA, *Europe's Myths of Orient: Devise and Rule* (London, Macmillan, 1986).

KAHLER, MILES, *Decolonization in Britain and France: The Domestic Consequences of International Relations* (Princeton, NJ, Princeton University Press, 1986).

KAJMAN, MICHEL *et al.*, 'L'Algérie de la deuxième mémoire' (a series of articles to mark the thirtieth anniversary of the Évian accords), *Le Monde*, 17–23 March 1992.

KAUFFER, RENÉ, *OAS: Histoire d'une oganisation secrète* (Fayard, 1986).

KELLY, GEORGE ARMSTRONG, *Lost Soldiers: The French Army and Empire in Crisis, 1947–1962* (Cambridge, Mass., MIT Press, 1965).

KETTLE, MARTIN, *De Gaulle and Algeria, 1940–1960* (London, Quartet, 1993).

KIERNAN, VICTOR G., *The Lords of Human Kind: European Attitudes Towards the Outside World in the Imperial Age* (London, Weidenfeld and Nicolson, 1969).

KNAPP, BETTINA L. (ed.), *Critical Essays on Albert Camus* (Boston, Mass., G. K. Hall, 1988).

KNIEBIEHLER, YVONNE, and GOUTALIER, RÉGINE, *La Femme au temps des colonies* (Stock, 1985).

KOMOR, ANDRÉ-PAUL, 'L'Image de la Légion étrangère à travers la littérature française', *Revue historique des armées*, 8/3 (1981), 157–79.

LACOUTURE, JEAN, *1962: Algérie, la guerre est finie* (Brussels, Complexe, 1985).

LAFFONT, PIERRE, *Histoire de la France en Algérie* (Plon, 1980).

—— *L'Algérie des Français* (Bordas, 1981).

LANCELOT, MARIE-THÉRÈSE, *Organisation armée secrète* (2 vols., Fondation Nationale des Sciences Politiques, 1963).

LARRAIN, JORGE, *The Concept of Ideology* (London, Hutchinson, 1979).

LAURENT, JACQUES, *Mauriac sous de Gaulle* (La Table Ronde, 1964).

LEBEDEL, PIERRE, 'Polar: dix livres après', in Gervereau *et al.*, 240–1.

LECONTE, DANIEL, *Les Pieds-Noirs: histoire et portrait d'une communauté* (Seuil, 1980).

LEIF, JOSEPH, *Pièges et mystifications de la parole* (Nathan, 1982).

LEMALET, MARTINE, *Lettres d'Algérie, 1954–1962: la guerre des appelés, la mémoire d'une génération* (Jean-Claude Lattès, 1992).

LE MIRE, HENRI, *Histoire militaire de la guerre d'Algérie* (Albin Michel, 1982).

LENZINI, JOSÉ, *L'Algérie de Camus* (Aix-en-Provence, Edisud, 1987).

LOTTMAN, HERBERT, *Albert Camus: A Biography* (London, Weidenfeld and Nicholson, 1979).

LERICHE, J., *Les Algériens parmi nous* (Éditions Sociales, 1959).

LUSINCHI, PAUL, 'L'Idéologie du roman de masse', *Cahiers internationaux de sociologie*, 65 (July-Dec. 1978), 347–58.

LUSTICK, IAN, *State-Building Failure in British Ireland and French Algeria*, Institute of International Studies, UC, Berkeley, Research Series 63 (Berkeley, Calif. 1985).

MACMASTER, NEIL, 'The "dark age" of colonialism? Algeria 1920–1954', *Bulletin of Francophone Africa*, 1 (Spring 1992), 106–11.

MAIER, CHARLES S., and WHITE, DAN S. (eds.), *The Thirteenth of May: The Advent of de Gaulle's Republic* (New York, Oxford University Press, 1968).

MANNONI, OCTAVE, *Psychologie de la colonisation* (Seuil, 1950).

MARAN, RITA, *Torture and the Role of Ideology: The French-Algerian War* (London, Greenwood Press, 1989).

MARSEILLE, JACQUES, *Empire colonial et capitalisme français: histoire d'un divorce* (Albin Michel, 1986).

—— *L'Age d'or de la France coloniale* (Albin Michel, 1986).

MARSHALL, BRUCE D., *The French Colonial Myth and Constitution Making in the Fourth Republic* (New Haven, Conn., Yale University Press, 1973).

MARTIN, CLAUDE, *Histoire de l'Algérie française, 1830–1962* (Éditions des Quatre Fils Aymon, 1963).

——*L'Empire renaissant, 1789–1871* (Denoël, 1987).

MASCHINO, MAURICE, *Le Refus* (Maspero, 1960).

——*L'Engagement* (Maspero, 1961).

——and M'RABET, FADÉLA, *L'Algérie des illusions: la révolution confisquée* (Robert Laffont, 1972).

MASSU, JACQUES, *La Vraie Bataille d'Alger* (Plon, 1971).

MATHIEU, MARTINE (ed.), *Le Roman colonial* (L'Harmattan, 'Itinéraires et contacts de cultures', 7, 1987).

MAURIAC, FRANÇOIS, *Bloc-notes: 1952–1957* (Flammarion, 1958).

——*Le Nouveau Bloc-notes: 1958–1960* (Flammarion, 1961).

——*Le Nouveau Bloc-notes: 1961–1964* (Flammarion, 1965).

——*L'Imitation des bourreaux de Jésus-Christ* (Desclée de Brouwer, 1984). (Writings on torture; edited, with introduction, by Jean Lacouture and Alain de la Morandais).

MCCARTHY, PATRICK, *Camus: A Critical Study of his Life and Work* (London, Hamish Hamilton, 1982).

MCCULLOCH, JOCK, *Black Soul White Artifact: Fanon's Clinical Psychology and Social Theory* (Cambridge, Cambridge University Press, 1983).

MELLING, PHIL, and ROPER, JON, *America, France and Vietnam: Cultural History and Ideas of Conflict* (Aldershot, Avebury, 1991).

MEMMI, ALBERT, *Portrait du colonisé précédé du portrait du colonisateur* (Corréa, 1957; Gallimard/NRF, 1985).

——'Camus ou le colonisateur de bonne volonté', *La Nef*, 12 Dec. 1957, 95–6.

——(ed.) *Anthologie des écrivains maghrébins d'expression française* (Présence Africaine, 1964).

——(ed.) *Anthologie des écrivains français du Maghreb* (Présence Africaine, 1969).

——(ed.) *Écrivains francophones du Maghreb: anthologie* (Seghers, 1985).

MEYER, JEAN *et al.*, *Histoire de la France coloniale* (2 vols., Armand Colin, 1991).

MICHEL, MARIE, '"It really makes you sick!": Jean-Luc Godard's *À bout de souffle* (1959)', in Hayward and Vincendeau, 201–15.

MICHEL-CHICH, DANIELLE, *Déracinés: les pieds-noirs aujourd'hui* (Éditions Plume, 1990).

MILBURY-STEEN, SARA L., *European and African Stereotypes in Twentieth-Century Fiction* (New York, New York University Press, 1981).

MONTAGNON, PIERRE, *La Guerre d'Algérie: genèse et engrenage d'une tragédie* (Pygmalion/Gérard Watelet, 1984).

——*La France coloniale*, i: *La Gloire de l'Empire* (Pygmalion, 1988).

——*La France coloniale*, ii: *Retour à l'hexagone* (Pygmalion, 1990).

MONTHERLANT, HENRY DE, *Romans et œuvres de fiction non-théâtrales* (Gallimard, 1982).

MOROT-SIR, EDOUARD, 'Humor and Exile', in Rizzuto, 53–70.

MOUNIER, EMMANUEL, 'Impossibilités algériennes ou le mythe des trois départements', *Esprit*, July 1947.

MULTEAU, NORBERT, 'Le cinéma et la guerre d'Algérie', *Le Spectacle du Monde/Réalités*, 241 (Apr. 1982), 101–6.

MUS, PAUL, *Guerre sans visage* (Seuil, 1961).

NORA, PIERRE, 'Pour une autre explication de *L'Étranger*', *France observateur*, 7 Jan. 1960, 16–17.

—— *Les Français d'Algérie* (Julliard, 1961).

—— (ed.) *Les Lieux de mémoire*, i: *La République* (Gallimard, 1984).

O'BALLANCE, EDGAR, *The Algerian Insurrection, 1954–1962* (London, Faber and Faber, 1967).

O'BRIEN, CONOR CRUISE, *Camus* (Glasgow, Collins, 1970).

OBUCHOWSKI, CHESTER W., 'Algeria: The Tortured Conscience', in his *Mars on Trial* (Madrid, José Porrúa Turanzas, 1978). (Previously published in the *French Review*, 42 (1968–9), 90–103).

O'CONNELL, DAVID, 'Jean Lartéguy: A Popular Phenomenon', *French Review*, 45/6 (May 1972), 1087–97.

—— 'Jules Roy, Albert Camus, and *Les Chevaux du soleil*', *Revue Celfan/Celfan Review*, 6/2–3 (Feb.-May 1987), 15–19.

ORR, ANDREW, *Ceux d'Algérie: le silence et la honte* (Payot, 1990).

ORY, PASCAL, 'L'Algérie fait écran', in Rioux, J.-P., *La Guerre d'Algérie et les Français* (Fayard, 1990), 572–81.

—— and SIRINELLI, JEAN-FRANÇOIS, *Les Intellectuels en France, de l'affaire Dreyfus à nos jours* (Armand Colin, 1986).

PAILLAT, CLAUDE, *Vingt ans qui déchirèrent la France*, ii: *La Liquidation, 1954–1962* (Robert Laffont, 1972).

PARET, PAUL, *French Revolutionary Warfare from Indochina to Algeria: The Analysis of a Political and Military Doctrine* (New York, Praeger, 1964).

PASCAL, MICHEL, and SLAMA, ALAIN-GÉRARD, '"Ils y ont laissé une part de leur jeunesse"', *Le Point*, 22 Feb. 1992, 58–9.

PEILLARD, JEAN, *La Pacification de l'Algérie et la conscience française* (Algiers, Baconnier, n.d.).

PÉJU, MARCEL, *Le Procès du réseau Jeanson* (Minuit, 1961).

PÉLÉGRI, JEAN, 'Libres propos', in Henry *et al.*, 215–23.

PERRAULT, GILLES, *Les Parachutistes* (Seuil, 1961).

PERVILLÉ, GUY, 'Historiographie de la guerre d'Algérie', *Annuaire de l'Afrique du Nord* (CNRS, 1976 onwards).

—— *De l'Empire français à la décolonisation* (Hachette, 1991).

PETITFILS, JEAN-CHRISTIAN, *La Droite en France de 1789 à nos jours* (PUF, 1973).

PLANCHAIS, JEAN, *Le Malaise de l'armée* (Plon, 1958).

—— *Une histoire politique de l'armée*, ii: *1940–1967, De de Gaulle à de Gaulle* (Seuil, 1967).

—— 'Les Vétérans de la guerre d'Algérie', 1: 'La Volonté d'oublier', *Le Monde*, 5 July 1985, 1, 10; 2: 'Un autre ciel', *Le Monde*, 6 July 1985, 8.

——*L'Empire embrasé (1946–1962)* (Paris, Denoël, 1990).

——(ed.) 'L'Algérie depuis 1945', *Le Monde: Dossiers et Documents*, 203 (Oct. 1992).

Prochaska, David, *Making Algeria French* (Cambridge, Cambridge University Press and Éditions de la Maison des Sciences de l'Homme, 1990).

Quilliot, Roger, *La Mer et les prisons: essai sur Albert Camus* (Gallimard, 1970).

Randau, Robert, *Les Colons* (Algiers, Sansot, 1907).

Ray, William, *Literary Meaning: From Phenomenology to Deconstruction* (Oxford, Blackwell, 1984).

Reboux, Paul, *Notre (?) Afrique du Nord: Maroc, Algérie, Tunisie. La Valise . . . ou le cercueil!* (Brussels, Éditions de Chabassol, 1946).

Redfern, Walter D., *Georges Darien: Robbery and Private Enterprise* (Amsterdam, Rodopi, 1985).

Ridley, Hugh, *Images of Imperial Rule* (London, Croom Helm, 1983).

Rinaldi, Angelo, 'Le Faible cri d'une mémoire blessée', *L'Express*, 1477 (3 Nov. 1979), 86–7.

Rioux, Jean-Pierre, *La France de la Quatrième République* (2 vols., Seuil, 1980; 1983).

——'La colonie, ça s'apprend à l'école!', *L'Histoire* (special number on 'Le Temps des colonies'), 69 (1984), 49–55.

——(ed.) *La Guerre d'Algérie et les Français* (Fayard, 1990).

——(ed.) 'Les Fins d'empires', *Le Monde* (special edn.), Sept. 1992.

——and Sirinelli, Jean-François (eds.), *La Guerre d'Algérie et les intellectuels français* (Brussels, Éditions Complexe, 1991). (First publ. in *Les Cahiers de l'Institut d'Histoire du Temps Présent*, 10, Nov. 1988).

Rizzuto, Anthony (ed.), *Albert Camus' L'Exil et le royaume: The Third Decade* (Toronto, Paratexte, 1988).

Robbe-Grillet, Alain, *Pour un nouveau roman* (Minuit, 1963).

Robin, Maurice *et al.*, 'Remarques sur l'attitude de Camus face à la Guerre d'Algérie', in Guérin, 185–202.

Robin, Régine, 'Towards Fiction as Oblique Discourse', *Yale French Studies*, 59 (1980), 230–42.

Roblès, Emmanuel (ed.), *Les Pieds-Noirs* (Lebaud, 1982).

Roche, Anne, 'La Posture ethnographique dans quelques textes à compte d'auteur de Français sur l'Algérie', in Henry *et al.*, 165–74.

Roelens, Maurice, 'Un texte, son "histoire" et l'histoire. "L'Hôte" d'Albert Camus', *Revue des sciences humaines*, 42/165 (Jan.-Mar. 1977), 5–22.

Rose, Marilyn Gaddis, 'Roger Ikor's Moral Metaphor', *French Review*, 39/2 (Nov. 1965), 220–9.

Rotman, Patrick, and Tavernier, Bertrand, *La Guerre sans nom: les appelés d'Algérie, 1954–1962* (Seuil, 1992).

Roux, Michel, *Les Harkis: les oubliés de l'histoire* (La Découverte, 1991).

ROY, JULES, *J'accuse le général Massu* (Seuil, 1972).

—— 'Le Mythe d'une Algérie heureuse', *Le Monde*, 4 June 1982, 19.

RUSCIO, ALAIN, *La Décolonisation tragique, 1945–1962* (Messidor/Éditions Sociales, 1987).

SAADI, YACEF, *La Bataille d'Alger* (Témoignage Chrétien, 1982).

SAID, EDWARD W., *Orientalism* (London, Routledge and Kegan Paul, 1978).

SAINT-HAMONT, DANIEL, 'Pourquoi je continuerai à vivre dans le pays de ma mémoire', *Les Nouvelles littéraires*, 2729 (20–27 Mar. 1980), 23.

SAND, SHLOMO, 'Les Représentations de la Révolution dans l'imaginaire historique du fascisme français', *Mil neuf cent: revue d'histoire intellectuelle*, 9 (1991), 29–47.

SAROCCHI, JEAN, 'L'Autre et les autres', in Rizzuto, 95–104.

SARTRE, JEAN-PAUL, 'Orphée noir', in *Situations*, iii (Gallimard/NRF, 1949). (First publ. as a preface to Léopold Sedar Senghor's *Anthologie de la nouvelle poésie nègre et malgache*, Presses Universitaires, 1948.)

—— *Situations*, v: *colonialisme et néo-colonialisme* (Gallimard, 1964).

SCHALK, DAVID L., *War and the Ivory Tower* (New York, Oxford University Press, 1991).

SCHNEIDER, WILLIAM H., *An Empire for the Masses: The French Popular Image of Africa, 1870–1900* (Westport, Conn., Greenwood Press, 1982).

SCHOLES, ROBERT, *Semiotics and Interpretation* (New Haven, Conn., Yale University Press, 1982).

SHOWALTER, ENGLISH JNR., '*The Guest*: The Reluctant Host, Fate's Hostage', in his *Exiles and Strangers: A Reading of Camus's Exile and the Kingdom* (Columbus, Ohio State University Press, 1984), 73–87.

SIBLOT, PAUL, 'Retours à "l'Algérie heureuse" ou les mille et un détours de la nostalgie', in Henry *et al.*, 151–64.

—— 'Pères spirituels et mythes fondateurs de l'Algérianisme', in Mathieu, 29–59.

SIGG, BERNARD, *Le Silence et la honte: névroses de la guerre d'Algérie* (Messidor/Éditions Sociales, 1989).

SILVERMAN, MAXIM, 'The Racialization of Immigration: Aspects of Discourse from 1968–1981', *French Cultural Studies*, 1/2, 2 (June 1990), 111–28.

SIMON, PIERRE-HENRI, *Contre la torture* (Seuil, 1957).

SIRINELLI, JEAN-FRANÇOIS, *Intellectuels et passions françaises: manifestes et pétitions au XXe siècle* (Fayard, 1990).

SLAMA, ALAIN-GÉRARD, 'La guerre d'Algérie en littérature ou la comédie des masques', in Rioux, J.-P. (ed.), *La Guerre d'Algérie*, 582–602; 676–82.

SMITH, TONY, 'Idealism and People's War: Sartre on Algeria', *Political Theory*, 1 (Nov. 1973), 426–49.

—— 'The French Colonial Consensus and People's War, 1946–1958', *Journal of Contemporary History*, 9/4 (1974), 217–47.

—— *The End of European Empire: Decolonization after World War II* (Lexington, Mass., Heath, 1975).

—— *The French Stake in Algeria: 1954–1962* (London, Cornell University Press, 1978).

SORLIN, PIERRE, 'The Fanciful Empire: French Feature Films and the Colonies in the 1930s', *French Cultural Studies*, 2/2, 5 (June 1991), 135–51.

—— 'French Opinion and the Algerian War', *Bulletin of Francophone Africa*, 1 (Spring 1992), 49–57.

SORUM, PAUL CLAY, *Intellectuals and Decolonization in France* (Chapel Hill, University of North Carolina Press, 1977).

SOUMILLE, M., 'La Notion de race chez les Français d'Algérie à la fin du XIXème siècle', in Guiral and Témime, 242–5.

STOCKWELL, SHIRLEY A., 'French Literary Reaction to the Algerian War: A Study of Texts Produced by Intellectuals and Writers of French Expression, 1954–1962', unpubl. Ph.D. thesis (University of Reading, 1980).

STORA, BENJAMIN, *Histoire de l'Algérie coloniale, 1830–1954* (La Découverte, 1991).

—— *La Gangrène et l'oubli: la mémoire de la guerre d'Algérie* (*La Découverte, 1992*).

—— 'Indochine, Algérie, autorisations de retour', *Libération*, 1 May 1992, 5.

SUTHER, JUDITH D. (ed.), *Essays on Camus's Exile and the Kingdom* (University of Mississippi, Romance Monographs 41, 1980).

TAILLART, CHARLES, *L'Algérie dans la littérature française: essai de bibliographie méthodique et raisonnée jusqu'à l'année 1924* (Champion, 1925).

TALBOTT, JOHN, 'French Public Opinion and the Algerian War: A Research Note', *French Historical Studies*, 9 (Fall 1975), 354–61.

—— 'The Myth and Reality of the Paratrooper in the Algerian War', *Armed Forces and Society*, 3 (Fall 1976), 69–86.

—— 'Terrorism and the Liberal Dilemma: The Case of the Battle of Algiers', *Contemporary French Civilization*, 2/2 (Winter 1978), 177–89.

—— *The War Without a Name: France in Algeria, 1954–1962* (London, Faber and Faber, 1981).

TARROW, SUSAN, *Exile from the Kingdom: A Political Rereading of Albert Camus* (Alabama, University of Alabama Press, 1985).

THODY, PHILIP, *French Caesarism from Napoleon I to Charles de Gaulle* (London, Macmillan, 1989).

THOMPSON, LEONARD, *The Political Mythology of Apartheid* (New Haven, Conn., Yale University Press, 1986).

TILLION, GERMAINE, *Les Ennemis complémentaires* (Minuit, 1960).

TODOROV, TZVETAN, *On Human Diversity: Nationalism, Racism, and Exoticism in French Thought* (Cambridge, Mass., Harvard University Press, 1993).

TREIL, C., *L'Indifférence dans l'œuvre d'Albert Camus* (Sherbrooke, Quebec, Editions Cosmos, 1971).

TRIPIER, PHILIPPE, *Autopsie de la guerre d'Algérie* (Éditions France-Empire, 1972).

TRISTAN, ANNE, *Le Silence du fleuve: ce crime que nous n'avons toujours pas nommé* (Au nom de la mémoire, 1991).

VACHER, MICHEL-ALAIN, 'L'Idéologie dans le roman colonial algérien, 1900–1940', unpubl. doctoral thesis (Université d'Aix-Marseille, 1977).

VATIN, JEAN-CLAUDE, *L'Algérie politique: histoire et société* (Armand Colin and Fondation Nationale des Sciences Politiques, 1974).

—— and LUCAS, PHILIPPE, *L'Algérie des anthropologues* (Maspero, 1975).

VIANSSON-PONTÉ, PIERRE, *Histoire de la République gaullienne*, i: *la fin d'une époque, mai 1958–juillet 1962* (Fayard, 1970).

VIDAL-NAQUET, PIERRE, *L'Affaire Audin* (Minuit, 1958).

—— *La Raison d'État: la répression en Algérie (1954–1962)* (Minuit, 1962).

—— *La Torture dans la République* (Minuit, 1972).

—— 'Une Fidélité têtue: la Résistance française à la guerre d'Algérie', *Vingtième siècle*, 10 (Apr.-June 1986), 3–18.

VIGNY, ALFRED DE, *Servitude et grandeur militaires* (1st edn. 1835; Paris, Nelson, 1952).

VINCENT, GÉRARD, *Les Français 1945–1975: chronologie et structures d'une société* (Masson, 1977).

VITTORI, JEAN-PIERRE, *Nous, les appelés d'Algérie* (Stock, 1977; Messidor/ Temps Actuels, 1983).

—— *Confessions d'un professionnel de la torture* (Ramsay, 1980).

WAARDENBURG, JEAN-JACQUES, *L'Islam dans le miroir de l'occident* (Mouton, 1963; 3rd edn. 1970).

WANSBOROUGH, JOHN, 'The Decolonization of North African History', *Journal of African History*, 9 (1968), 643–50.

WEBER, EUGEN, *My France: Politics, Culture, Myth* (Cambridge, Mass., Belknap/Harvard University Press, 1991).

WILLIAMS, ALAN, *Republic of Images: A History of French Filmmaking* (Cambridge, Mass., Harvard University Press, 1992).

WILLIAMS, PHILIP, *Crisis and Compromise: Politics in the Fourth Republic* (London, Longman, 1964).

—— *Wars, Plots and Scandals in Post-War France* (Cambridge, Cambridge University Press, 1970).

WINOCK, MICHEL, *La République se meurt: chronique 1956–1958* (Seuil, 1978).

—— 'La Guerre d'Algérie', *Libération*, 26 June 1984, 22–4.

—— *La Fièvre hexagonale* (Calmann-Lévy, 1986).

WOLF, WILLIAM, *Landmark Films: The Cinema and Our Century* (New York, Paddington Press, 1979).

YACONO, XAVIER, *Les Étapes de la décolonisation française* (PUF, 1971).

—— *Histoire de la colonisation française* (PUF, 1979).

YOUNG, ROBERT, *White Mythologies: Writing History and the West* (London, Routledge, 1990).

ZREHEN, RICHARD, 'Écrit au soleil: la littérature de 1830 à 1962', in Elia, 112–13.

Alphabetical List of Films Cited

À bout de souffle (Jean-Luc Godard, 1960)
Adieu Philippine (Jaques Rozier, 1963)
Algérie en flammes (René Vautier, 1958)
Avoir vingt ans dans les Aurès (René Vautier, 1972)
La Bataille d'Alger (Gillo Pontecorvo, 1965)
La Belle Vie (Robert Enrico, 1963)
Certaines nouvelles (Jacques Davila, 1979)
Le Chagrin et la Pitié (Marcel Ophuls, 1971)
Cher Frangin (Gérard Mordillat, 1989)
Cléo de cinq à sept (Agnès Varda, 1962)
Le Combat dans l'île (Alain Cavalier, 1962)
Le Complot (René Gainville, 1973)
Le Coup de sirocco (Alexandre Arcady, 1978)
Le Crabe-Tambour (Pierre Schoendoerffer, 1977)
Dien Bien Phu (Pierre Schoendoerffer, 1992)
Élise ou la vraie vie (Michel Drach, 1970)
Français, si vous saviez (André Harris and Alain de Sédouy, 1972)
La Guerre sans nom (Bertrand Tavernier and Patrick Rotman, 1992)
L'Honneur d'un capitaine (Pierre Schoendoerffer, 1982)
L'Insoumis (Alain Cavalier, 1964)
Le Joli Mai (Chris Marker, 1963)
Liberty Belle (Pascal Kané, 1983)
Lost Command (Mark Robson, 1966)
Muriel ou le temps d'un retour (Alain Resnais, 1963)
Nuit et Brouillard (Alain Resnais, 1955)
Octobre à Paris (Vérité-Liberté collective, 1962)
Les Oliviers de la justice (James Blue, 1962)
Outremer (Brigitte Rouan, 1990)
Les Parapluies de Cherbourg (Jacques Demy, 1964)
Le Petit Soldat (Jean-Luc Godard, 1960)
La Question (Laurent Heynemann, 1976)
RAS (Yves Boisset, 1973)
Réfugiés algériens (Pierre Clément, 1958)
Sakiet Sidi Youssef (Pierre Clément, 1958)

Secteur postal 89 098 (Philippe Durand, 1959)
Les Statues meurent aussi (Alain Resnais and Chris Marker, 1953)
Z (Costa-Gavras, 1969)
58 2/B (Guy Chalon, 1959)
La 317e Section (Pierre Schoendoerffer, 1965)

INDEX